IMAGES
of America

FLORENCE

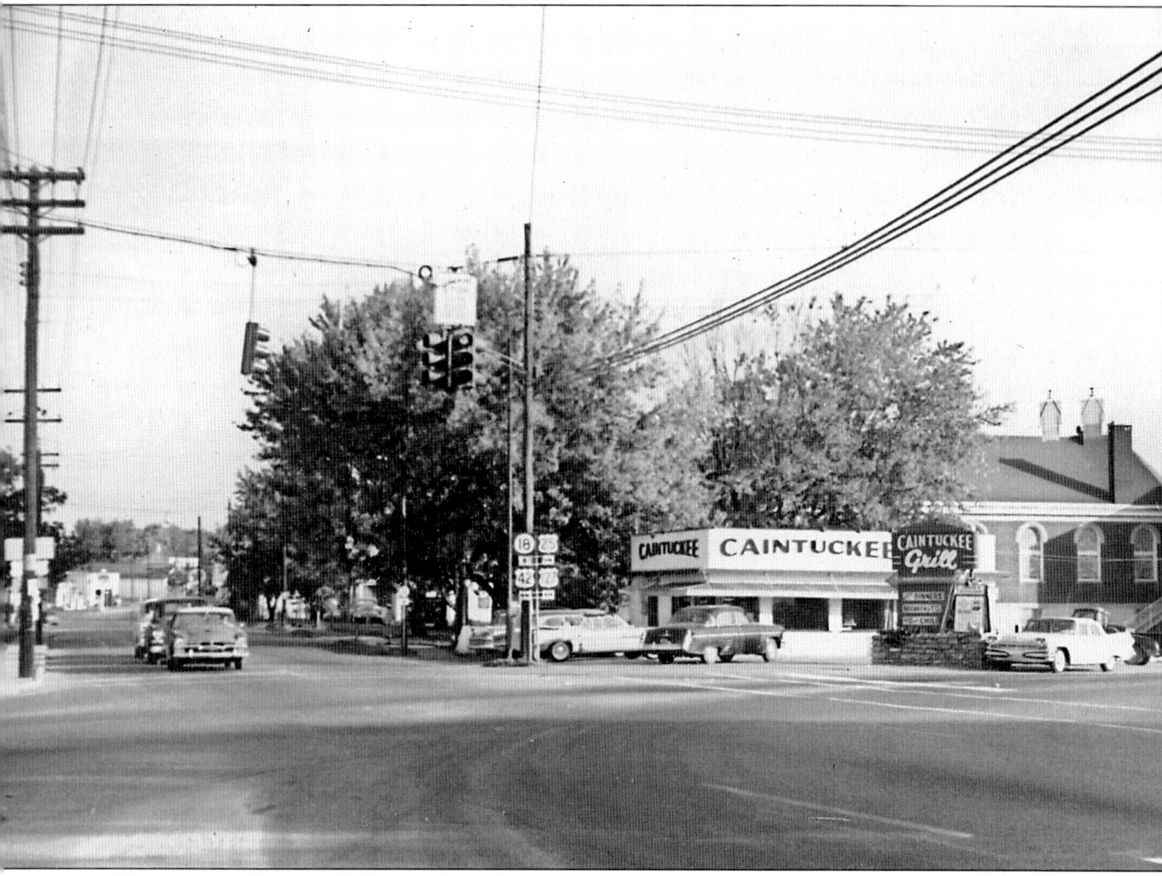

The Caintuckee Grill, located at the intersection of U.S. 25 and U.S. 42, was a community gathering place when this picture was taken in the 1960s. Before the construction of I-75, locals as well as travelers shared good food and conversation at this popular Florence landmark. The name of the grill was a combination of the owner's last name and Kentucky.

IMAGES
of America

FLORENCE

Michael D. Rouse and Tim Moore

ARCADIA
PUBLISHING

ISBN 978-0-7385-4194-5

Published by Arcadia Publishing
Charleston, South Carolina

Printed in the United States of America

Library of Congress Catalog Card Number: 2005929300

For all general information contact Arcadia Publishing at:
Telephone 843-853-2070
Fax 843-853-0044
E-mail sales@arcadiapublishing.com
For customer service and orders:
Toll-Free 1-888-313-2665

Visit us on the Internet at www.arcadiapublishing.com

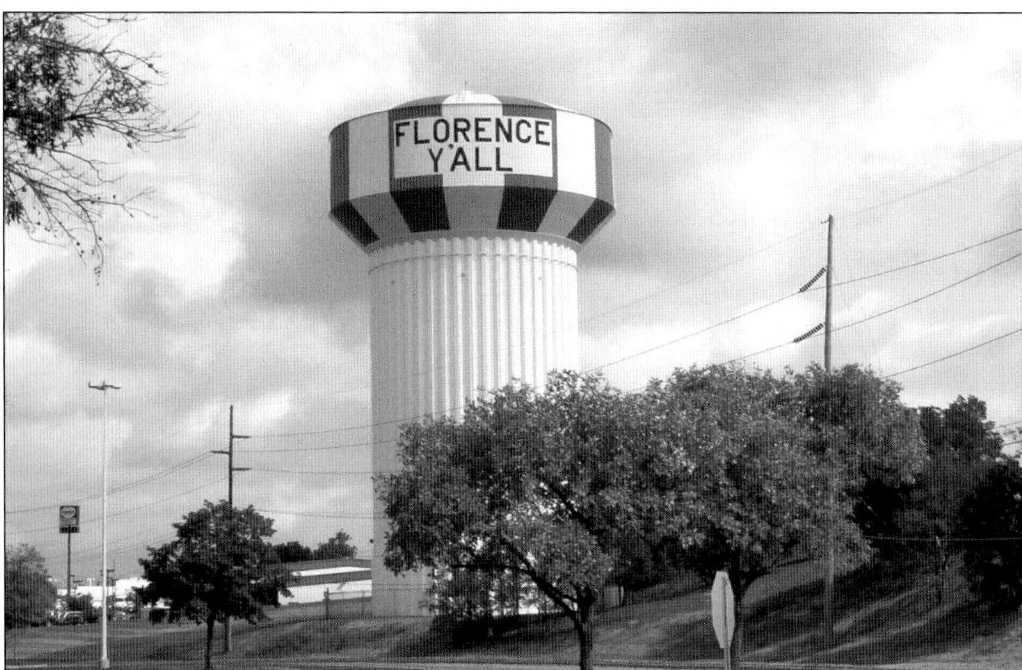

For over 30 years, the Florence Y'all water tower has served as a visual reminder to southbound travelers on I-75 that they have officially crossed the border between North and South. Built in 1974 to announce the future opening of the Florence Mall, the water tower had to be altered to its now-legendary slogan to comply with federal regulations prohibiting advertising along the interstate highway system for a facility that was yet to open.

Contents

ACKNOWLEDGMENTS

This book could not have been completed without the generous support and encouragement of the staff of the Boone County Public Library. The authors would like to particularly acknowledge the assistance Mrs. Bridget Stricker rendered by meticulously copying the numerous photographs selected by the authors from the Fitzgerald Collection and making them readily available. Similarly, the authors would like to thank the staff of the John Uri Lloyd Library and Museum in Cincinnati, Ohio, for their help and assistance with the pictures and information related to Mr. Lloyd and his tenure in Florence.

Closer to home, the authors would like to thank the following friends and relatives who took time out of their busy schedules to sift through countless photographs stored in the top of their closets or attics for the many photographs we requested. This book is a tribute to their love and dedication to the city of Florence. Many contributors will notice no doubt that some of the pictures they offered were not incorporated into the book. As with any work of this type, the authors had to make some very difficult decisions when it came to deciding which photographs to include or exclude from the book. The selection of photographs for inclusion was based primarily on how they related to a particular chapter heading or on the overall quality of the photograph. In many instances, there were just too many photographs to include in a particular chapter.

Charles Aylor
Louise Aylor
Donald Beemon
Boone County Public Library
Kathy Caminiti
Irvin Carpenter
Karen Cutebirth
Alice Conrad
Betsy Coppage
Barbara Crume
Rosetta Dringenburg
Bob England
Kay Garnett
Nellie Garnett
Marilyn Goley
Grace Episcopal Church
Virginia Nestor Kohl
Fay Kirkpatrick
Virginia Lainhart
Lloyd Library, Cincinnati, Ohio
Don and Elain Markesbery
Terry Roberts Moffitt
Linda Moore
Sherry Noel
Imogene Regenbogen
Perry Renaker
Wanda Riegler
Katherine Rouse
Jim Rowland
Barbara Sharp
Bridget Striker
Thelma Sturgeon
Dr. George R. Tanner
Bob Taylor
Wayne Trego
Ella Pearl Utz
Tom Utz
Russ Wilmhoff
Debbie Wood
Kathleen Woods
Mary Lou Wright

INTRODUCTION

To countless Northern tourists traveling south along the I-75 corridor, Florence represents their first visual reminder that they have crossed that wonderful border separating North and South. While the Ohio River just a few miles north and west of Florence officially represents the boundary, few take notice of this actual border crossing until they come face to face with the now famous Florence water tower with its unique "Florence Y'all" logo.

Built in 1974 to support a growing suburban infrastructure, the water tower was originally painted with the words "Florence Mall" to herald the future opening of one of the Greater Cincinnati area's premier shopping facilities. Following a blunt reminder from federal highway engineers concerning the illegality of advertising along the interstate highway system for a facility that was yet to open, quick-thinking local officials creatively modified the M pending the completion of the mall. The modifications soon attracted local, regional, and even national attention to the extent that the decision was finally made to make the change permanent. Some would later say that the water tower actually put Florence on the map. Today the tower is closely associated with the identity of Florence and has even been incorporated into the city's logo.

Florence's location in the early 19th century at the intersection of two prominent county roads leading from Burlington and Union with the then-Ridge Road (U.S. 25) gave the small collection of homes and businesses clustered around the intersection the early name of Crossroads. The eventual completion of the Covington to Lexington Turnpike in 1836 quickly spurred additional growth. During these early, formative years, Florence underwent several name changes reflecting the influence of some of the early founding fathers. Formally laid out in 1821 by Thomas Madden, the town was labeled Maddentown or Maddensville. When Madden eventually moved on in 1828, the town was renamed Connersville after Jacob Conner, another prominent early settler to the area. Since an earlier community in nearby Harrison County had laid claim to the name Connersville, the decision was made in 1830 to rename the town Florence after Conner's wife. Lewis Collins's 1847 *History of Kentucky* described Florence as a town containing two churches, three doctors, two stores, two taverns, two schools, four mechanics' shops, and a population of 200.

To local residents born and raised in Florence since 1900, the community, however, will always be known affectionately as Stringtown after John Uri Lloyd's popular turn-of-the-century novel *Stringtown on the Pike*. Lloyd was a celebrated chemist and novelist who grew up in Boone County during the turbulent Civil War and postwar Reconstruction era. His eight novels about the region and numerous contributions to the pharmaceutical industry would bring him national recognition as both an accomplished author and scientist, but he will always be locally remembered first and foremost for capturing and preserving the quaint rural traditions of Boone County.

Those cherished traditions faced a serious challenge following the postwar economic boom generated by World War II. The construction of the Greater Cincinnati/Northern Kentucky International Airport in 1947, coupled with the opening of the Northern Kentucky Industrial

Park in 1959 and the completion of I-75 in 1963, transformed Florence from a sleepy farming community into the bustling suburban hub it is today. Subdivisions and strip malls mushroomed virtually overnight as economic growth and development gravitated away from Main Street Florence toward the thriving junction of Route 18 and I-75. Between 1950 and 1960, with Florence in the forefront, Boone County as a whole grew 68 percent, and the growth rate has continued at no less than 25 percent per decade since 1960.

With a population rapidly approaching 25,000 people, Florence is one of the fastest growing communities in the commonwealth of Kentucky. The challenge facing city and county planners today is how to manage the seemingly limitless expansion radiating outward from Florence without destroying the quality of life that has traditionally made Florence, and Boone County in general, a wonderful place to live and raise a family.

While this book represents a pictorial history of Florence from the Civil War through the early 1960s, to many it no doubt represents little more than a nostalgic glimpse of the past. Admittedly, it does reflect the simplicity of growing up in small-town America during the first half of the 20th century. Perhaps it even reflects the authors' subconscious desire to recapture their own identity with the lifestyle of the 1950s and early 1960s they still so vividly recall. More importantly, however, this book represents a caution to future generations of Northern Kentuckians as to the dangers of advancing the banner of progress too rapidly without thoroughly understanding or preserving their past.

One

STRINGTOWN ON THE PIKE
The Story of John Uri Lloyd

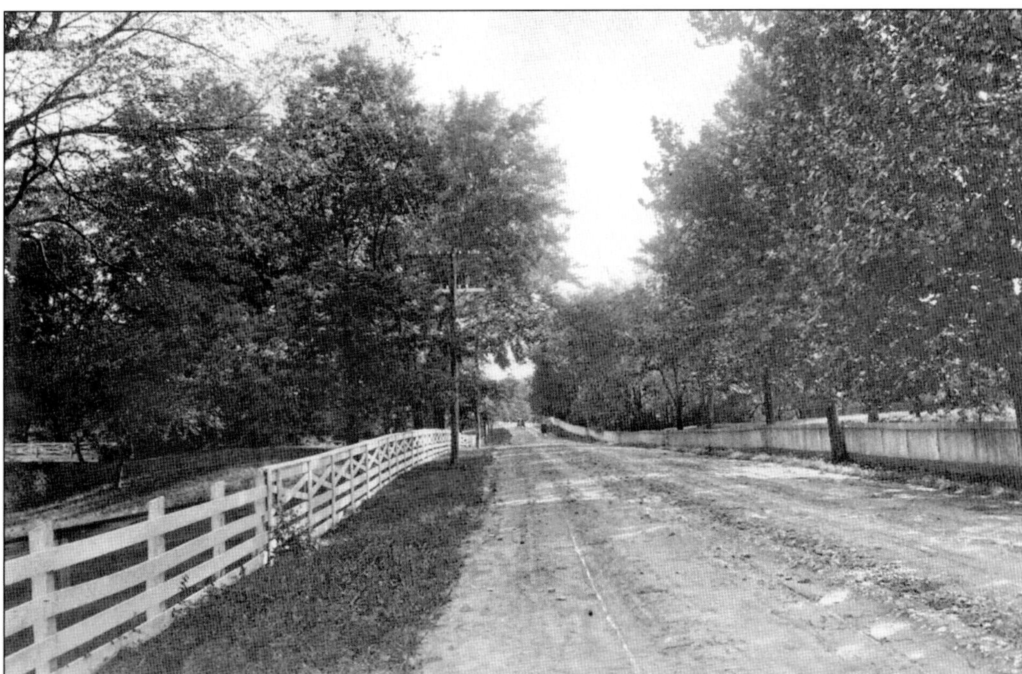

"I love the dust of that old Pike." This statement refers to the Lexington Pike, which ran through Florence and gave rise to John Uri Lloyd's novel *Stringtown on the Pike* in 1900. In a newspaper interview at that time, Lloyd recorded that he chose the name after viewing the town of Florence from a distance, strung out, as he said, along the pike—thus the name Stringtown. He further related that he decided against using Florence in the title, as it sounded too Italian. (Courtesy of Lloyd Library and Museum, Special Collection 106, Box 2, Folder 2.)

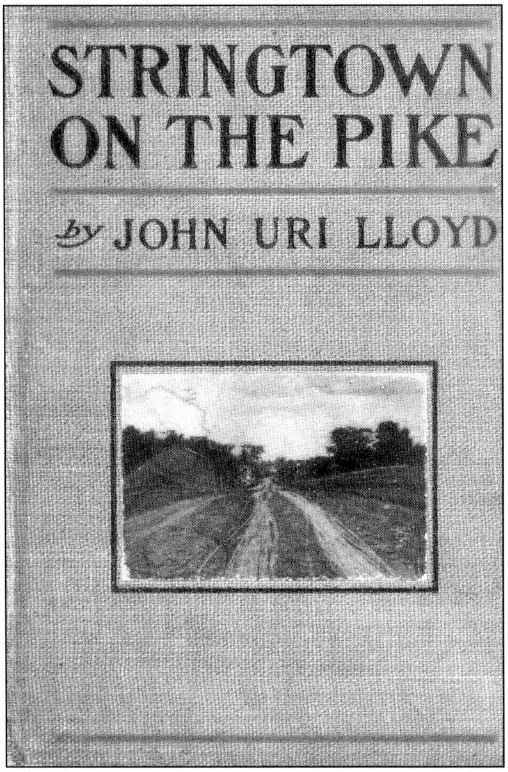

The most famous novel written by John Uri Lloyd was *Stringtown on the Pike*. Published in 1900, the novel reflects Lloyd's interest in local folklore and superstition, while utilizing Northern Kentucky dialect. Although Lloyd would pen eight novels, including *Warwick of the Knobs*, *Red Head*, and *Our Willie*, *Stringtown on the Pike* would remain his most popular work and give Florence its nickname.

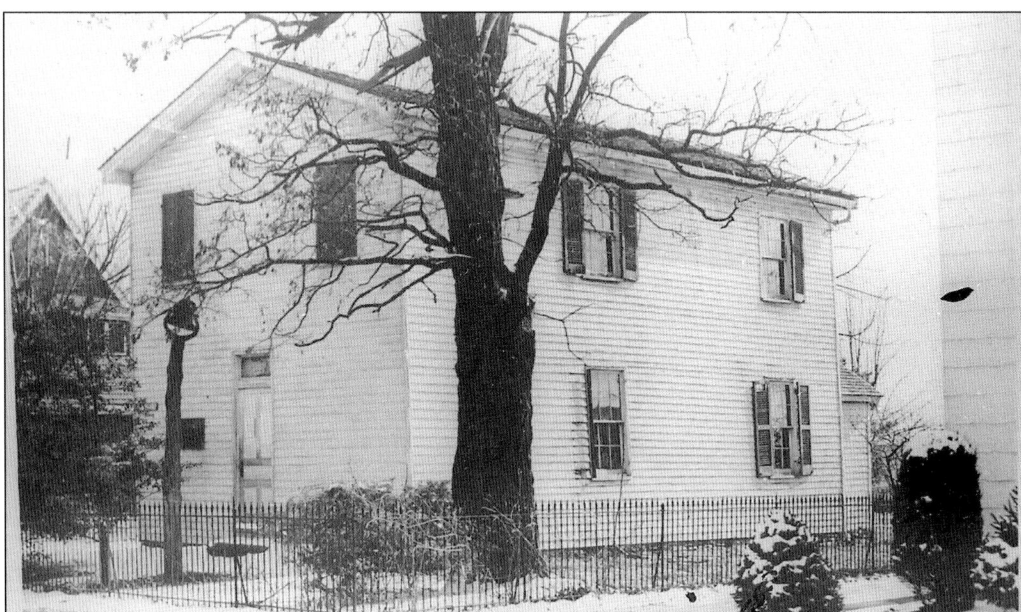

For over 100 years, the old Florence Town Hall stood on the corner of Dortha and Main Streets. Records show that until 1892, the Good Faith Lodge No. 95 F&AM (Free and Accepted Masons) occupied the second floor. The first floor was used as a private school when John Uri Lloyd's father taught there. Over the years, it has been used for meetings by various community groups as well as a polling place.

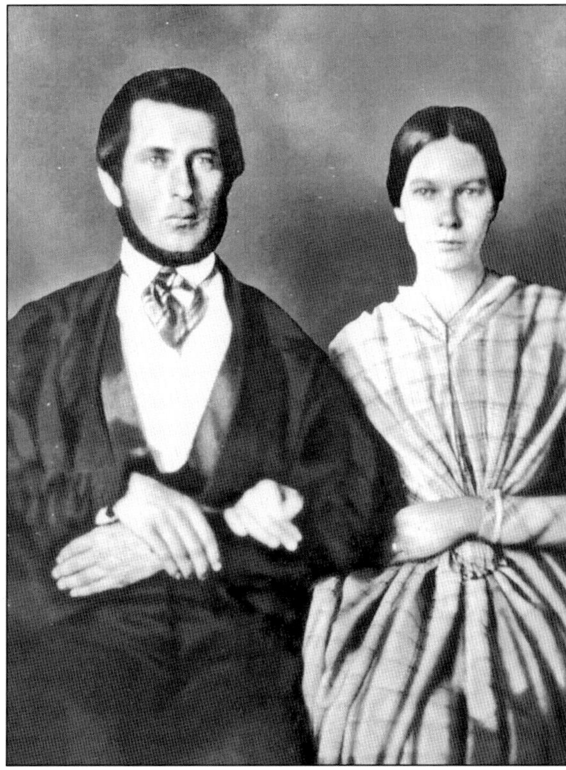

Pictured are Nelson Marvin Lloyd and Sophia Webster Lloyd, the parents of John Uri Lloyd. Mr. Lloyd was a civil engineer and teacher. Arriving in Kentucky from New York in 1853, the family eventually settled in Boone County. Living first in Burlington, and then in Petersburg, the family finally moved to Florence. Nelson conducted a private school in the old town hall during the Civil War era. (Courtesy of Lloyd Library and Museum, Special Collection 106, Box 1.)

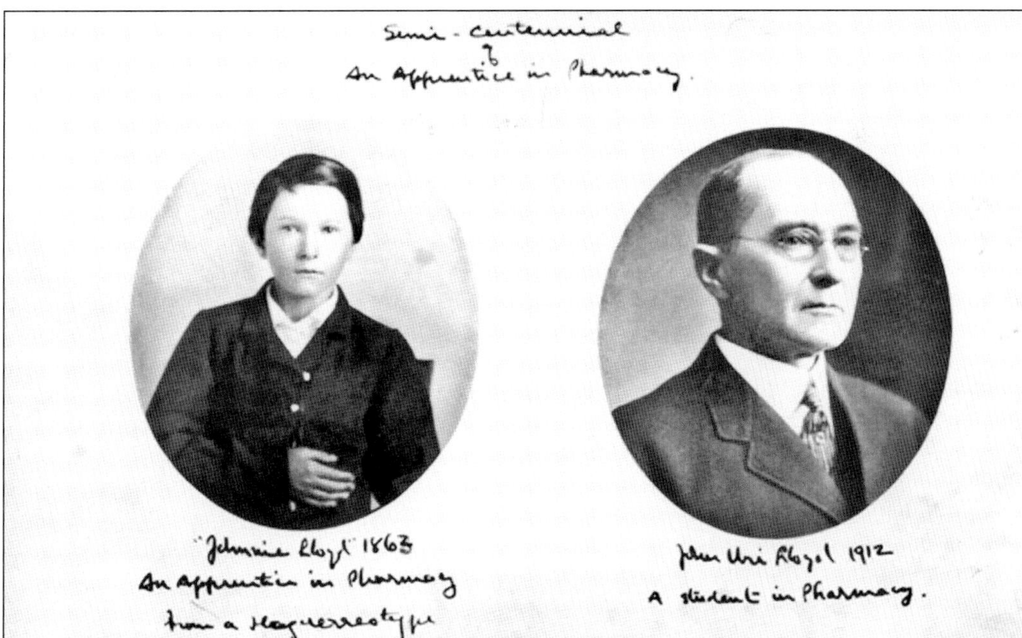

This photo captures a glimpse of a young and a mature John Uri Lloyd. The photo at right was taken in 1863 at the height of the Civil War, when he was a pharmaceutical apprentice. Forty-nine years later, Lloyd was a nationally recognized chemist and author. (Courtesy of Lloyd Library and Museum, Special Collection 106, Box 1.)

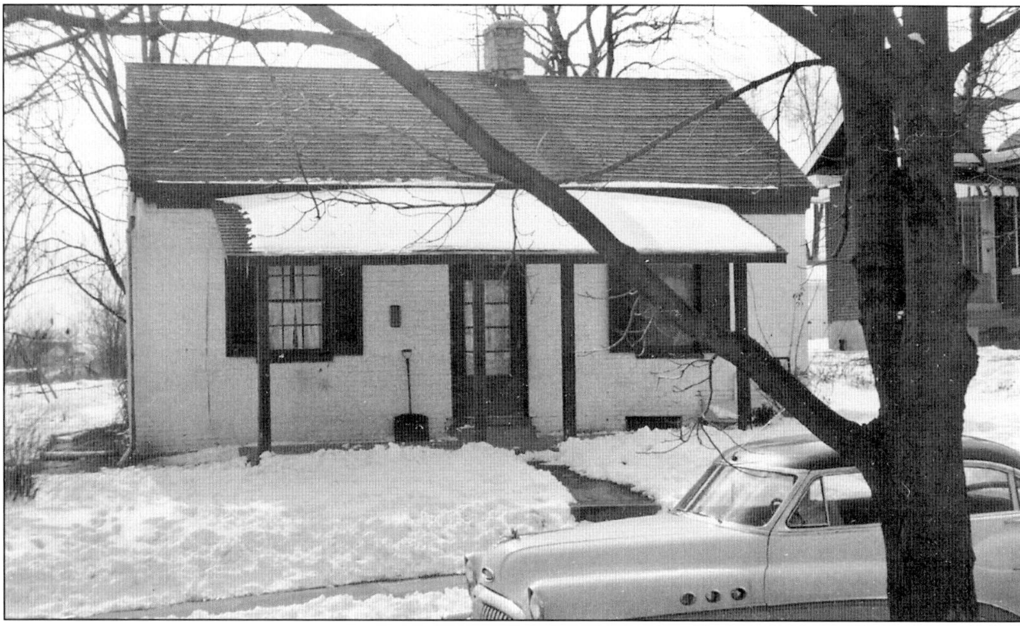

This small antebellum house on Shelby Street was home to Nelson and Sophia Webster Lloyd and their son, John Uri Lloyd. The rich childhood memories from this home provided the nucleus of John Uri Lloyd's book *Stringtown on the Pike*. The front porch seen here in the 1950s was added long after the Lloyd family moved from the home. Soon after this picture was taken, the house was demolished to make way for the Florence Post Office.

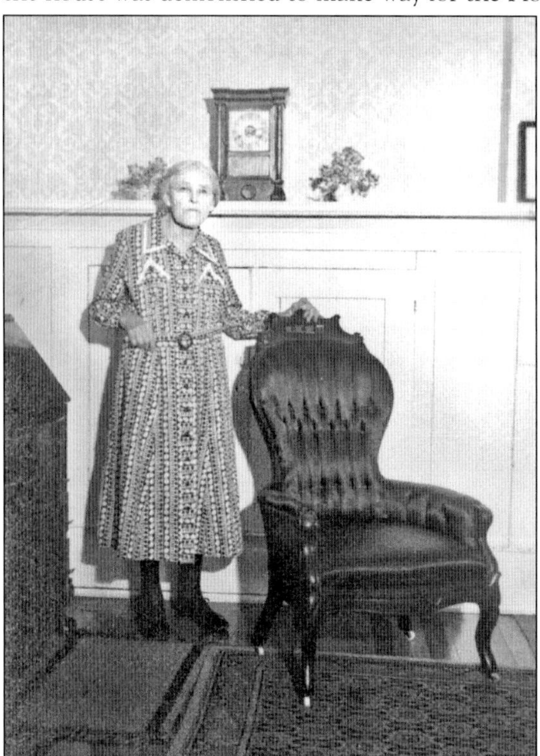

Located on Shelby Street, John Uri Lloyd's boyhood home was maintained by the Lloyd Society. During the weekly meetings held there, members would quilt and enjoy a light lunch. The home was cared for by Mrs. Fannie Clutterbuck, pictured here. Several pieces of Lloyd family memorabilia can also be seen in the picture.

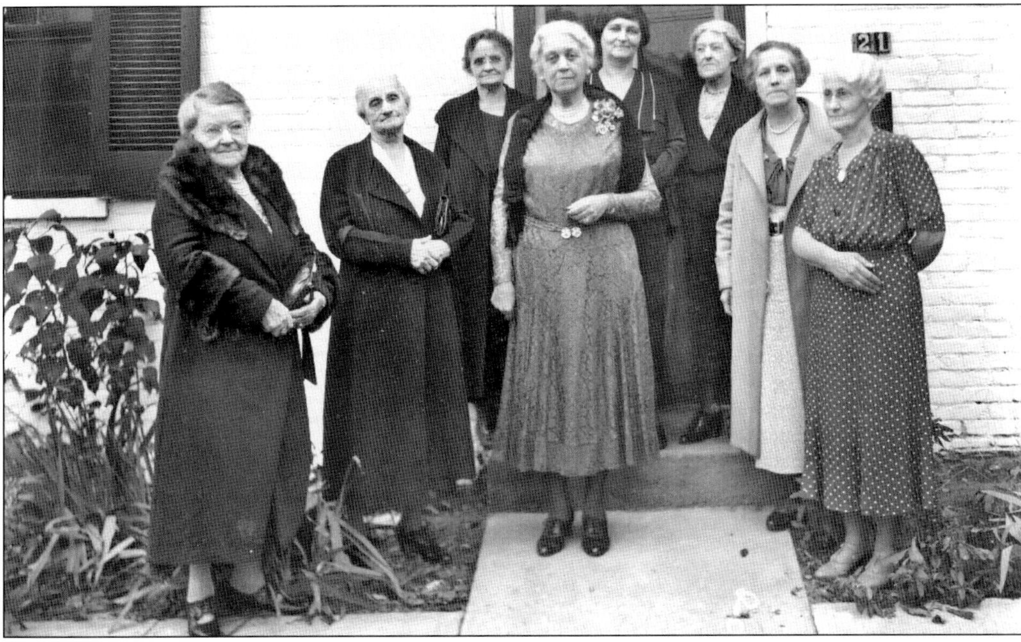

Posing in front of the John Uri Lloyd home at 21 Shelby Street are members of the Lloyd Society. The society's membership was composed of ladies who had been students of John Uri Lloyd's parents, Nelson and Sophia Lloyd, at their school in the old town hall. The society met weekly during the 1930s.

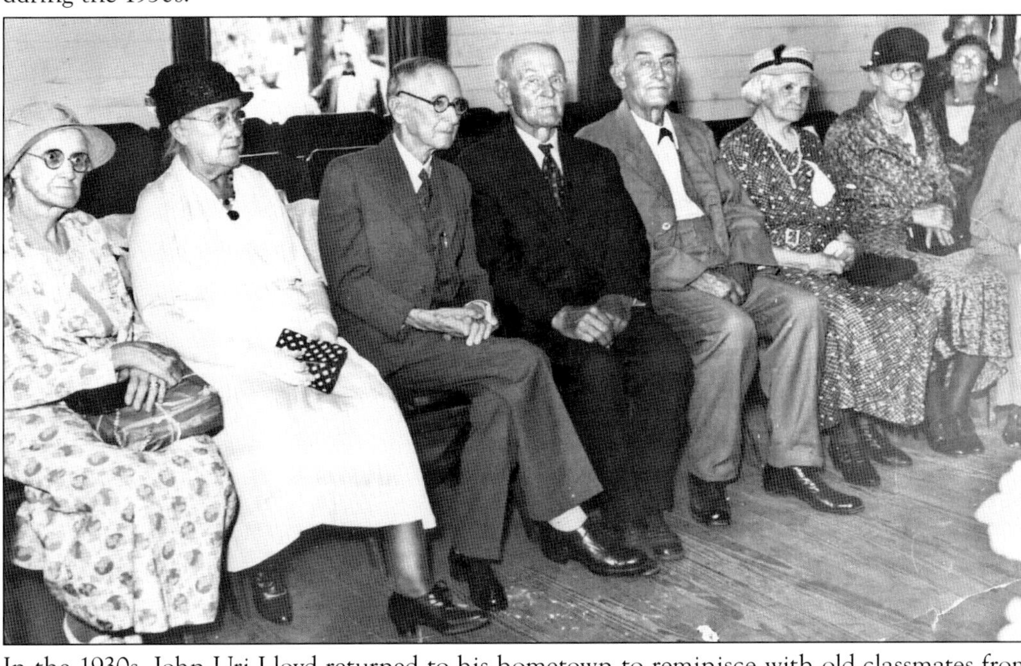

In the 1930s, John Uri Lloyd returned to his hometown to reminisce with old classmates from his father's school. They are seen here in the old town hall that had once functioned as a schoolhouse. Seated from left to right are Fannie Goodridge, Anna G. Price, John Uri Lloyd, Spencer Tanner, B. H. Tanner, Rachael Jones, Mary Lathan, and Nannie C. Hedges. (Courtesy of the Lloyd Library and Museum, Special Collection 106, Box 2, Folder 2.)

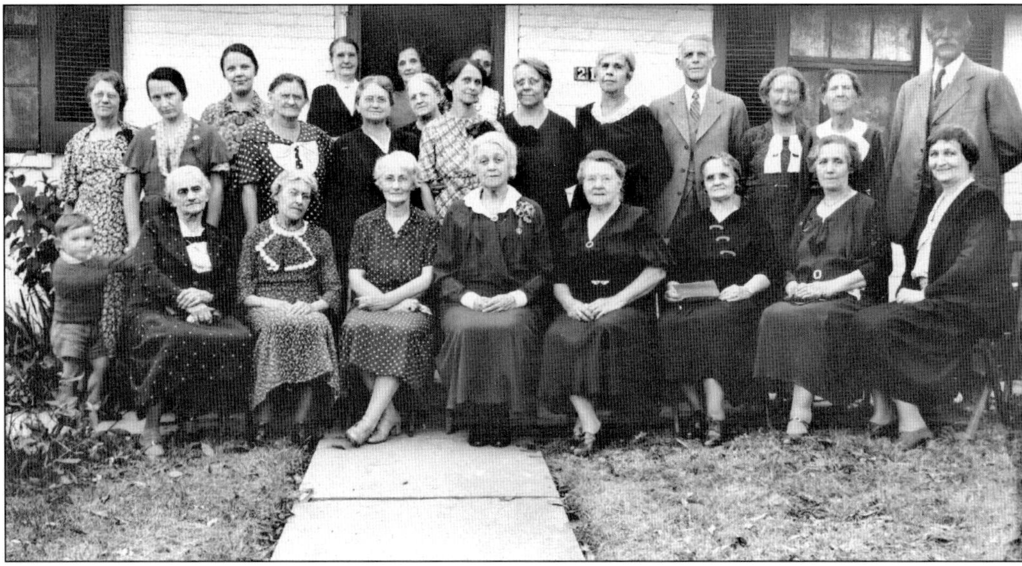

Gathered in front of the John Uri Lloyd home are the members of the Lloyd Society. Founded to honor local scientist and author John Uri Lloyd, the society would meet for years in the original family home on Shelby Street. The society often entertained members of the community at their weekly meeting. Seen here on the bottom left-hand corner of the picture is young Billy Ray Markesbery. Billy would later go on to become Dr. Bill Markesbery, a respected Lexington physician. (Courtesy of Lloyd Library and Museum, Special Collection 106, Box 2, Folder 2.)

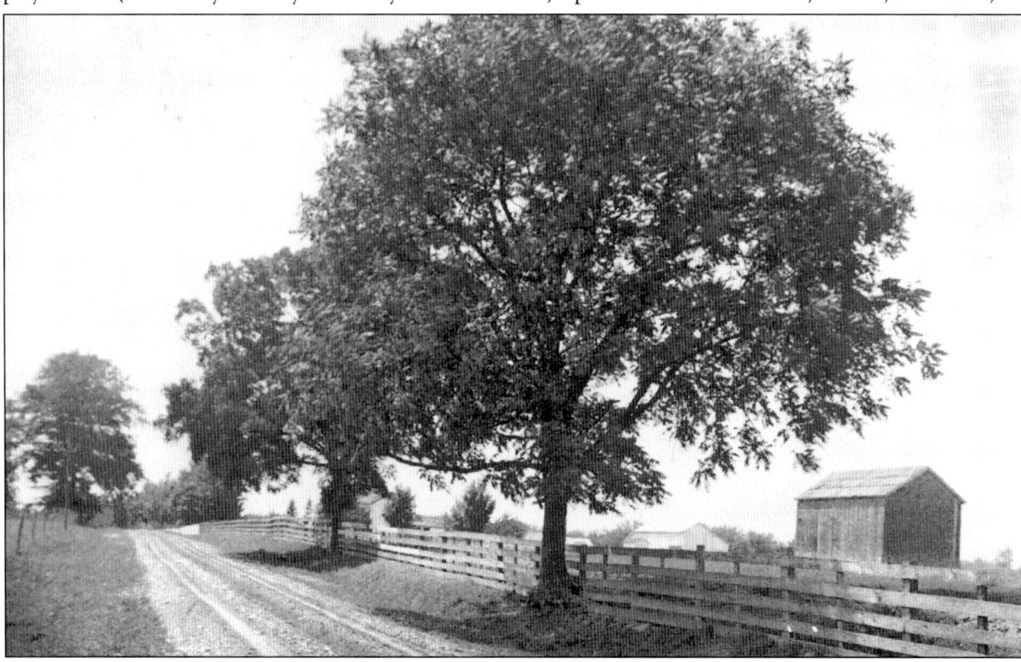

In preparation for his book *Stringtown on the Pike*, John Uri Lloyd snapped this picture, which he labeled the "Hangman's Tree." Lloyd's affection for his boyhood home and surrounding area was incorporated into several of his books. *Stringtown on the Pike* (1900) would give Florence its nickname. In *Our Willie*, he described the Florence fair, while his book *Felix Moses* captured the life and adventures of the popular local Jewish merchant.

Two

War Between the States

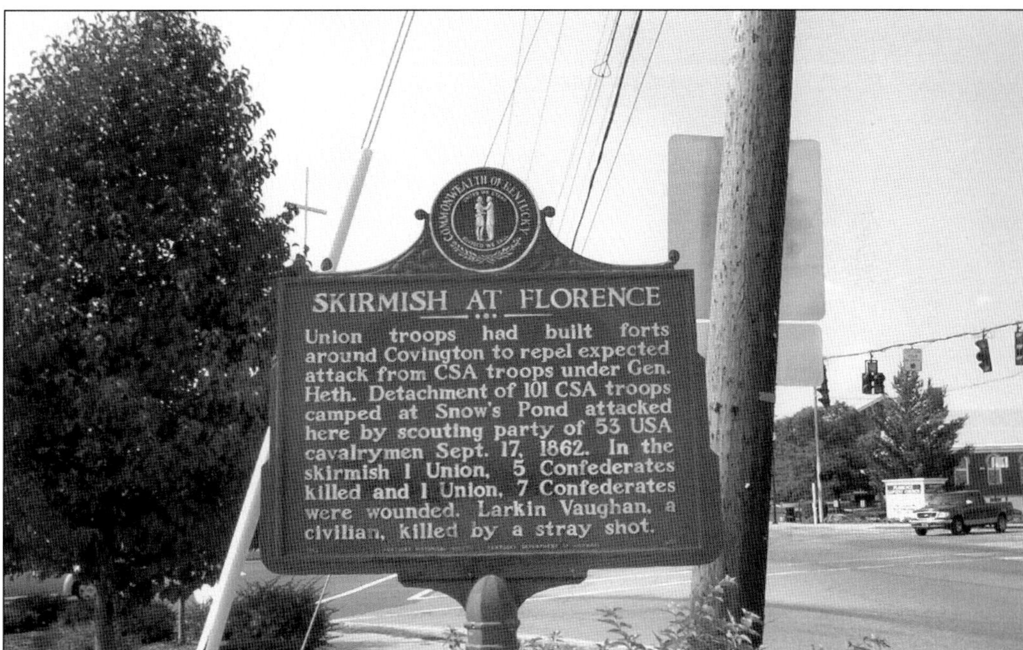

On September 17, 1862, the Civil War came home to the people of Florence, when Union and Confederate forces clashed along the streets of Florence. Confederate forces under Gen. Henry Heth moving north out of Lexington threatened Cincinnati, prompting a Union response. Forts were hastily erected in Northern Kentucky, and Union cavalry patrolled the Lexington Pike looking for the advancing Confederates. A chance encounter sparked a skirmish at the main intersection in town.

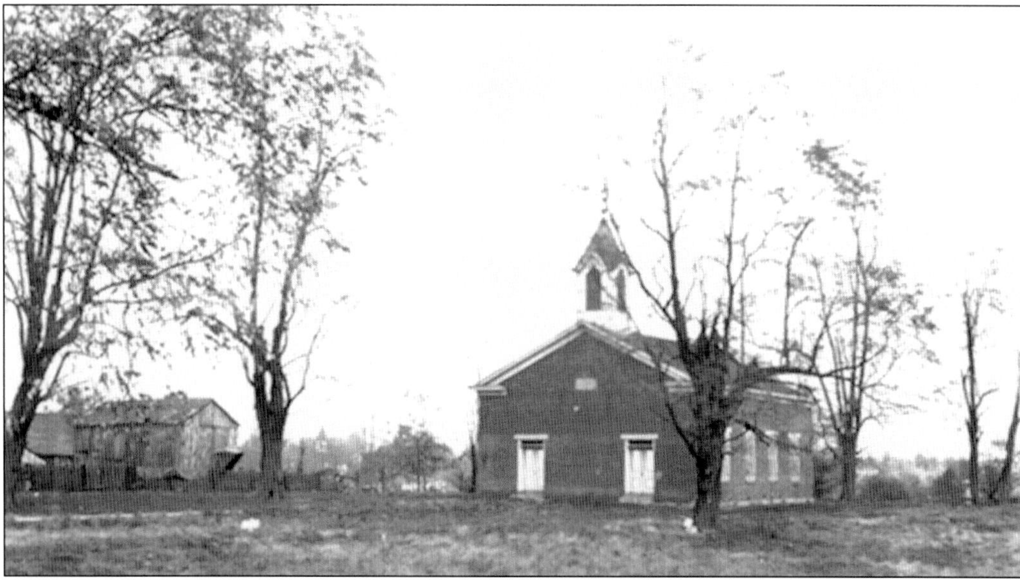

The Florence Baptist Church was barely seven years old when it witnessed the September 1862 skirmish between Union and Confederate troops along the Lexington Pike. During the 1862 invasion of Kentucky, Confederate soldiers threatened strategically important Cincinnati, Ohio, prompting the construction of numerous forts and camps throughout Northern Kentucky. On the back of this photograph taken by John Uri Lloyd is written, "In this yard under the locust trees were laid the wounded of the Raiding and the Raiders."

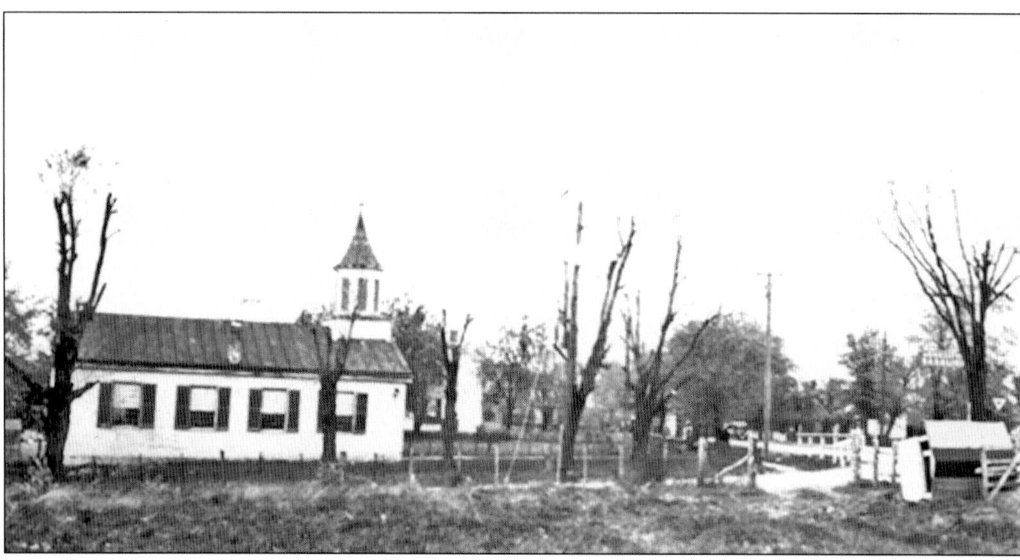

Located at the corner of the Union and Lexington Pikes opposite the Florence Baptist Church, the Florence Christian Church also played a role in the skirmish of Florence. This chance encounter between elements of the 10th U.S. Cavalry and Confederate troops under the command of Gen. Henry Heth resulted in the death of one Union and five Confederate soldiers. Casualties were laid in the grass around the church. General Heth went on to become famous at the Battle of Gettysburg. (Courtesy of Lloyd Library and Museum, Special Collection 106, Box 2, Folder 2.)

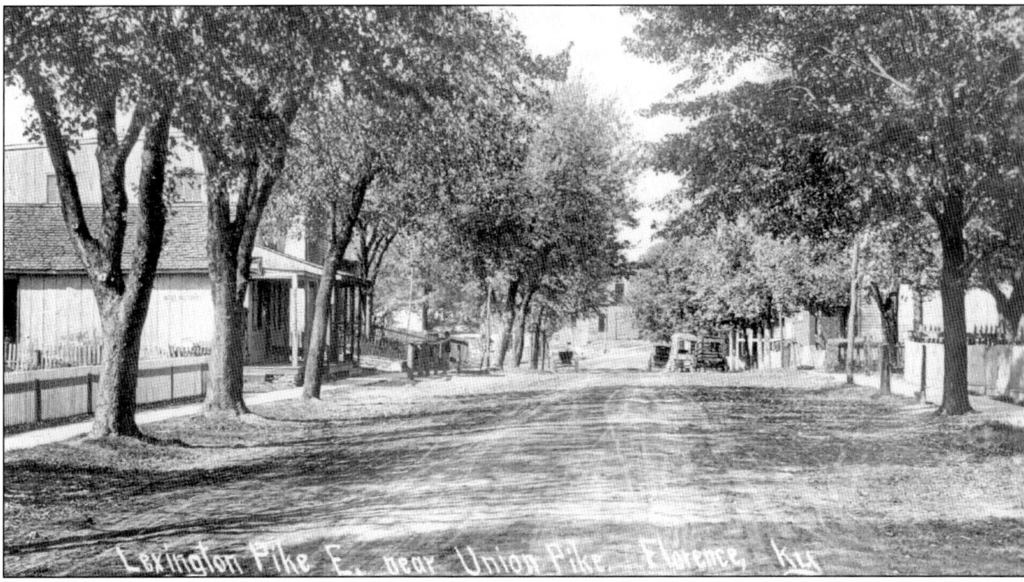

The photographer was standing near the site of the fighting in 1862 when he took this picture looking down Main Street. In the distance is the junction of Shelby Street where, according to some reports, Larkin Vaughn had taken cover in a barn during the skirmish on September 17. While in the barn, he was killed by a stray shot. Other versions of the story say he ventured out into the street during a lull in the fighting and was then shot. In any event, Larkin Vaughn was the only civilian casualty of the fighting. He was buried in the Vaughn family cemetery on Burlington Pike near Houston Road.

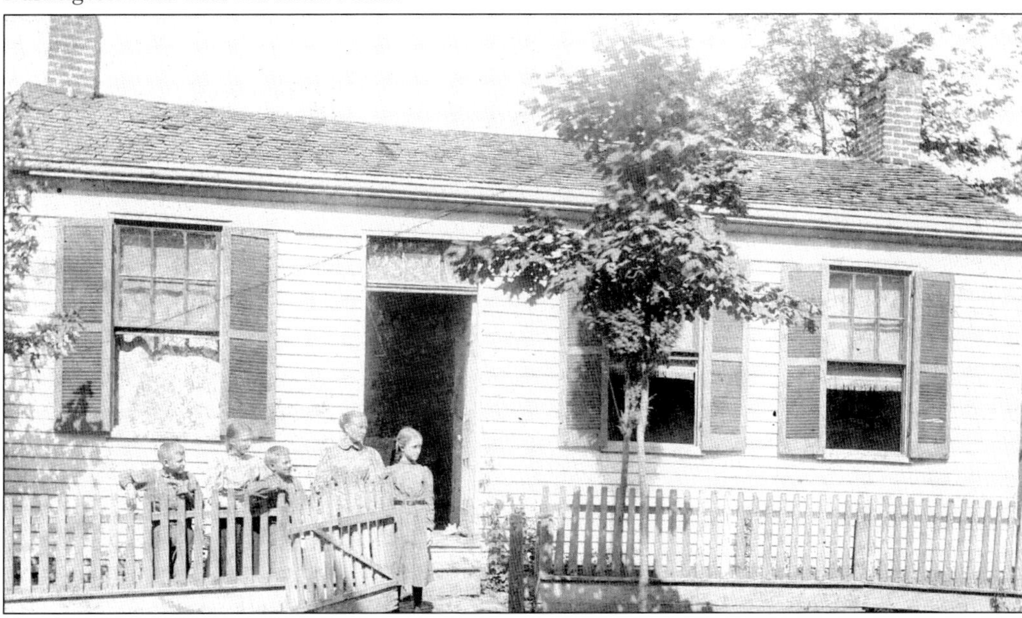

This house on Main Street was the home of Martin and Cora Blankenbeker when this photo was taken in the 1890s. Standing at the gate are Cora and her daughter Maud. In September 1862, as the fighting was raging nearby, the house was struck by stray shots. Thirty years later, bullet holes from those shots could still be seen in the shutters of the house. Today this site is part of the Florence Baptist Church parking lot.

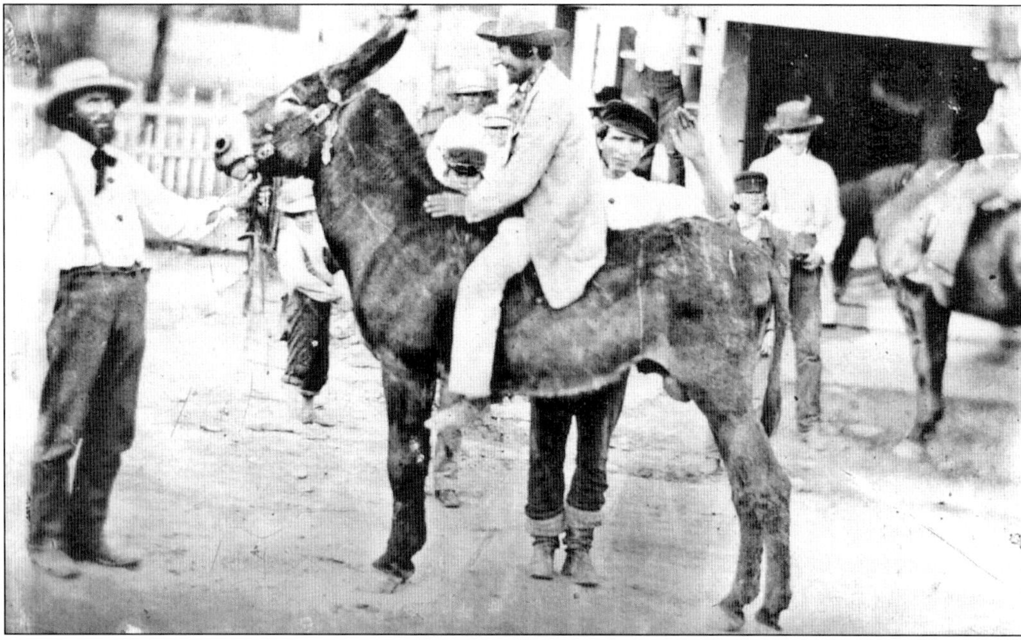

Seen here on the back of a mule is Felix Moses. Moses was an itinerate peddler who traveled the roads of Northern Kentucky. When the Civil War came, Felix joined the Confederate army along with many of the residents of Boone County. Not quite 60 years later, his story was recorded in John Uri Lloyd's historical novel *Felix Moses: The Beloved Jew of Stringtown on the Pike*. This photograph is the only known likeness of Felix. (Courtesy of Lloyd Library and Museum, Special Collection 106, Box 2, Folder 2.)

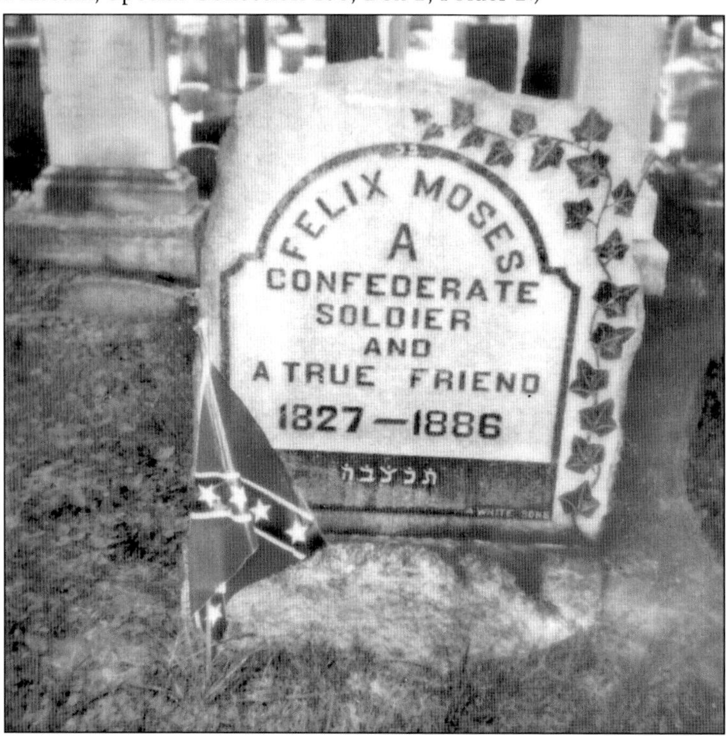

This stone marks the grave of Florence's beloved citizen Felix Moses. After he was found dead in the Ohio River on March 28, 1886, the town of Florence prepared to hold his funeral at the Florence Christian Church. However, several of his Jewish friends arrived from Cincinnati and took his body back to the city to be buried in the Walnut Hills Jewish Cemetery. In 1901, the Daughters of the Confederacy erected this monument in his honor.

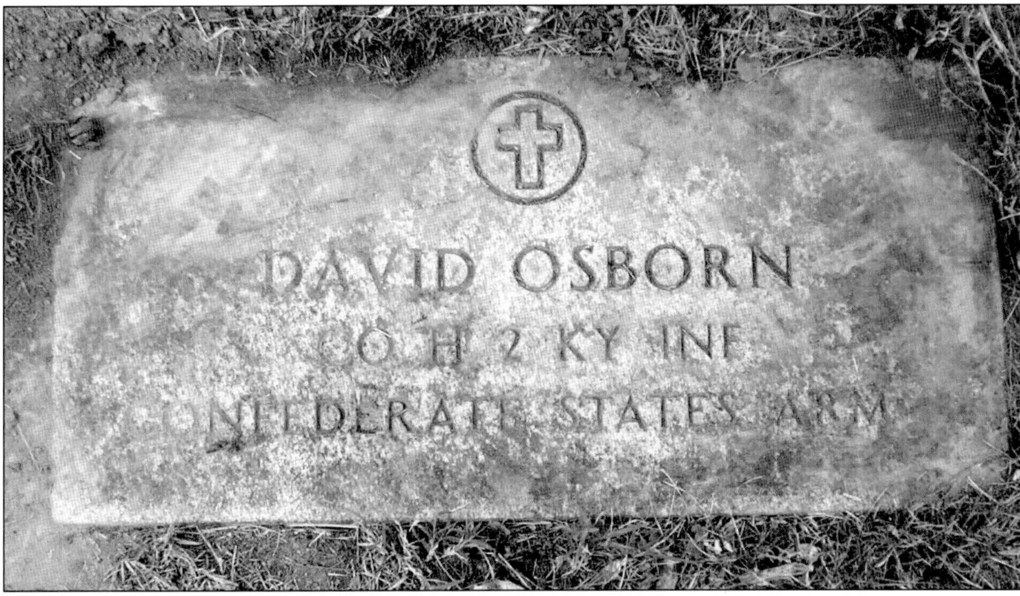

At the outbreak of the Civil War, David Osborn was 19 years old. Like many Boone County natives, his sympathies lay with the South. In September 1861, he joined the famous "Orphan Brigade" organizing just over the border in neighboring Tennessee. The Orphan Brigade, composed primarily of Kentuckians, amassed one of the most distinguished service records in the entire Confederate army. As a member of Company H, 2nd Kentucky Infantry, Osborn was wounded at the Battle of Fort Donelson in February 1862. Records indicate that he attended the 1886 funeral of Felix Moses, one of his comrades in arms. David Osborn is buried in Florence Cemetery.

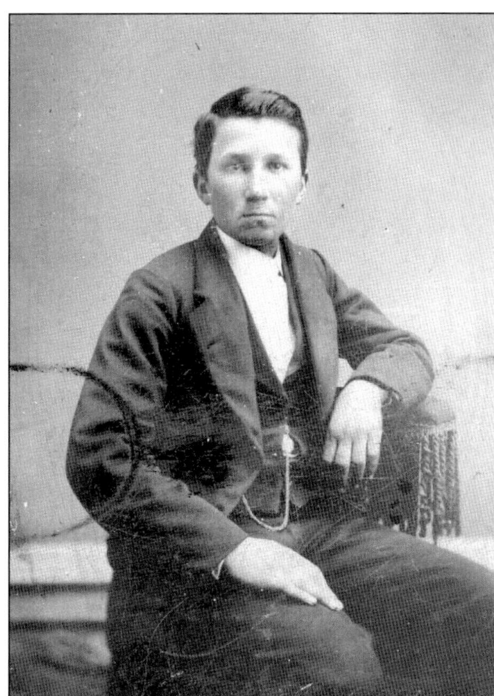

The inhabitants of Northern Kentucky reflected divided loyalties between North and South. Unfortunately, this division did not necessarily end with the surrender at Appomattox Court House. Lingering sympathies were often reflected in not so subtle ways. Seen here as a young man is Stonewall Jackson Clutterbuck.

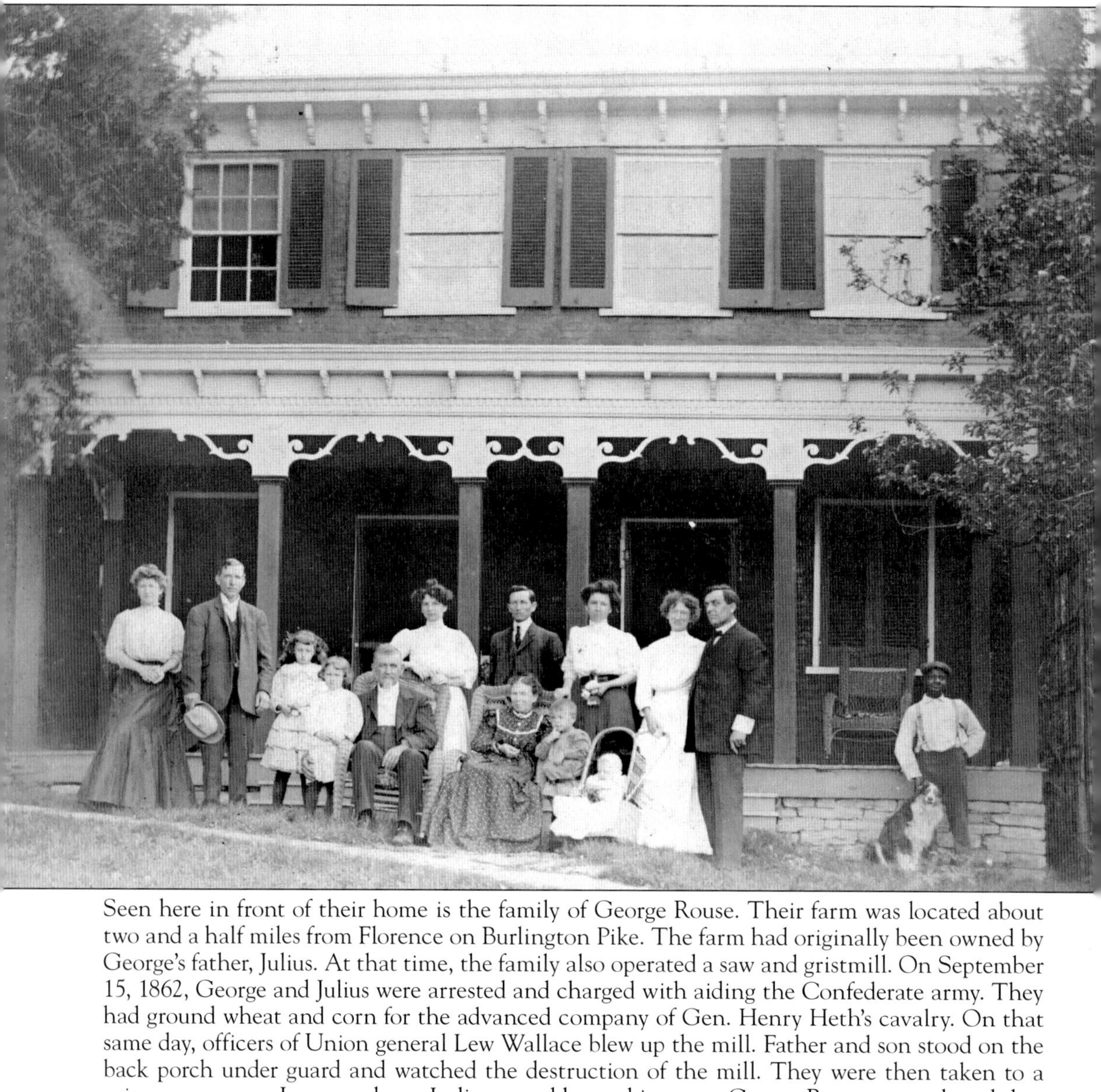

Seen here in front of their home is the family of George Rouse. Their farm was located about two and a half miles from Florence on Burlington Pike. The farm had originally been owned by George's father, Julius. At that time, the family also operated a saw and gristmill. On September 15, 1862, George and Julius were arrested and charged with aiding the Confederate army. They had ground wheat and corn for the advanced company of Gen. Henry Heth's cavalry. On that same day, officers of Union general Lew Wallace blew up the mill. Father and son stood on the back porch under guard and watched the destruction of the mill. They were then taken to a prison camp near Lawrenceburg, Indiana, and housed in tents. George Rouse remembered that every Sunday visitors would come and roam through the camp pulling back their tent flaps and staring at them as if they were wild animals. Eventually they took the oath of allegiance to the Union and were allowed to go home.

Three

MAIN STREET

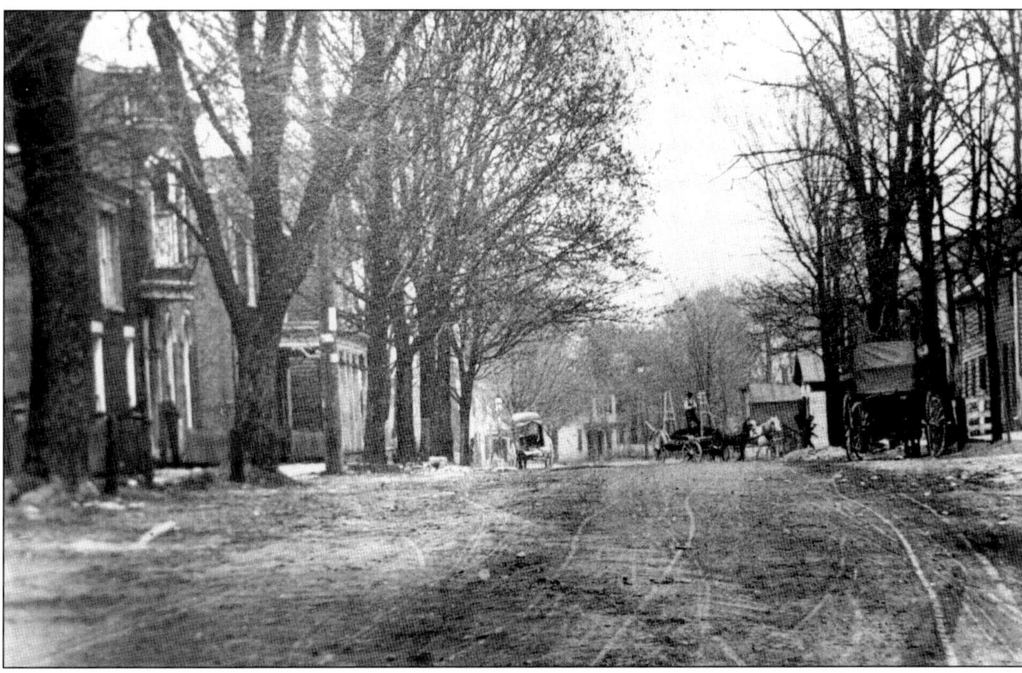

Buggy and wagon tracks mark this *c.* 1900 view of Main Street. The driver of the wagon in the center of the picture is thought to be a member of the Bauers family. Notice only three vehicles appear on the unpaved street.

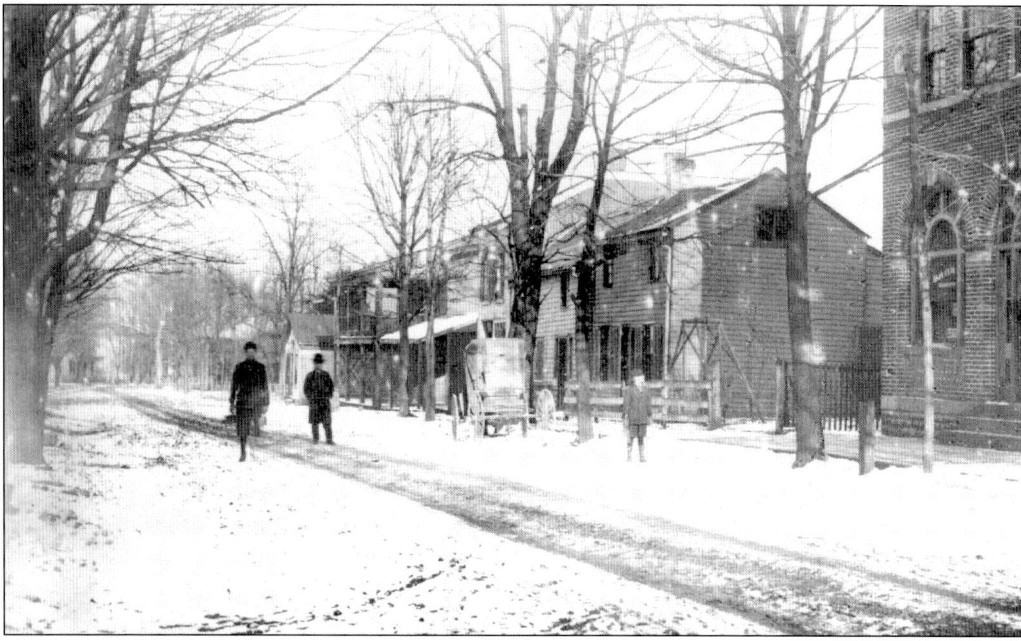

After a light snow, the photographer snapped this picture of central Main Street. As the Florence Deposit Bank building can be seen in the extreme right of the picture, it must be sometime after 1904. As was typical of the time, there is no rush of traffic on the street, and only three pedestrians venture out in the weather.

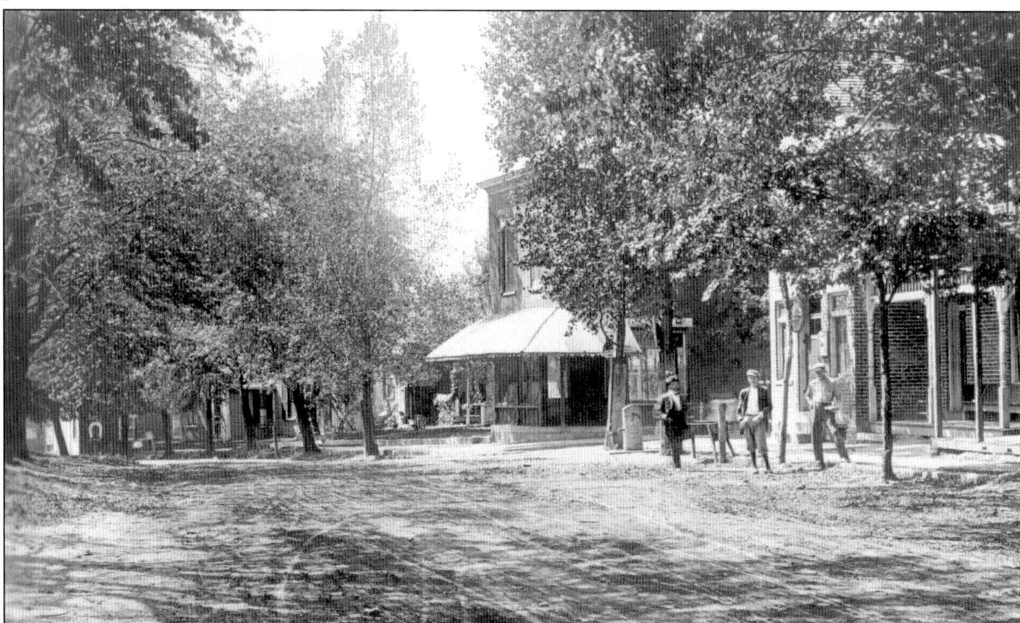

This view of the junction of Main and Girard remains one of the least changed today. Although the trees are gone, the two buildings on either side of Girard remain. During its history, the building to the left, with the awning, has housed numerous businesses, including several groceries, hardware stores, the post office, and a blacksmith. The building to the right has also housed the post office, a saloon, and various offices.

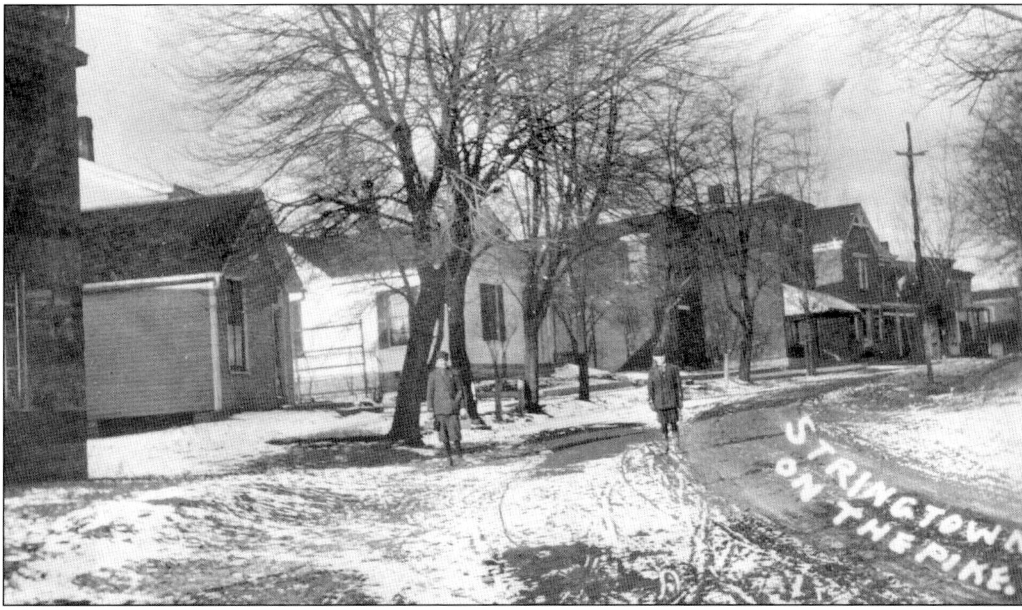

The view from the junction of Shelby and Main is from a series of postcards printed around 1910. The photographer has capitalized on the fame of John Uri Lloyd to label Main Street "Stringtown on the Pike." Just visible in the left-hand corner is Bradford Brothers Carriage Shop. Advertised in local papers as manufacturers of fine carriages, buggies, and phaetons, their ad stated that "their vehicles are made to stand the wear and tear of Boone County roads."

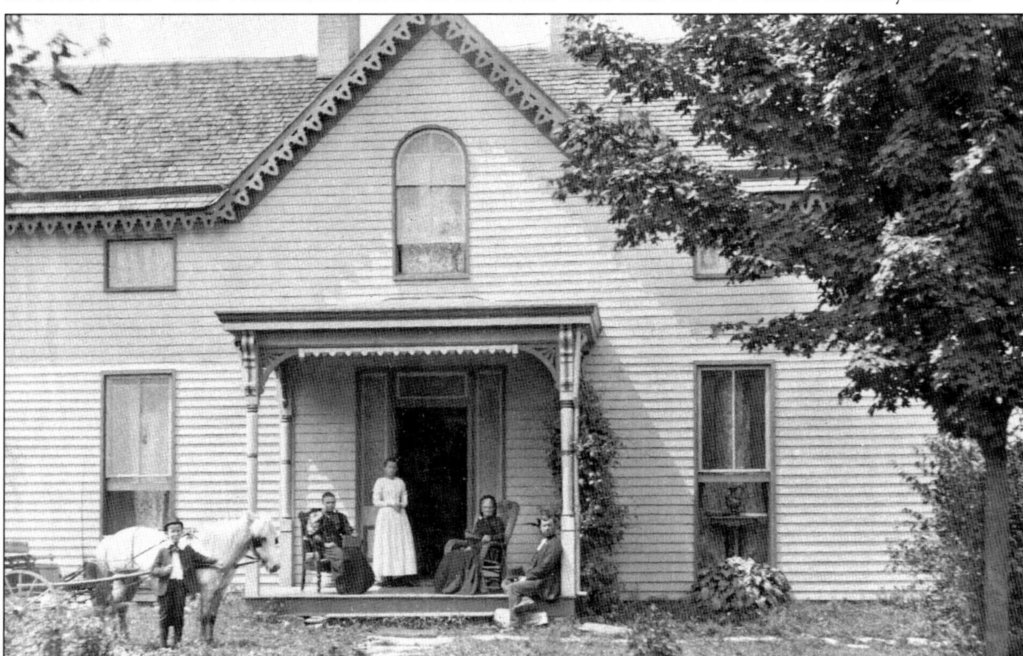

Seen here in front of their home on Main Street is the family of Jim Carpenter. A butcher by trade, Carpenter owned a butcher shop near where Denham's Drugstore would later stand. The Carpenter property included what would become the intersection of Turfway and Dixie Highway. Today the Florence Post Office is located on this site.

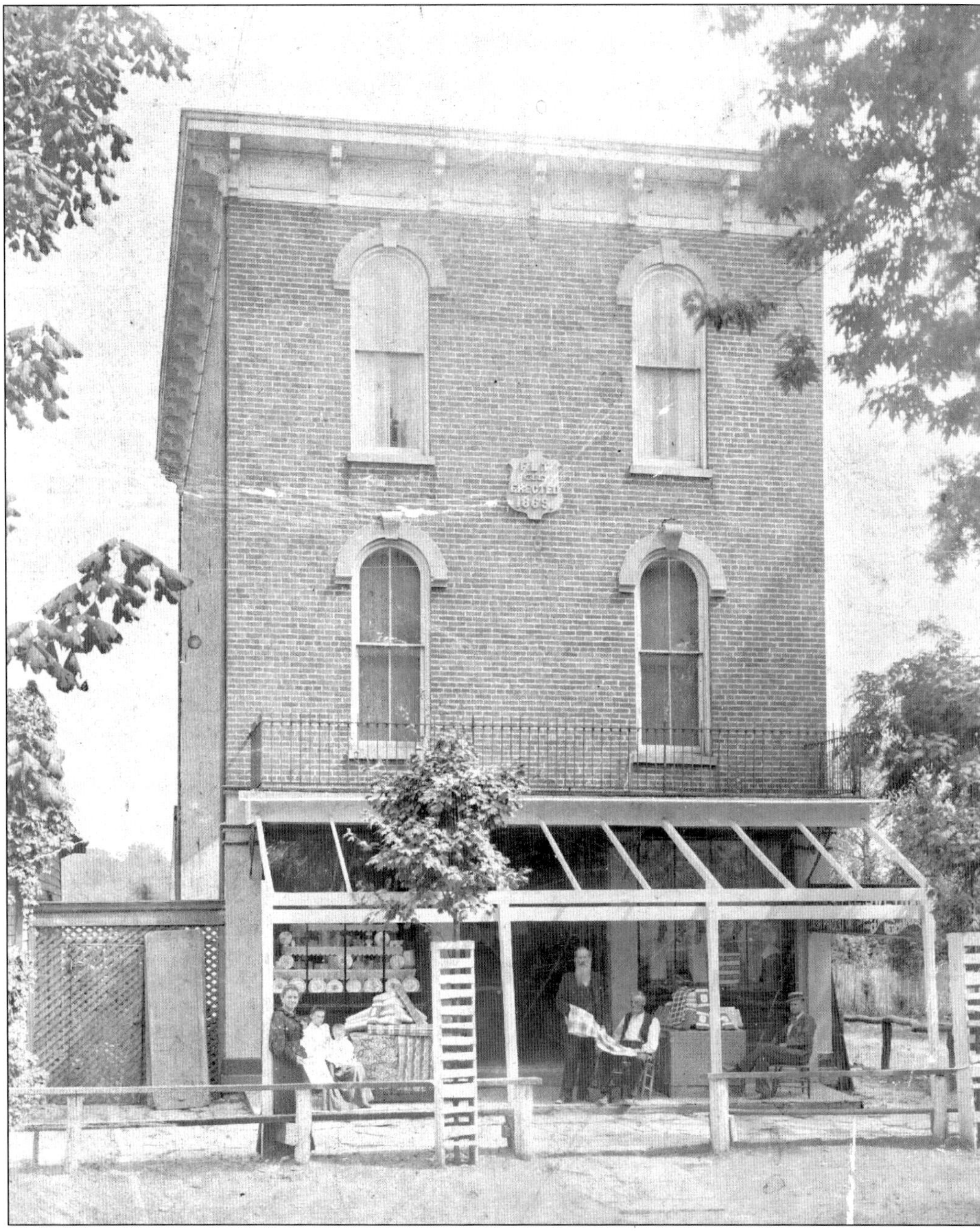

Built in 1869, the Odd Fellows Building has dominated the corner of Main and Youell for almost 140 years. The three-story building was for many years the tallest building in Florence. The first floor has been occupied by many businesses during this time. This photograph was taken around 1895. By the early 20th century, Henry Olsner and Son had their drugstore here. Later, Mentor Martin, followed by the Riddell family, sold groceries here. The second floor was used as an auditorium. Plays were staged, dances were held, and community dinners were prepared for various charitable events. The third floor was the exclusive domain of the Imperial Order of the Odd Fellows. An active organization at that time, its large membership of men met on Saturday nights. In short, the building was a longtime center of Florence community life.

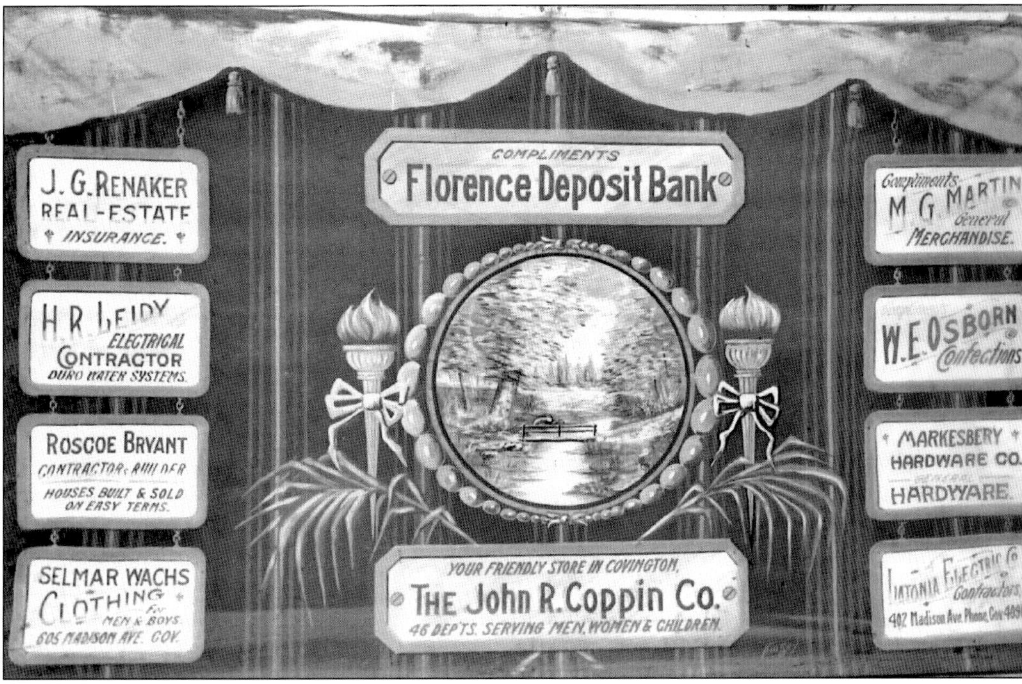

The second floor of the Odd Fellows Building was used as an auditorium. The curtain seen here hung at the back of the stage. Prominent among the Florence advertisers was the Florence Deposit Bank. Among other Florence merchants included were M. G. Martin, whose grocery occupied the first floor of the building; W. E. Osborn; Markesbery Hardware Company; and J. G. Reneaker.

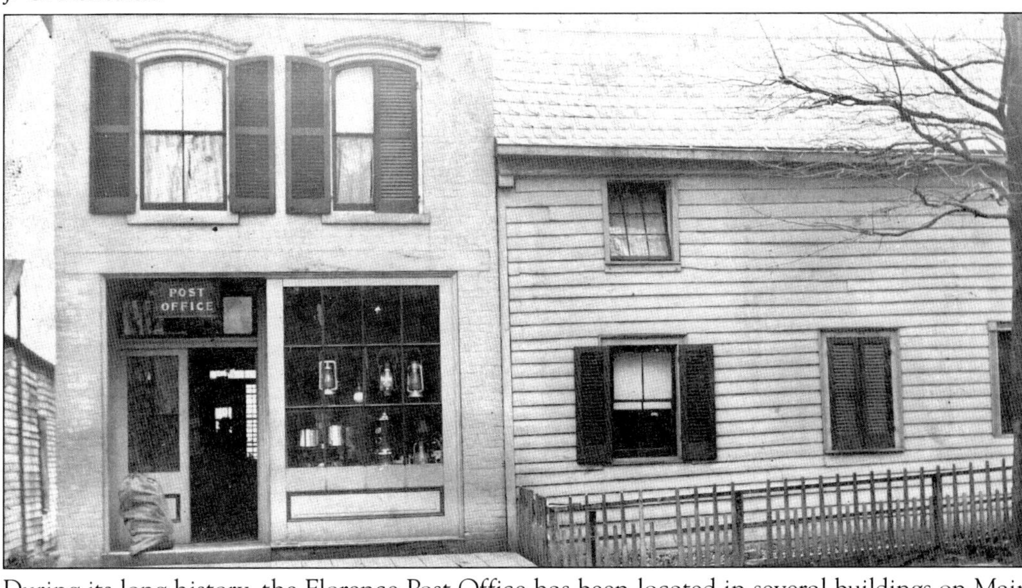

During its long history, the Florence Post Office has been located in several buildings on Main Street. Prior to the advent of rural free delivery, all mail was sent "General Delivery," which required patrons to pick up their mail at the post office. As a result, the post office became a community gathering place where locals exchanged news and gossip while they waited for the mail to be sorted. The post office seen here was housed in Jim Tanner's hardware store.

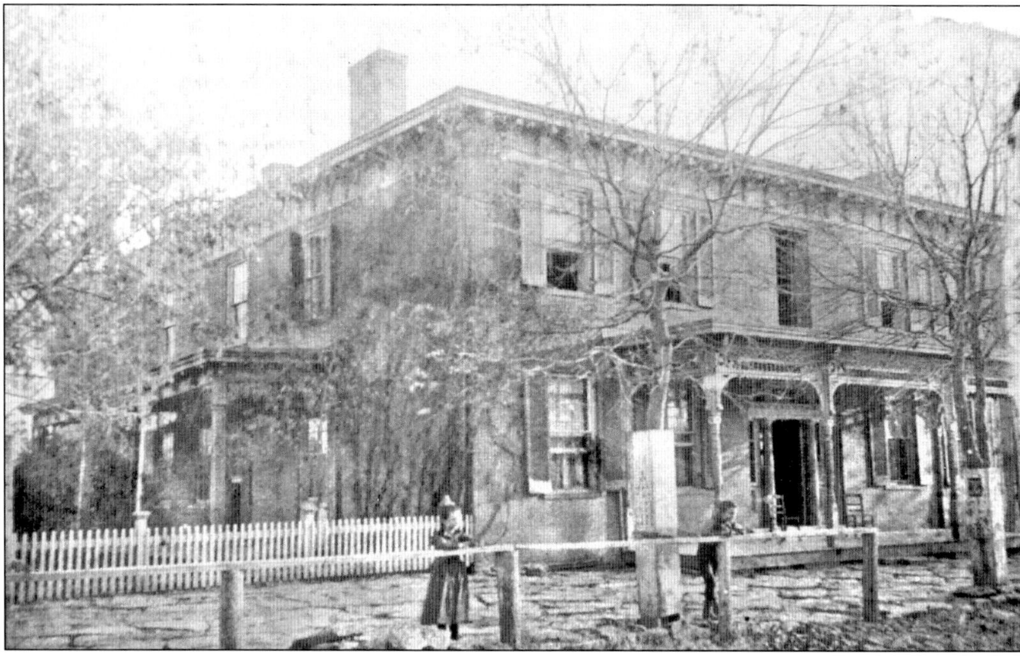

The Southern Hotel, on the corner of Main and Youell Streets, offered a touch of elegance to travelers staying overnight in Florence. In the 1883 *Atlas of Boone County*, Mrs. E. V. Grant is listed as the proprietor. The hotel was razed in the early part of the 20th century to make way for a new family home. Today descendants of Mrs. Grant still reside there.

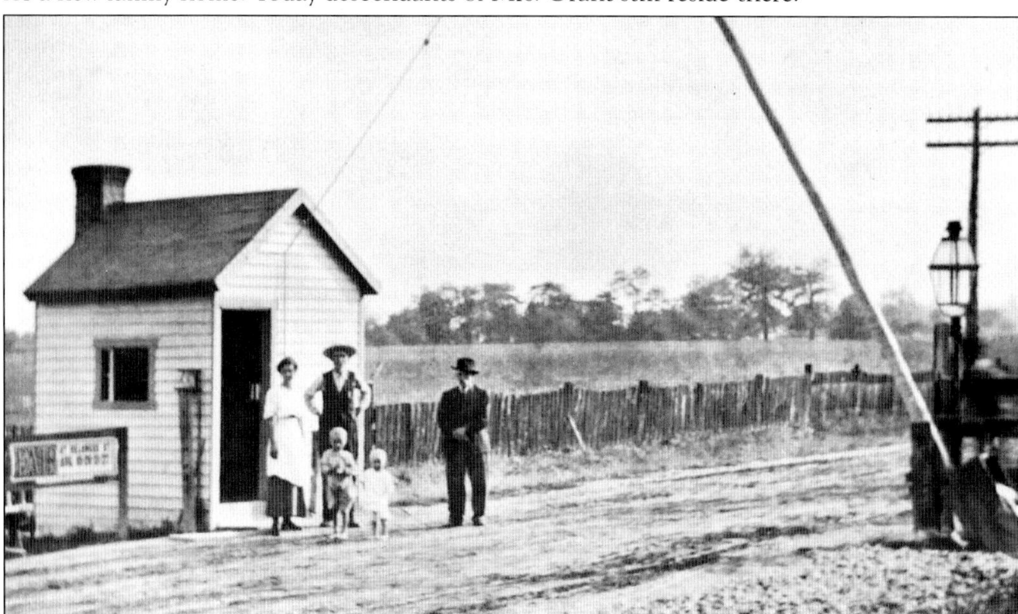

The early highway system in Kentucky was financed through the construction of toll roads. One of the first toll roads constructed was the present Dixie Highway, known then as the Covington-Lexington Turnpike. The road varied between 16 and 20 feet in width and was one of the few "macadamized" (crushed stone) roads in the commonwealth. The tollgate pictured here was near today's Goodridge Drive.

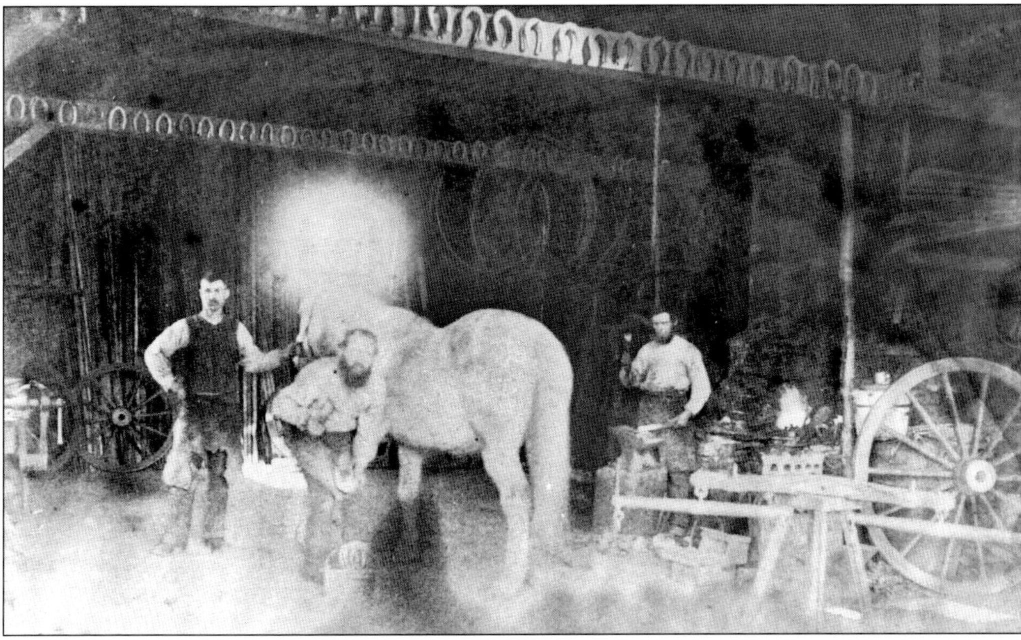

Seen here is the interior of Fred Reich's Blacksmith Shop located on Main Street. In the 1883 Florence business references, Reich's advertisement states that "horse-shoeing and repairing will receive prompt attention." In this picture, employee Mart Blankenbeker holds the horse's head, while Reich shoes the horse.

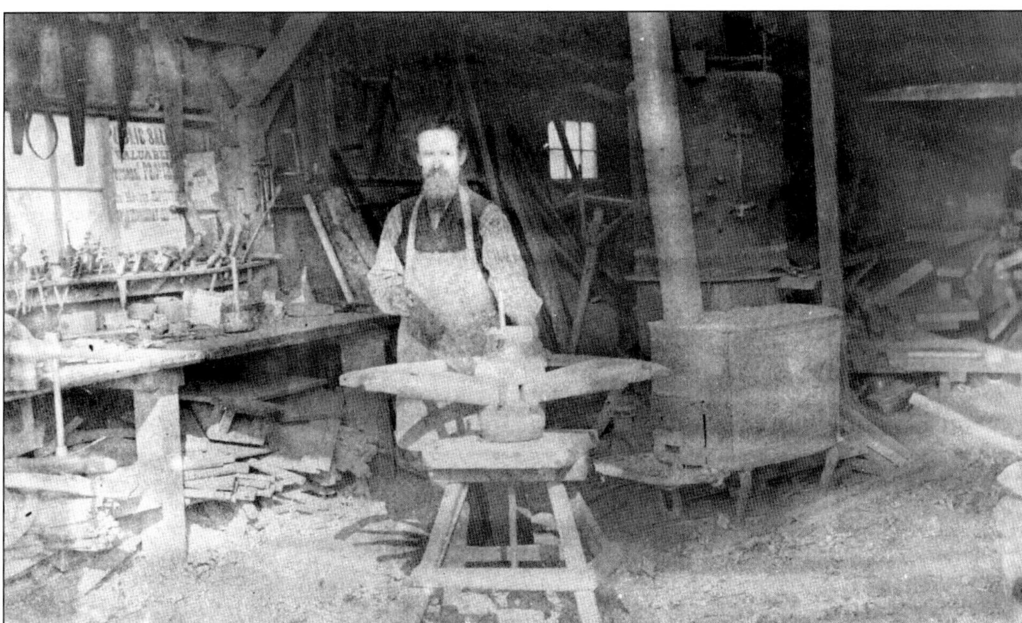

Working in his shop is wagon maker William Henry Tanner. Tanner's shop and his home were located on Main Street. According to a contemporary account, "a Tanner made wagon, denotes quality and long life of service." In addition to his work as a wagon maker, Tanner also served as Florence city clerk. Although he died in 1911, several of his wagons were still functioning well into the 1940s.

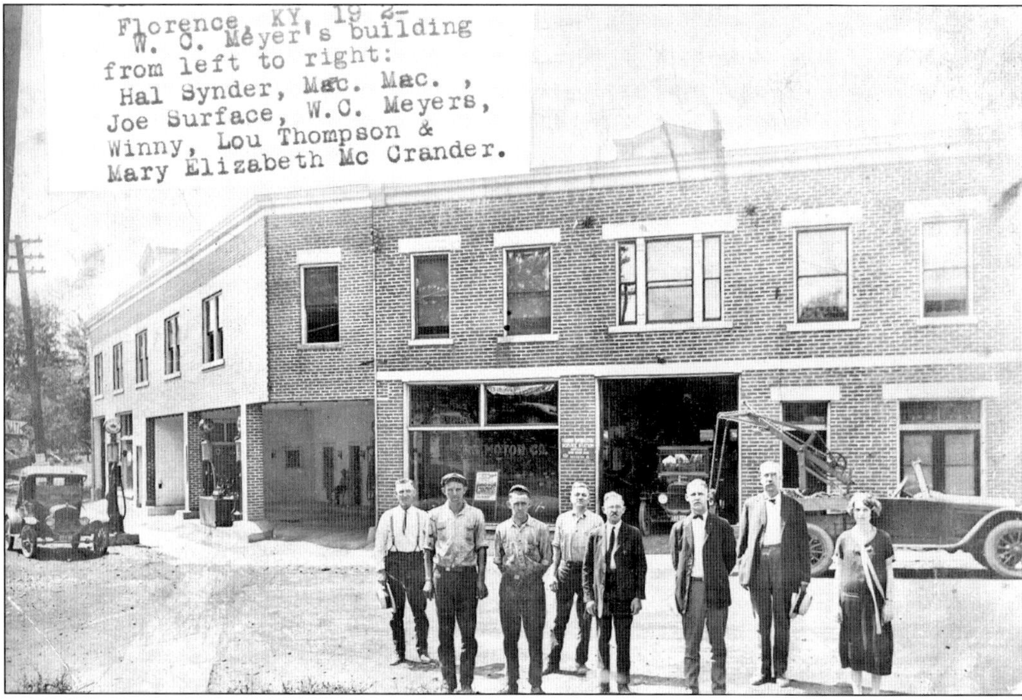

Seen here in the 1920s, the landmark Meyer's Building, at the corner of Main and Shelby, was home to the Meyers Motor Company. Pictured in front of the building are, from left to right, Hal Snyder, two unidentified employees, Joe Surface, W. C. Meyer, Winfield Meyer, Lou Thompson, and Mary Elizabeth McCrander. Notice the early tow truck and gas pumps behind the employees. Later occupants of the building included a market, a barbershop, and the offices of Dr. Harry Daughtery.

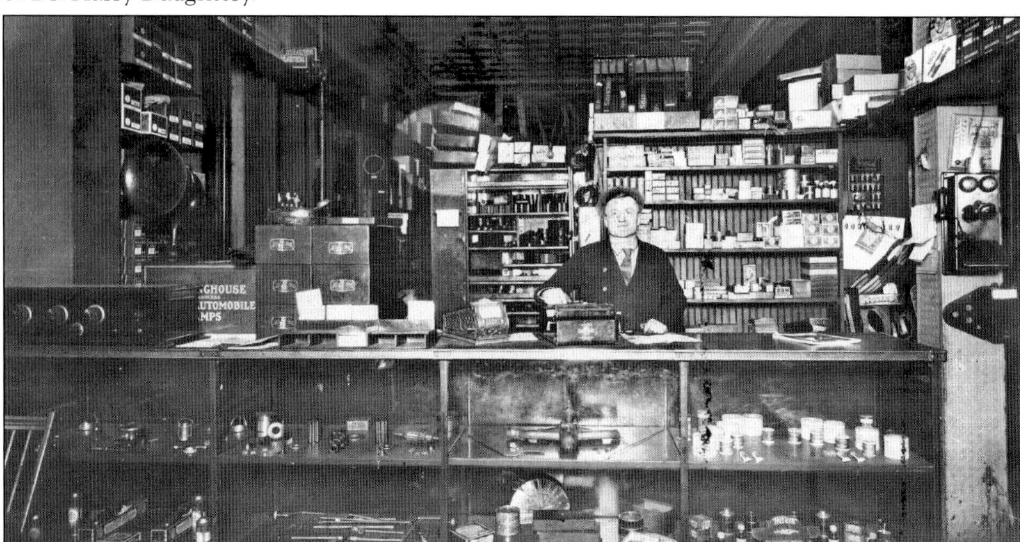

Seen here behind the counter of the parts department of Meyers Motor Company is Joe Surface. The company offered a full range of automotive services to the people of Florence. In an era when many people performed their own auto repairs, the Meyers garage proved to be a valuable asset to the community. It enjoyed a reputation of quality sales and service.

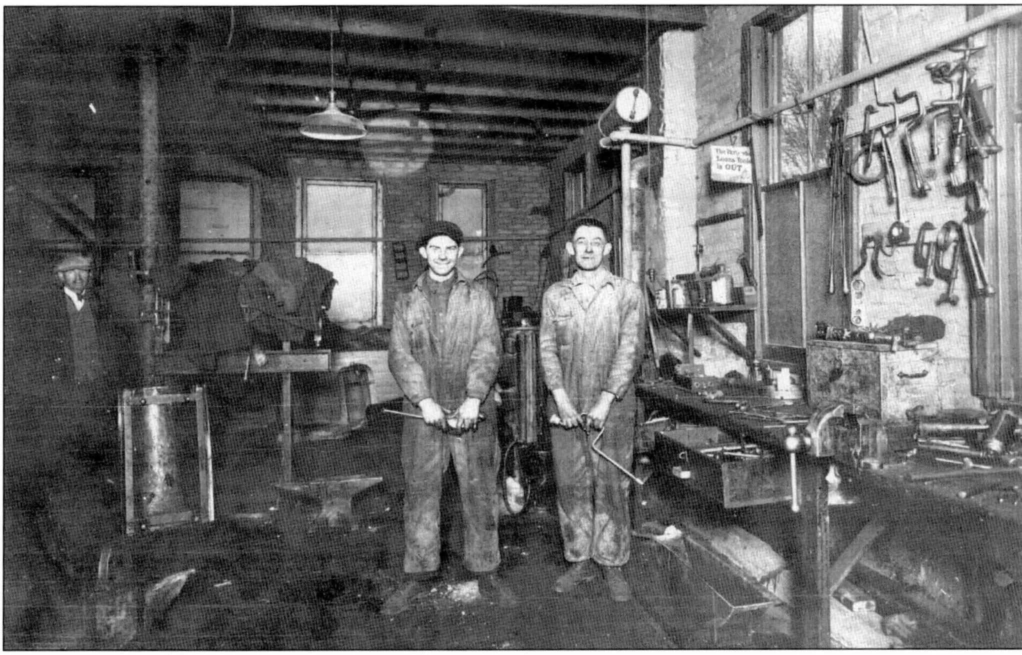

Garages in the late 1920s and early 1930s looked a lot different than today. Missing are all of the diagnostic machines required to repair today's computer-assisted engines. Mechanics relied on their own knowledge and experience to keep engines running. Around 1928, in the interior of Meyer's Garage, John Newman (left) and Henry Carpenter take a break from their work. The small sign visible on the right states humorously that "the party who loans tools is OUT."

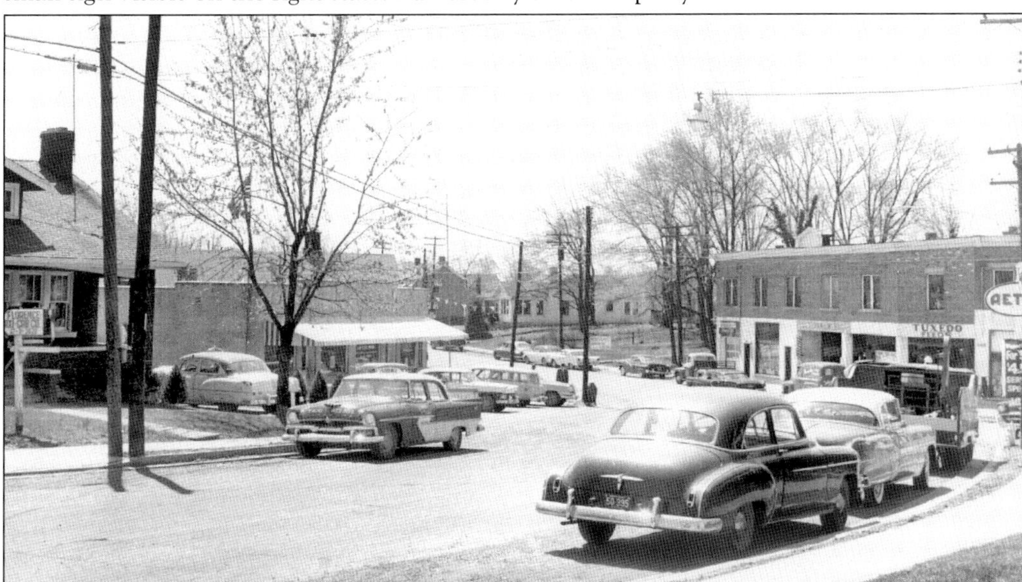

When this photograph was taken around 1960, the landmark Meyer's Building still stood at the corner of Main and Shelby Streets. Located on the second floor was the office of Dr. Harry R. Daughtery. Across Main Street was the yellow-brick building that housed the post office and the Florence Building and Loan. The post office remained here until it was relocated on Shelby Street in the early 1960s.

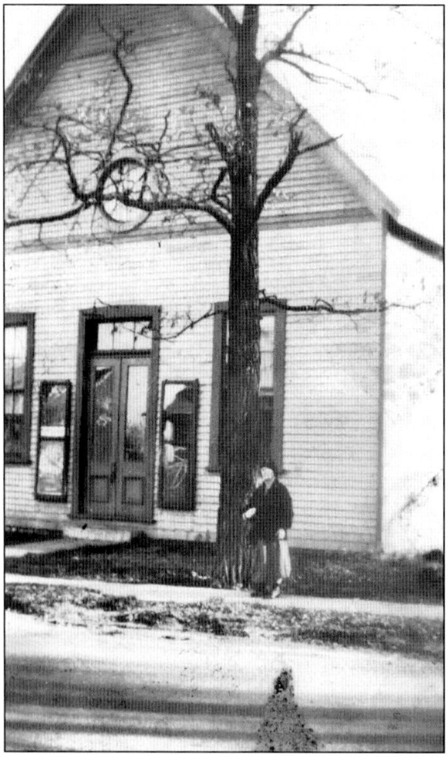

During the 1920s, the former Florence Presbyterian Church was converted into a silent movie theater. During the conversion, billboards were added to each side of the door. Known as the Rho-Albee Theater, this was where the 1929 Florence High School commencement ceremony took place. When the theater finally closed, it was converted into a private residence by Roy Lutes.

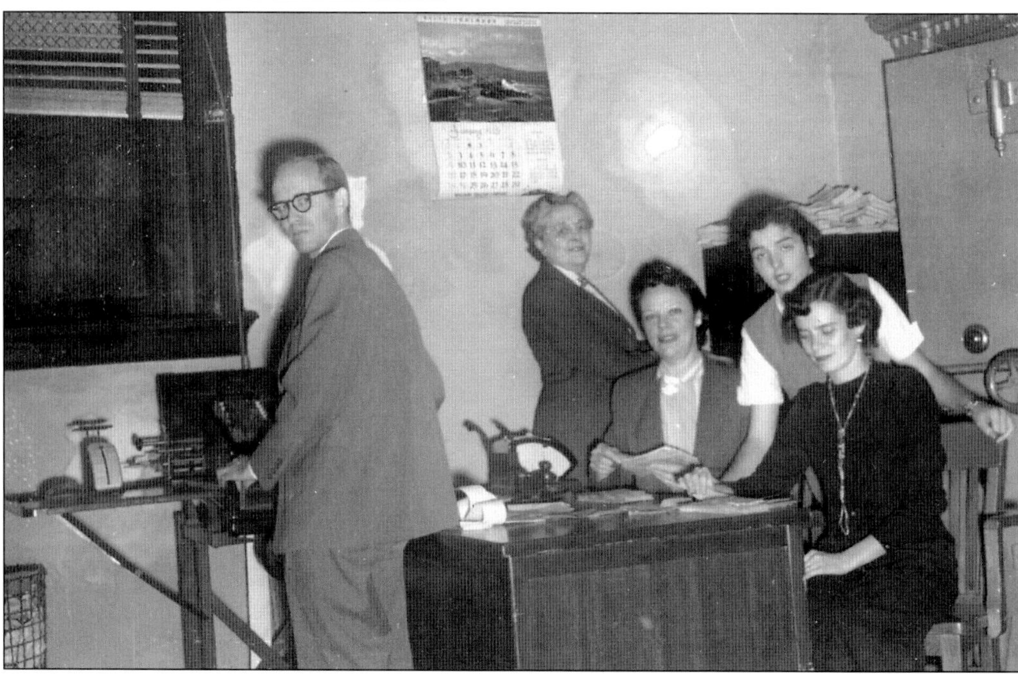

By the 1950s, the Florence Deposit Bank had grown to such an extent that the original building no longer met its needs. As a result, the bank acquired property along the bypass on Dixie Highway and relocated in 1955. Pictured from left to right inside the bank just before it moved are Art Tanner, Sibbia Reimer, Frances Berkshire, Joann Nussbaum, and unidentified.

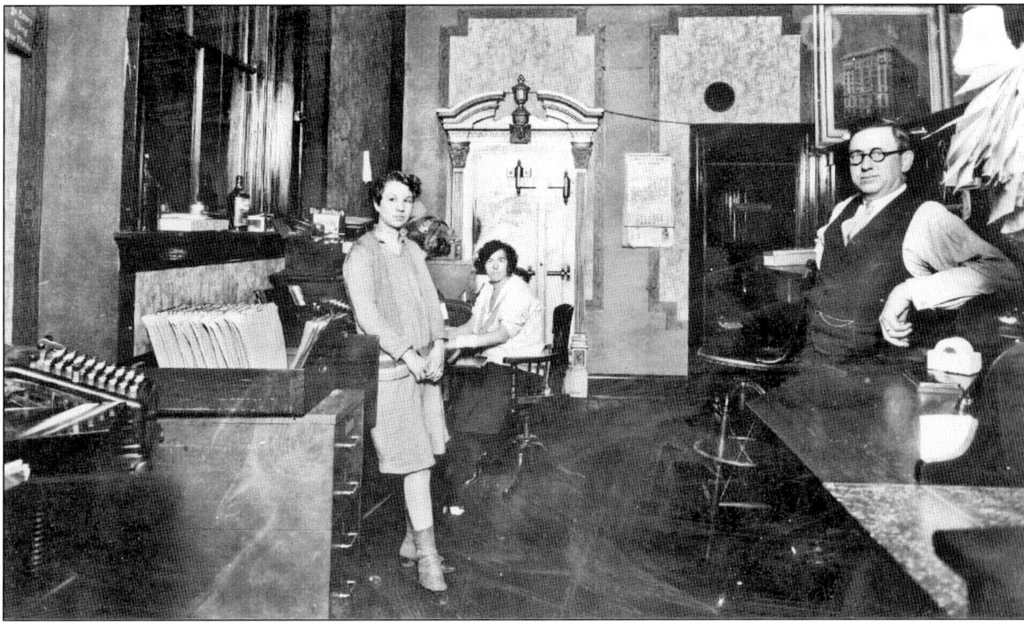

Founded in 1904, the Florence Deposit Bank was located on Main Street near the Odd Fellows Building. This December 1926 interior shot of the bank little resembles the modern banks of today. Seen here are Georgia Yealey Tanner (left), Eva Renaker (seated), and Garner Renaker. This bank building served the community for over 50 years, until the bank relocated on Dixie Highway.

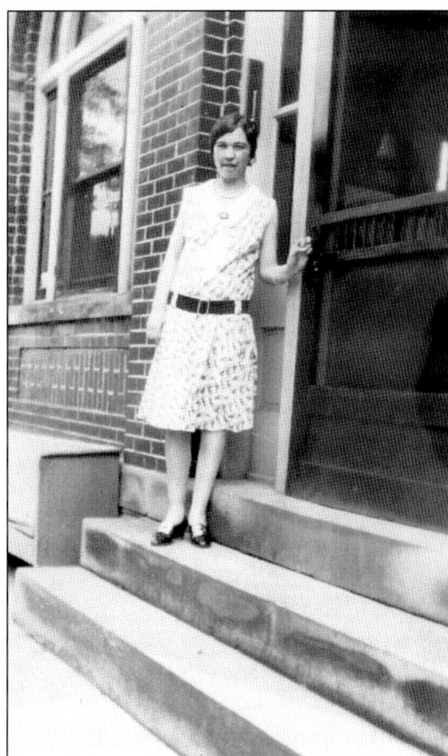

In simpler times, banks were more informal than they are today. Central air conditioning did not exist. During the summer months, the bank's door was left open to catch the summer breeze. Security concerns were not as pressing as they are today. Seen here next to the screen door of the Florence Deposit Bank is Georgia Yealey Tanner.

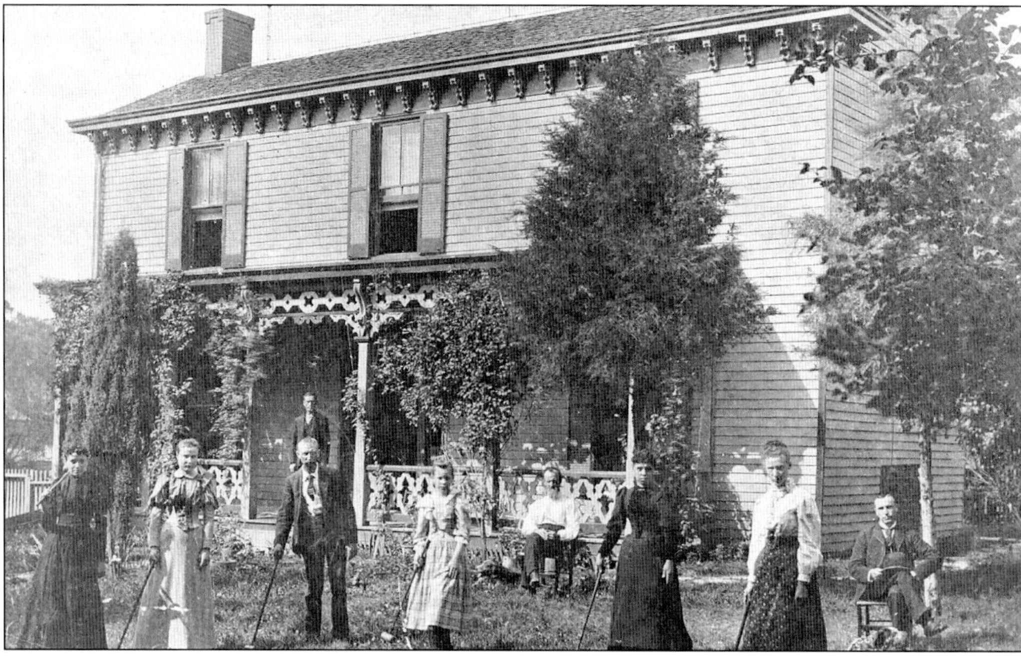

The home of Henry Olsner was located on Main Street next to the Christian church. In this *c.* 1890 photograph, members of the Olsner family are joined by members of the William Henry Tanner family in a game of croquet. The group includes, from left to right, Louise Olsner, Florence Tanner, Henry Olsner, unidentified girl, William Henry Tanner, Hannah Olsner, Carrie Goodridge, and John Goodridge. The man on the steps is unidentified. In the mid-20th century, the building housed Chambers and Grubbs Funeral Home.

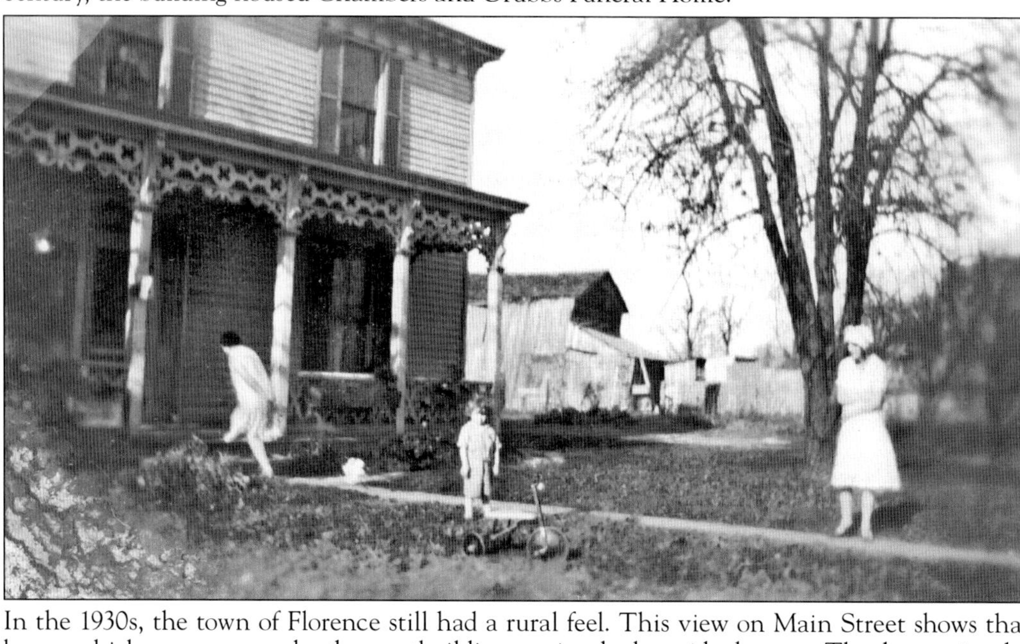

In the 1930s, the town of Florence still had a rural feel. This view on Main Street shows that barns, chicken coops, and other outbuildings existed alongside homes. The house in the foreground is the former Olsner home. The caption on the back of this photograph reads: "Rosie started to take this. Mom and I were dirty. I tried to get away but failed."

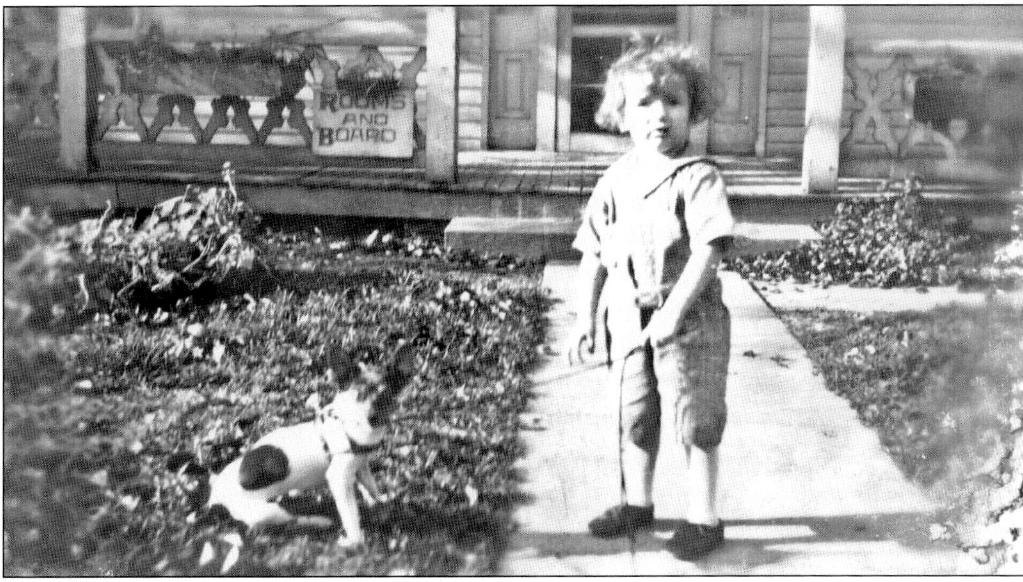

In this *c.* 1935 picture, Wendell Cooper and his dog pose in front of his grandmother Willa Carpenter's house on Main Street. In the late 19th century, the house had been the home of the Henry Olsner family. Note the sign on the porch railing stating that the home now offers room and board.

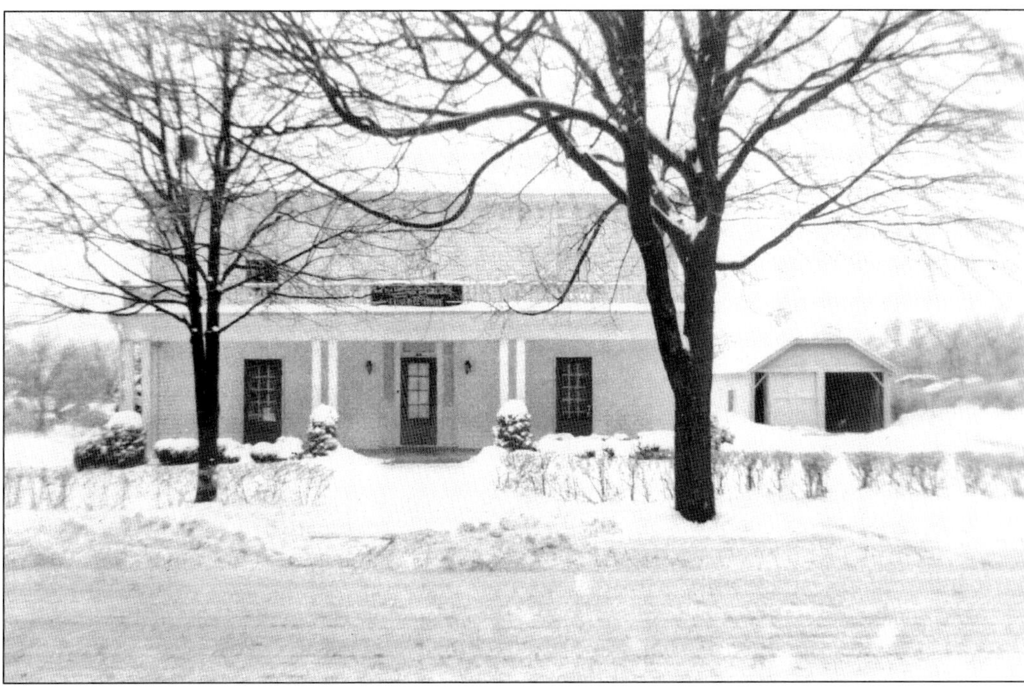

By the late 1940s, the one-time Henry Olsner home had become the Chambers and Grubbs Funeral Home. Seen here after a winter snowstorm, the home has a new front porch. A simpler, more modern design has replaced the elaborate Victorian trim. The house was later purchased by the Florence Christian Church and used as offices before being demolished.

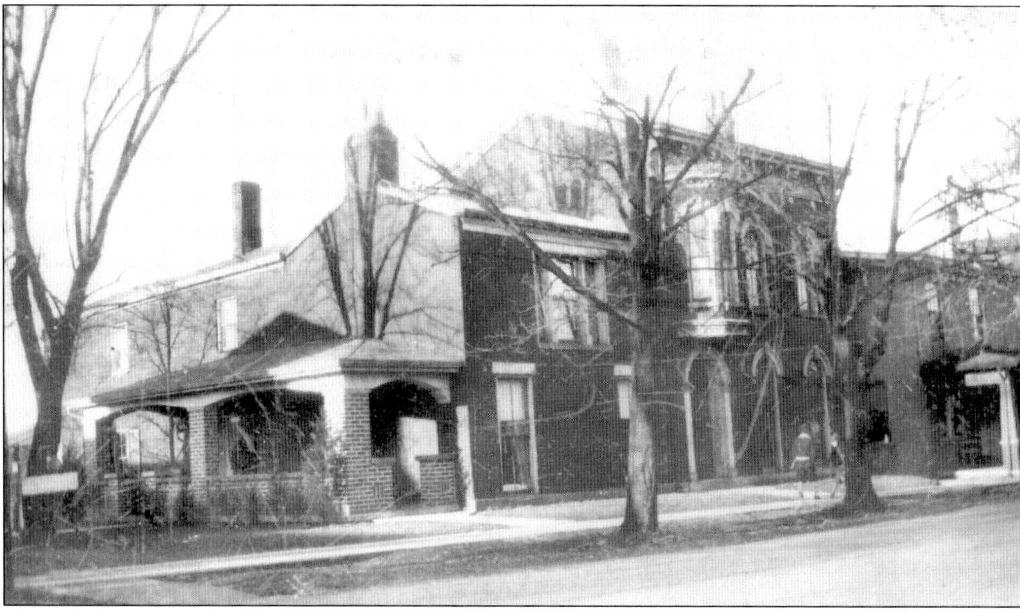

One of the most impressive houses on Main Street was the home of the Lewis and Rosa Aylor family when this picture was taken in the 1940s. Mr. Aylor had been a prosperous Boone County farmer before retiring and moving to Florence during World War I. A previous owner of the house was Dr. J. A. Corey, a prominent Florence physician in the late 19th century.

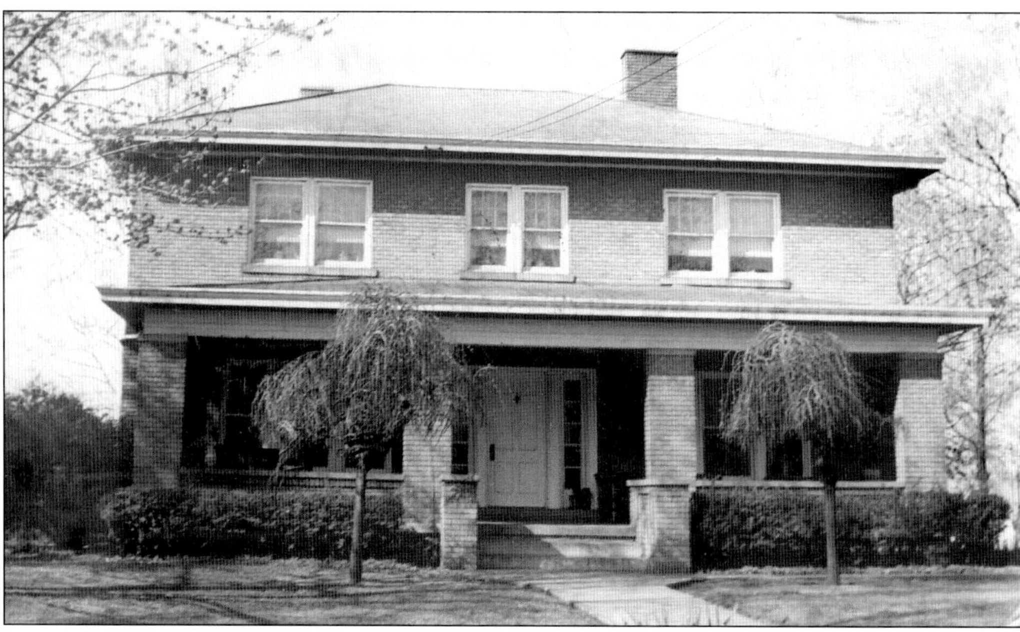

Located at the junction of Girard and Main Streets was the home of William and Virginia Goodridge. The home replaced the old Southern Hotel, which once stood nearby on the same acreage. The front door of the old hotel was incorporated into the family's new home and is clearly visible in this picture. Today descendants of Mr. and Mrs. Goodridge still occupy the home.

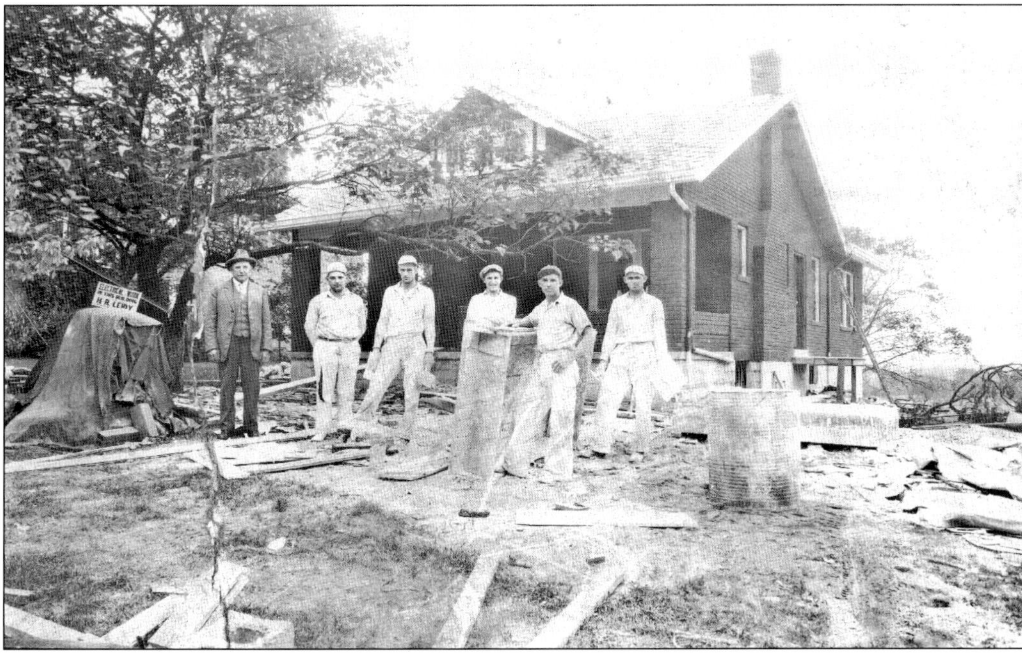

Construction on this house on Main Street was well underway when the workers took time out to have their picture taken. The sign visible to the left indicates that all of the electrical work was provided by H. R. Leidy, a local electrician. This house was later home to Walter and Sarah Huey, who founded Huey Motor Express.

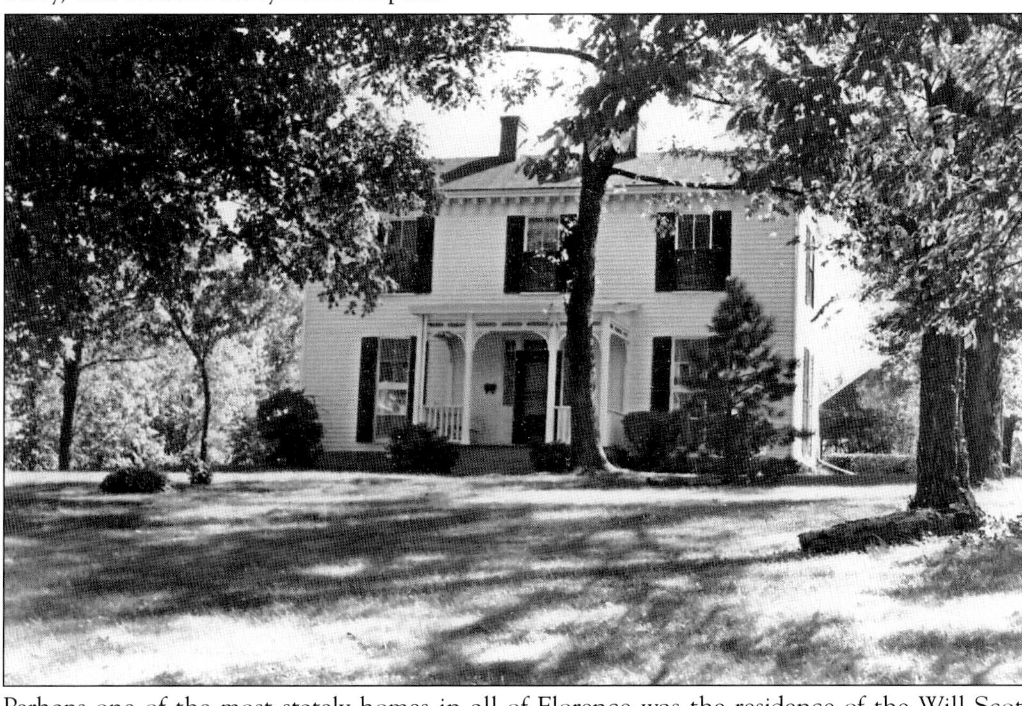

Perhaps one of the most stately homes in all of Florence was the residence of the Will Scott family. The home was located in the curve of Main Street near the old Meyer's Building. Sadly neither this home nor the Meyer's Building remains along Main Street today.

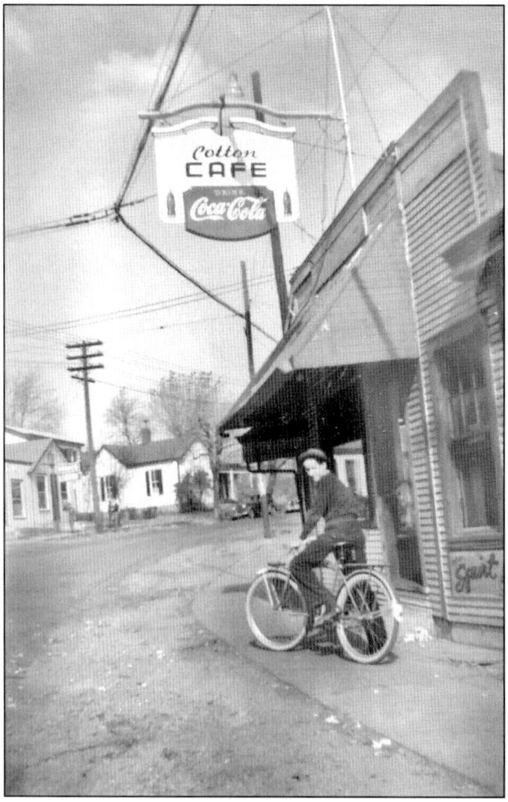

In the curve of Main Street across from the Meyers Building stood Cotton's Café. In the background to the left can be seen the local pharmacy. Pausing on his bicycle in front of Cotton's is Wendell Cooper. Today the Florence Firehouse stands on this site. Ironically Wendell would eventually serve the city of Florence as a volunteer fireman at this same location. Following Cotton's, the café would be owned by the Taylor family.

Lilly Taylor stands at the door of Taylor's Delicatessen on Main Street. The sign advertises "Home Cooking with a Plate Lunch" for 35¢ and a bottle of Pepsi-Cola for a nickel. Previously Cotton's Café occupied this site. Today the Florence Firehouse stands on this location.

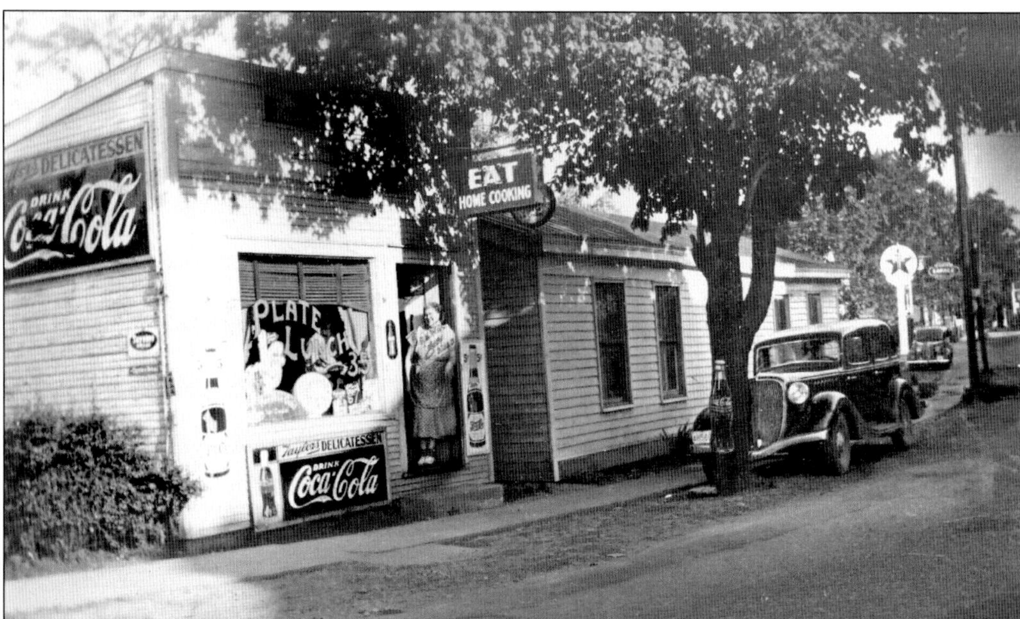

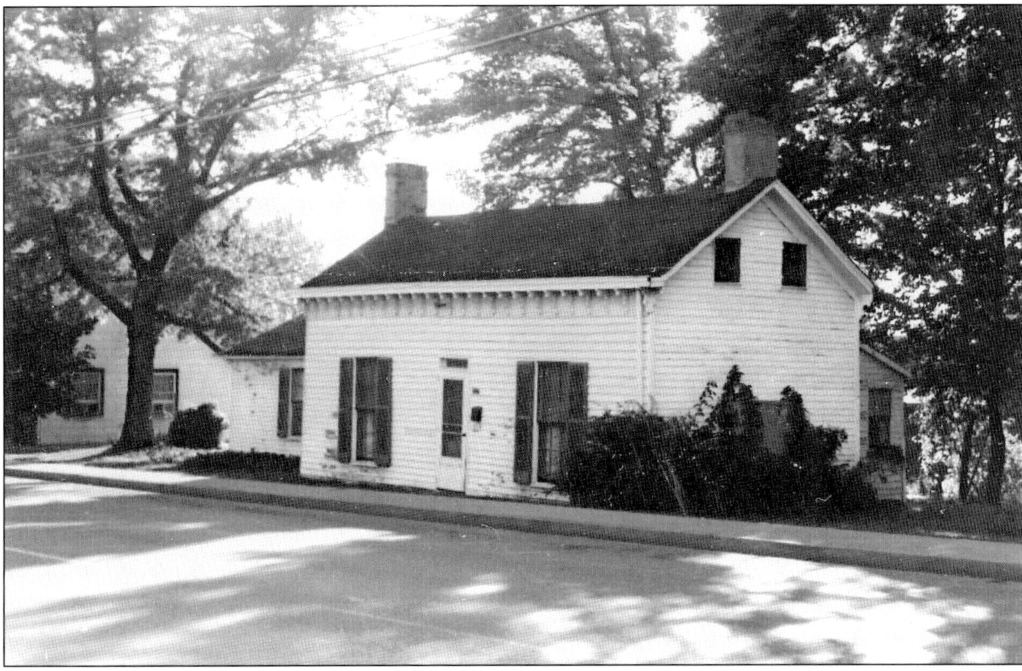

This quaint little house on Main Street was the home of Ed and Eva Osborn. Mr. Osborn was Florence's barber and had a store on Main Street. John Uri Lloyd used this house as the setting for his book *Our Willie*. The house no longer stands.

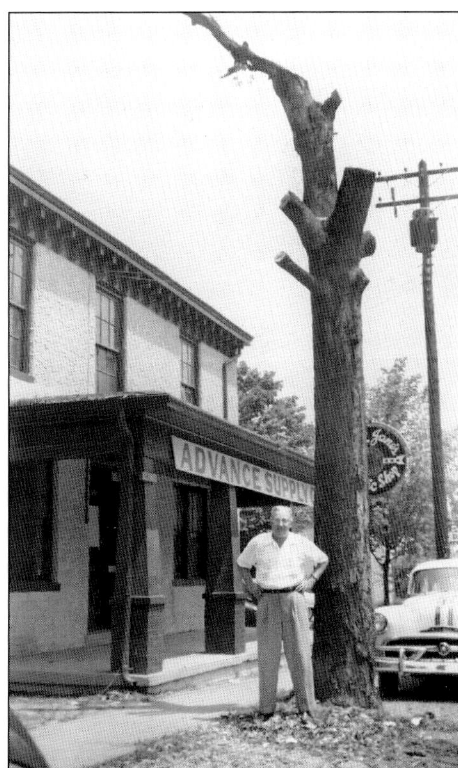

Visible in the background is the record-shaped sign of Mary Jane's Music Shop. At the time this picture was taken, her shop was in the basement of Denham's Drugstore. Eventually, the shop would move to the building seen in the foreground. Owner Mary Jane Kleemeier not only sold sheet music and records, but also gave music lessons to many of Florence's aspiring young piano students.

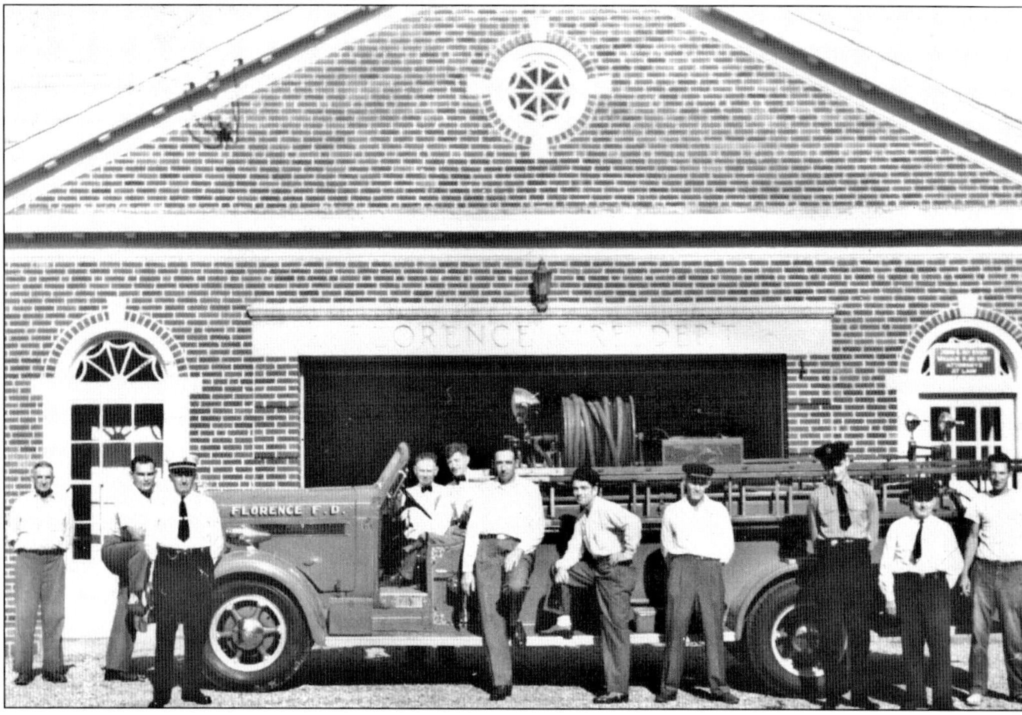

Standing in front of the firehouse in the early 1950s are several members of the Florence Volunteer Fire Department. In front of the truck from left to right are unidentified, Wilford "Fats" Tanner, Chief Al Hue, Roy Brooks, Vernon Smith, unidentified, Al Hue Jr., unidentified, and Francis Souther. The two men behind the truck are unidentified.

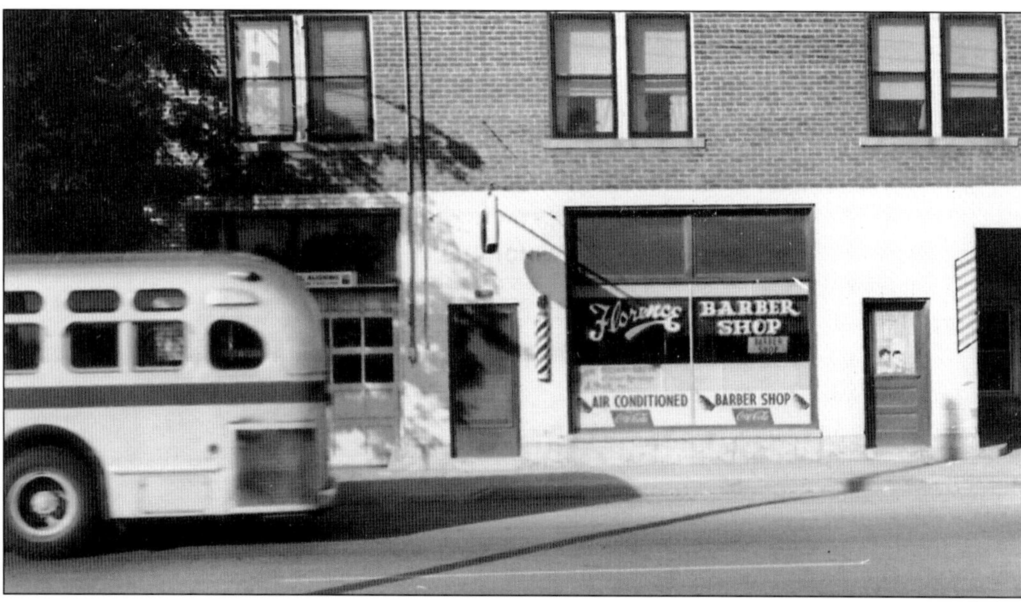

This snapshot of the Florence Barbershop records a familiar scene along Main Street. In the days before central air conditioning was common, the shop proudly advertises the fact that it is air conditioned. Clearly visible on the left-hand side of the picture is a Green Lines bus. Florence was the last stop on the Green Lines bus route between Cincinnati and Northern Kentucky.

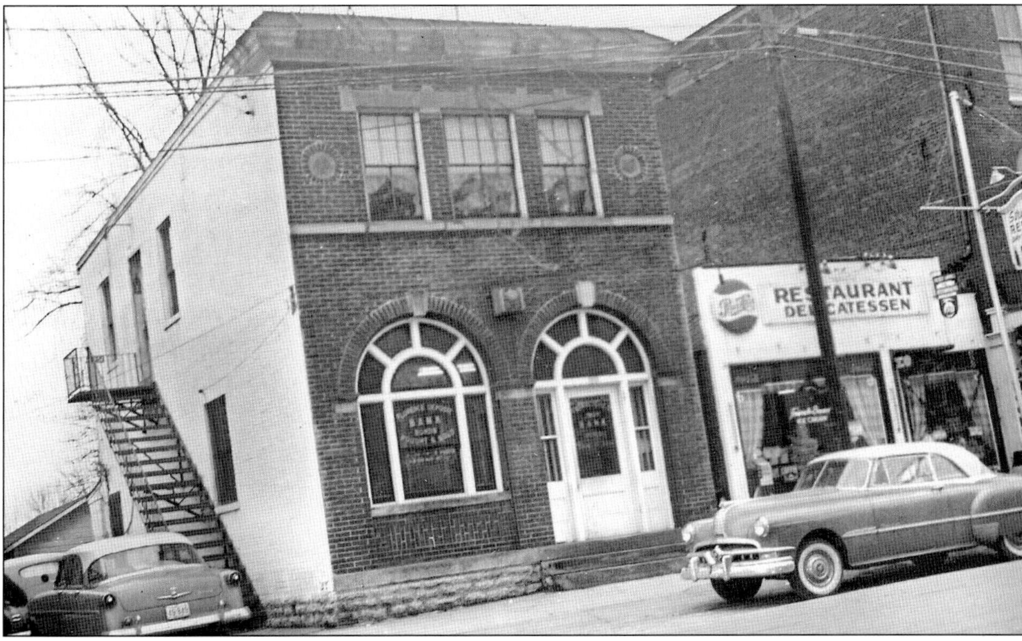

Just before 1955, a photographer captured this section of Main Street. The Stringtown Restaurant was housed in the small white building in the center. It was also the Greyhound bus stop for many years. The building to the right was Riddell's Grocery and today houses the Stringtown Restaurant. To the left is the Florence Deposit Bank, which was soon to relocate on Dixie Highway.

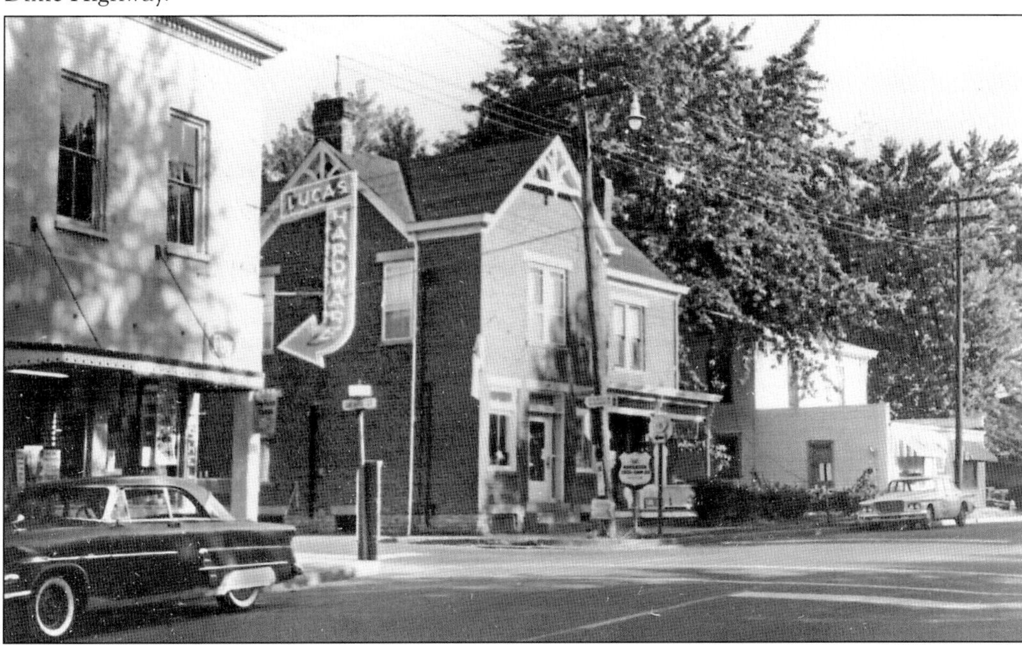

During its long history, this building at the corner of Girard and Main has housed many businesses. When this picture was taken in the early 1960s, it was the home of Lucas Hardware. At this time, the junction of Girard and Main was a three-way stop and Girard was still a two-way street.

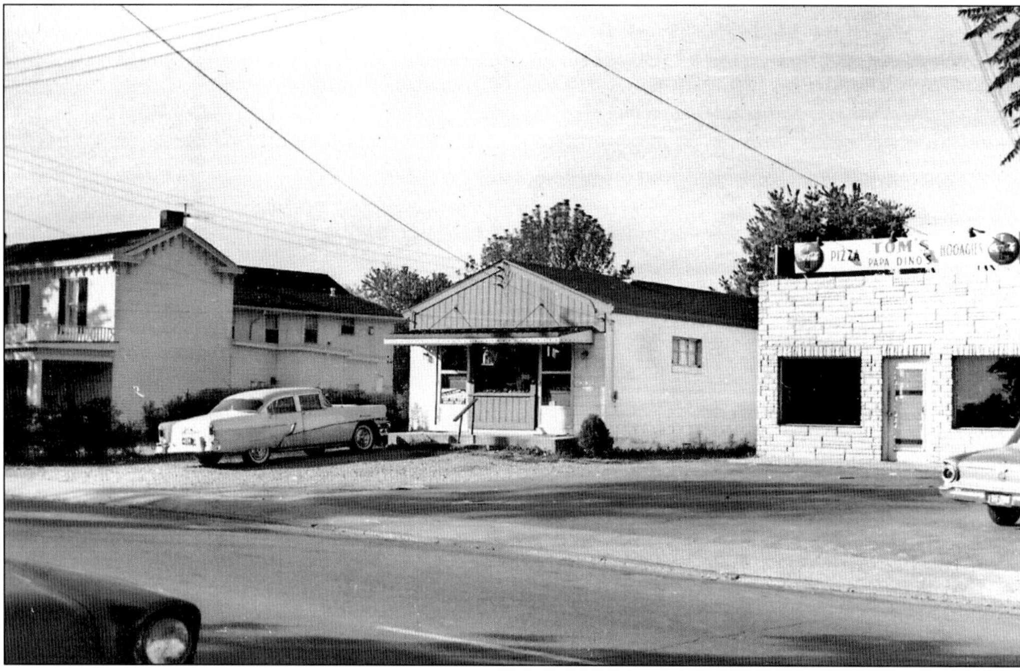

Number 292 Main Street, seen here in the center of the photograph, was the home of Joe Littrell's Shoe Repair Shop. To the right is Tom's Papa Dino's Pizza, while to the left can be seen Chambers and Grubbs Funeral Home. Although none of these three buildings survive today, the new Papa Dino's Restaurant occupies this space today.

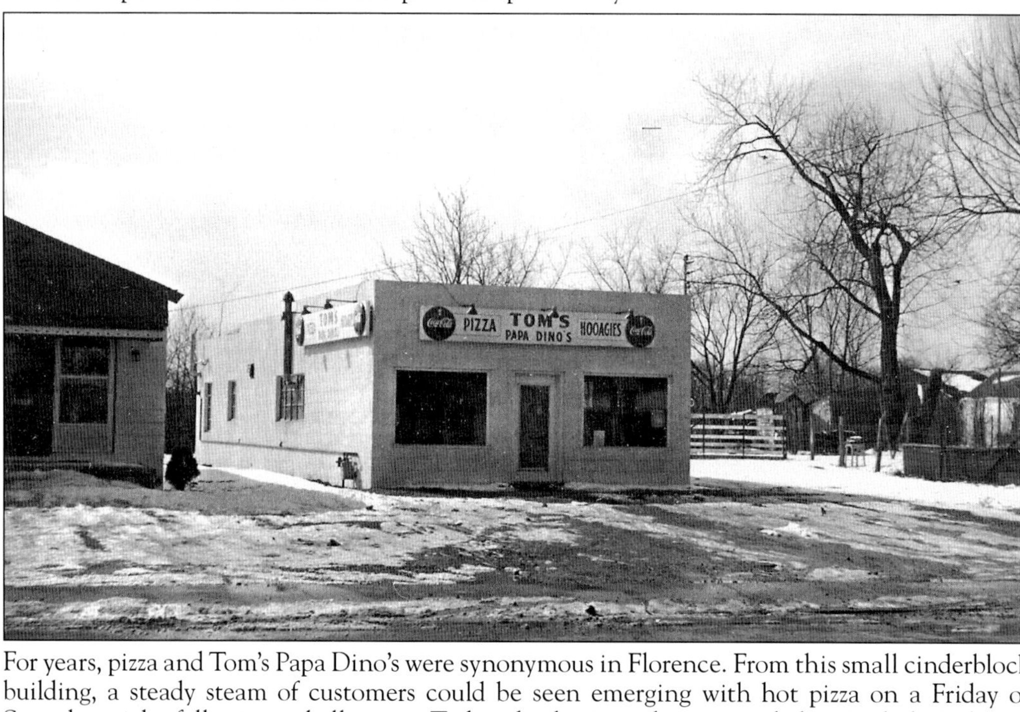

For years, pizza and Tom's Papa Dino's were synonymous in Florence. From this small cinderblock building, a steady steam of customers could be seen emerging with hot pizza on a Friday or Saturday night following a ball game. Today the business has expanded to include in-house dining as well as their popular carry-out service.

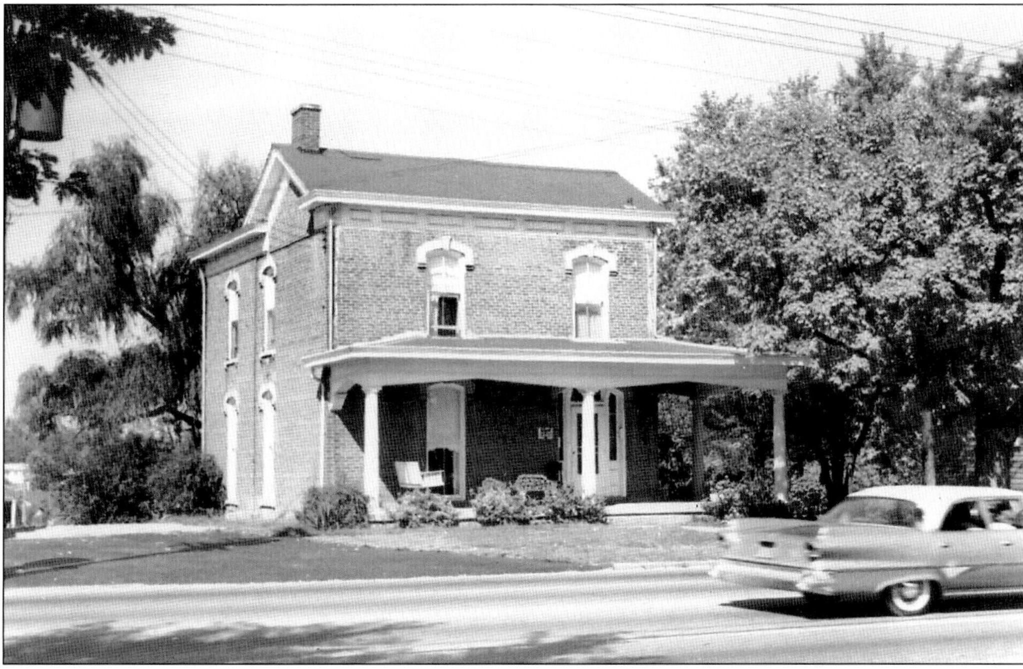

Seen here is the home of Carl and Pearl Anderson on Dixie Highway. Mrs. Anderson and daughter Alice founded Family Gardens Florist in a small shop next to the family home. For years, Family Gardens provided the citizens of Florence with flower arrangements for all occasions. The building still stands today, but it is no longer a residence.

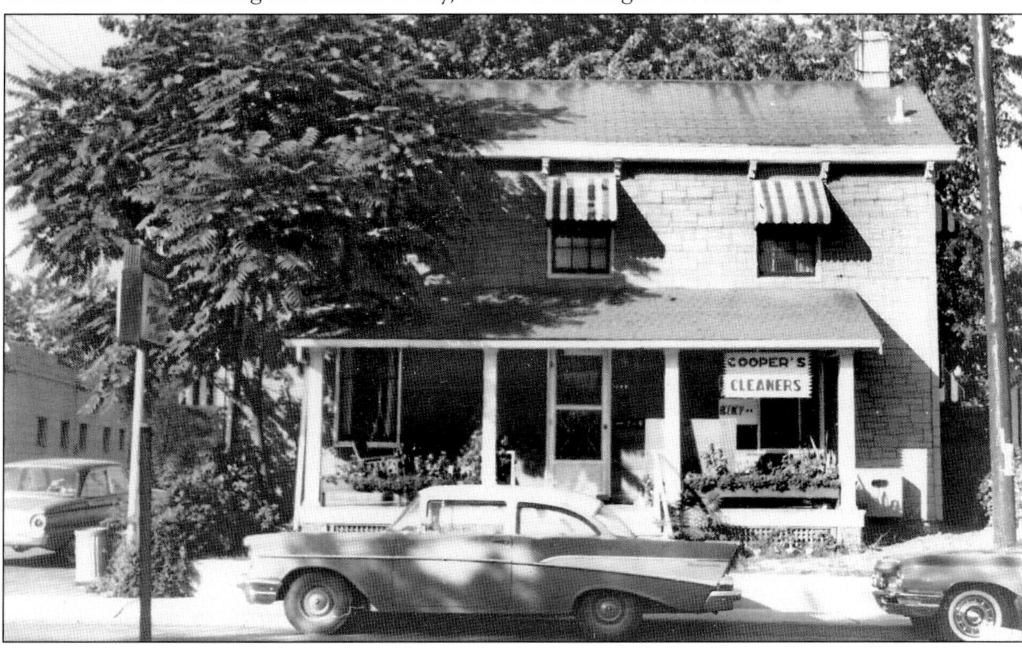

Cooper's Dry Cleaners was located on Main Street directly across from Martin Brothers Garage. Owner Ruth Cooper was a familiar face in Florence and served for many years as dispatcher for the Florence Police Department. Her son, Wendell Cooper, was a longtime member of the Florence Volunteer Fire Department.

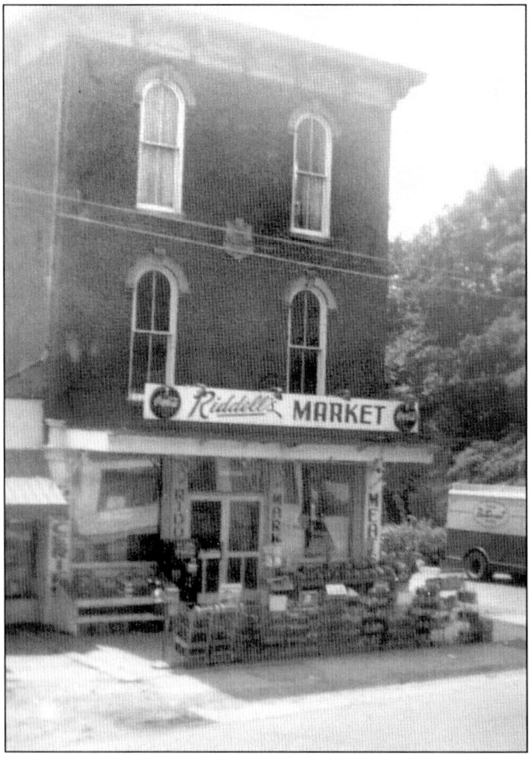

During much of the 20th century, a grocery occupied the first floor of the Odd Fellows Building. When this picture was taken in the 1950s, the store was owned by Lewis and Libby Riddell. Prior to that, the grocery was owned by Mentor Martin. In the first decade of the 20th century, the building housed a drug store owned by Henry Olsner and Son.

Parades through Florence invariably traveled down Main Street. Fire trucks can be seen passing the Odd Fellows Hall during this parade in the early 1960s. Memorial Day and the Fourth of July were often celebrated with a parade. After Boone County High School was opened in 1955, that school's homecoming parade annually wound its way through Florence.

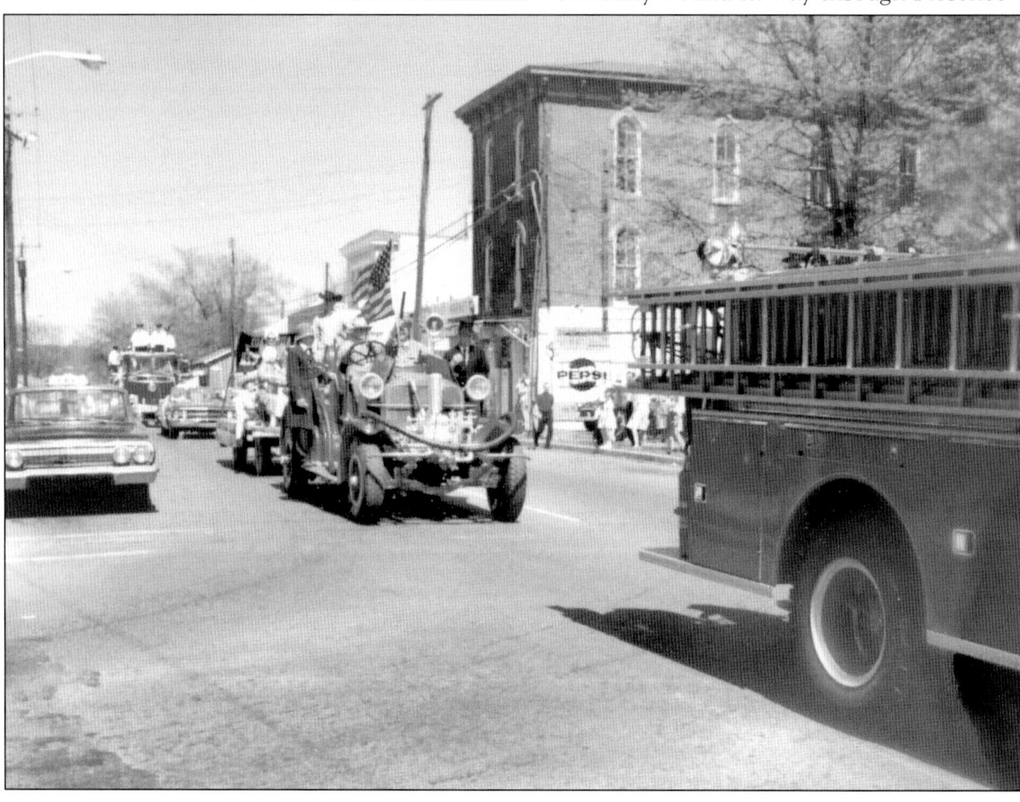

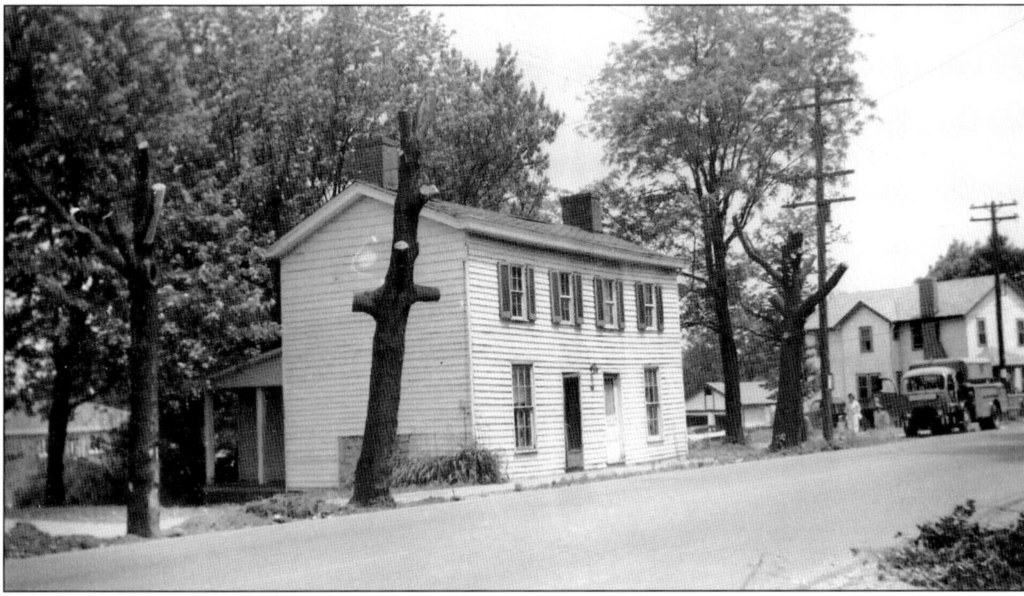

This picture of the David Osborn house was taken during the 1950s as the trees were being cut along Main Street. When this home was originally built, the land behind Main Street was open pastureland. By the 1950s, Lynn Street had been developed, the homes of which can be seen in the background.

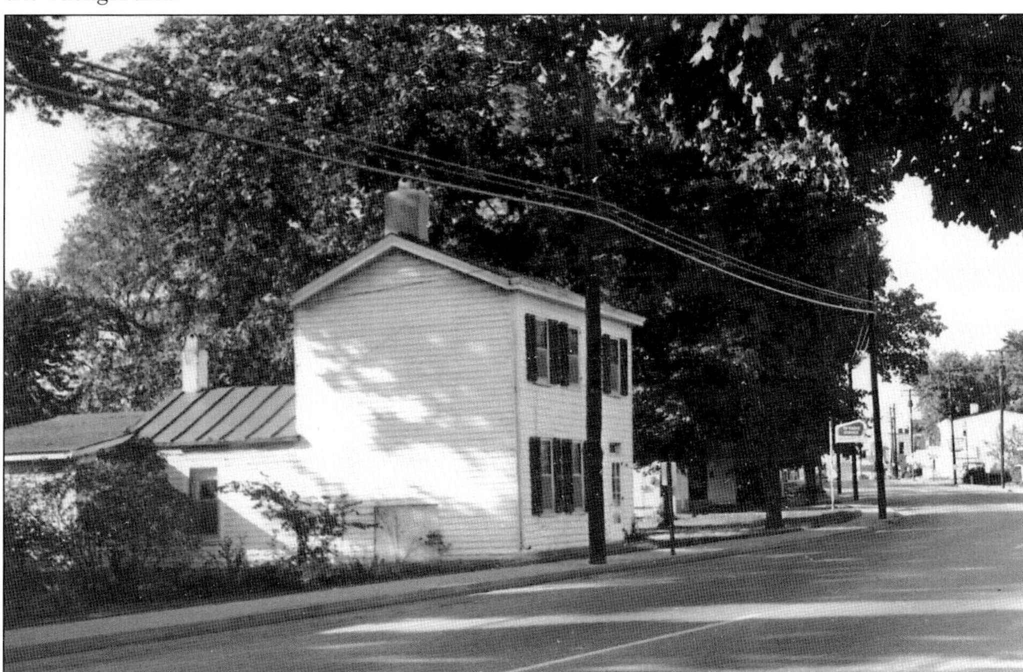

This picture of the Eades House on Main Street represents the quintessential view of small-town America in the 1950s. Just beyond the home can be seen the Television Repair Shop sign of C. A. England. With the growing popularity of television in the 1950s, television repair shops were in great demand. No young child of the 1950s wanted to miss an episode of *Superman* or the *Mickey Mouse Club*, while no teenager wanted to miss *American Bandstand*.

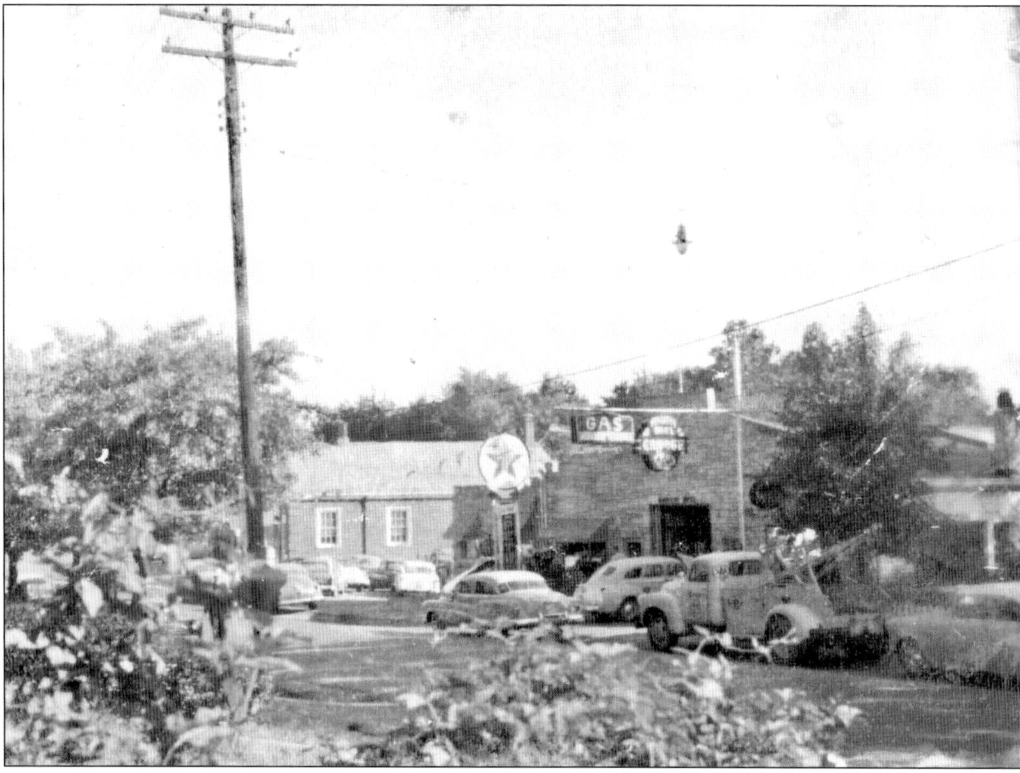

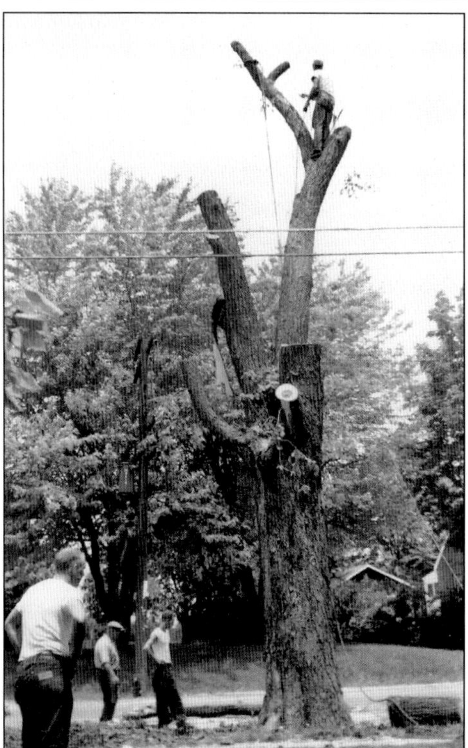

For many years, one of the most visible landmarks along Main Street was the Martin Brothers Garage. Founded by brothers Harold and Owen Martin, the garage was home to three generations of the Martin family. Before the construction of the firehouse on Main Street, the fire truck was housed in the Martin Brothers Garage. Owen also served as chief of the fire department.

During the 1950s, the beautiful trees lining Main Street were removed in order to widen the street for parking. Ironically the Dixie Highway bypass had been built around Main Street in the previous decade to preserve the traditional look along Main Street. Work was well under way when William Fitzgerald snapped this picture.

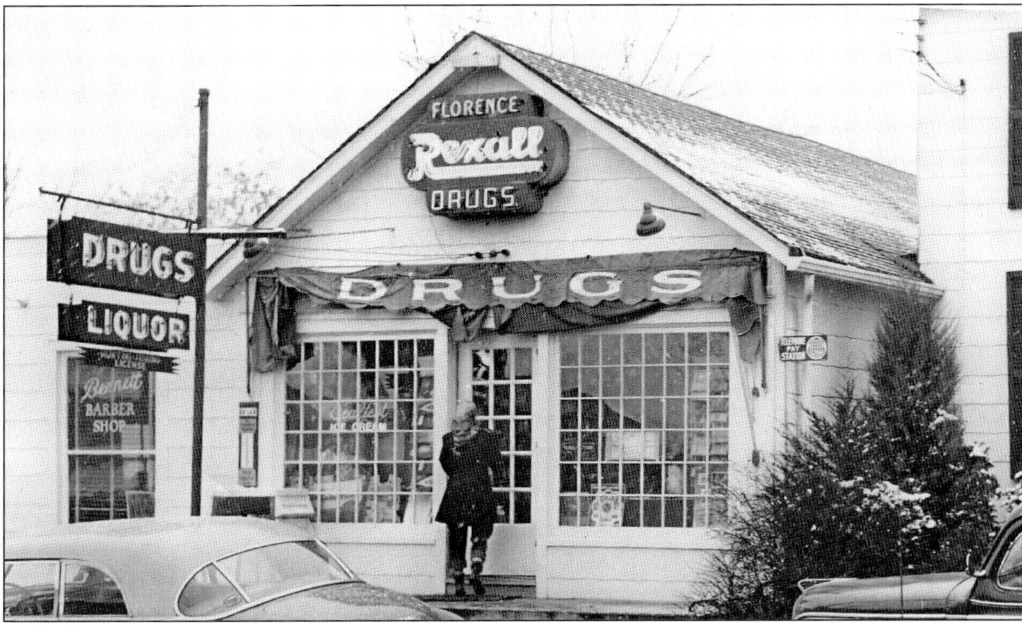

In 1948, Sam Denham operated the Florence Drug Store. Besides filling prescriptions, Mr. Denham offered a wide range of cards and sundries to the people of Florence. Hunting and fishing licenses could also be purchased there. Bennett's Barber Shop is visible in the left-hand corner of the picture.

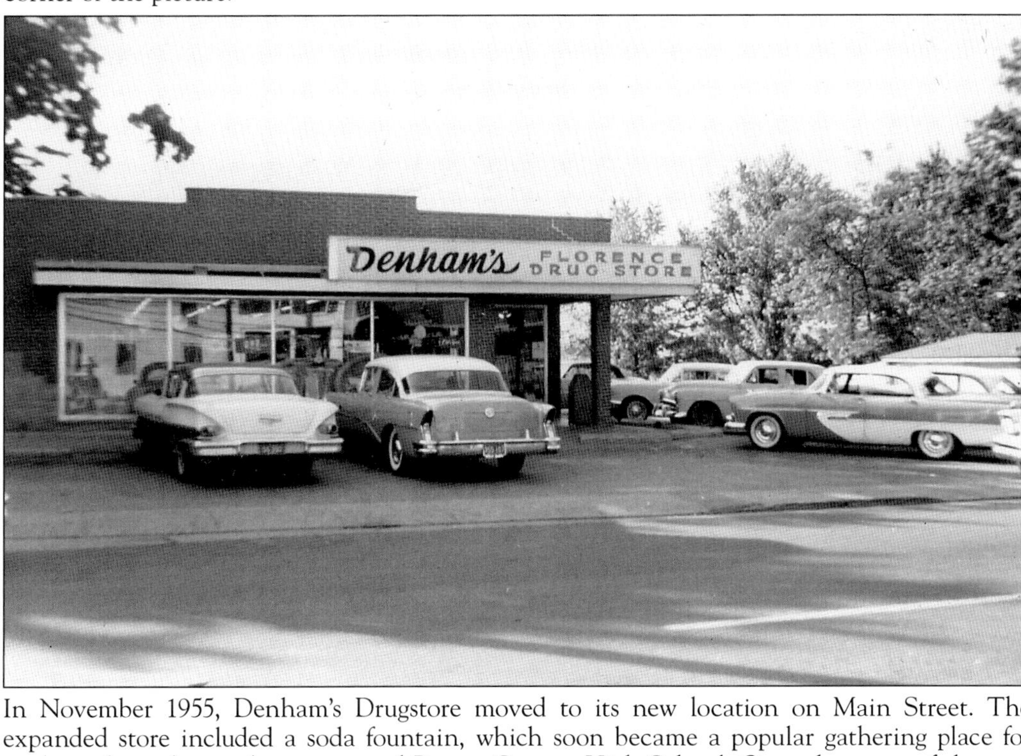

In November 1955, Denham's Drugstore moved to its new location on Main Street. The expanded store included a soda fountain, which soon became a popular gathering place for students from the newly constructed Boone County High School. One advantage of the new location was the large parking lot surrounding the store.

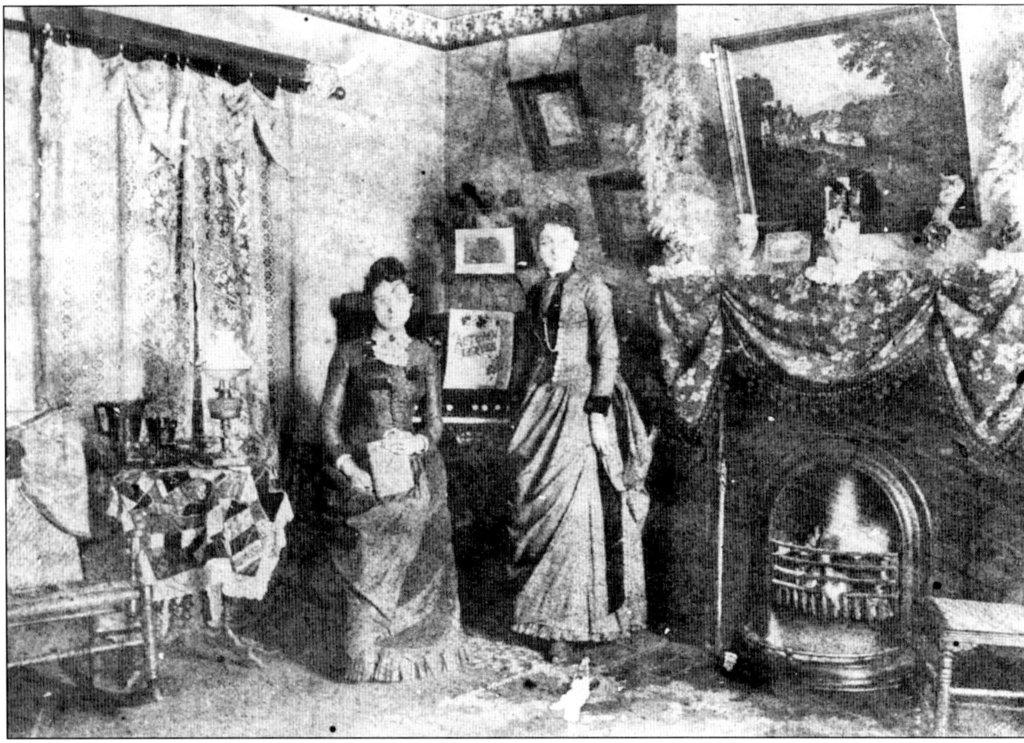

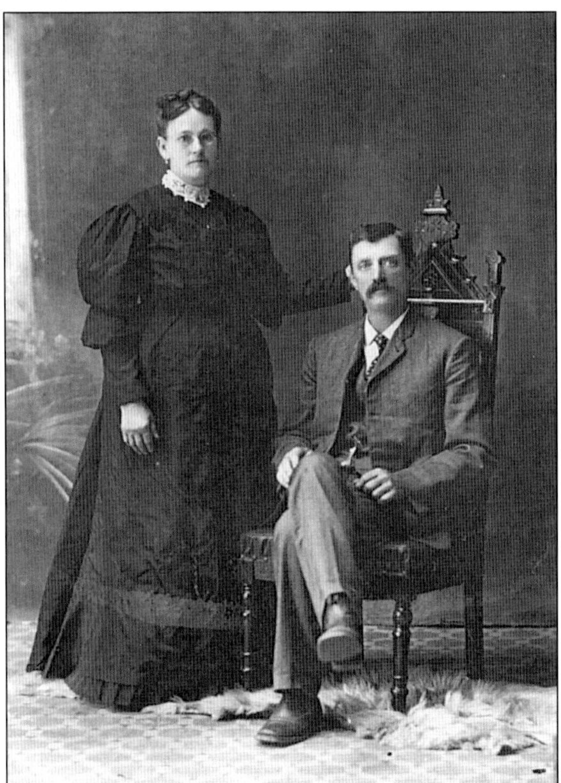

Wagon maker William Henry Tanner's home was located on Main Street next to the Baptist church. He and his wife, Lucy, had three daughters. Seen here in this lovely Victorian parlor are Carrie (left) and Cora Tanner. Both daughters eventually married local suitors. Carrie married John Goodridge, and Cora married Martin Blankenbeker.

Edward and Rhoda Snyder were longtime residents of Main Street. In the late 19th and early 20th centuries, they raised a large family. Their numerous descendants are part of the Florence community today. Their home was located on the site of the current parking lot of the Florence Baptist Church.

Four

Growing Up in Florence

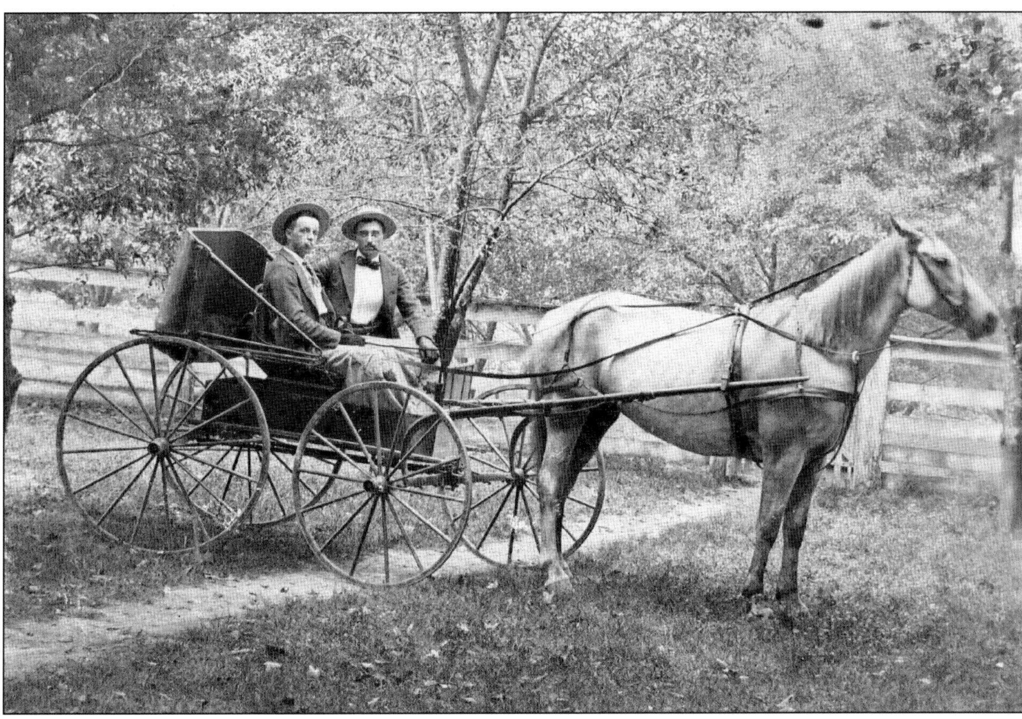

Smartly dressed for a summer drive, Eli Carpenter (left) and Henry Conner stop with their horse Duke to have their picture taken before proceeding on to Florence. It would be another 20 to 30 years before the automobile totally replaced the horse and carriage as the primary mode of transportation around town.

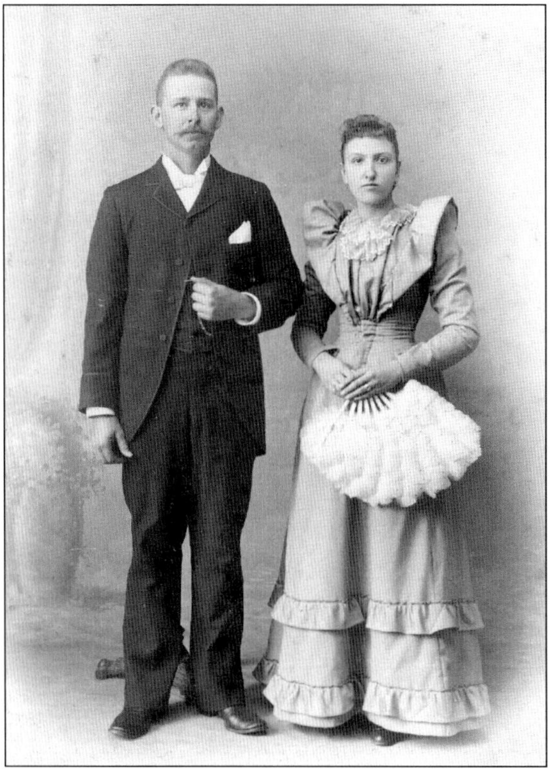

This distinguished-looking couple is Perry and Ella Barlow, seen here on their wedding day. Perry was one of the founding fathers of the Florence Deposit Bank in 1904. During the bank's long history on Main Street, Mr. Barlow was a member of the board of directors. He was present when the bank moved to its new location on Dixie Highway in 1955. Both Mr. and Mrs. Barlow were members of Hopeful Lutheran Church.

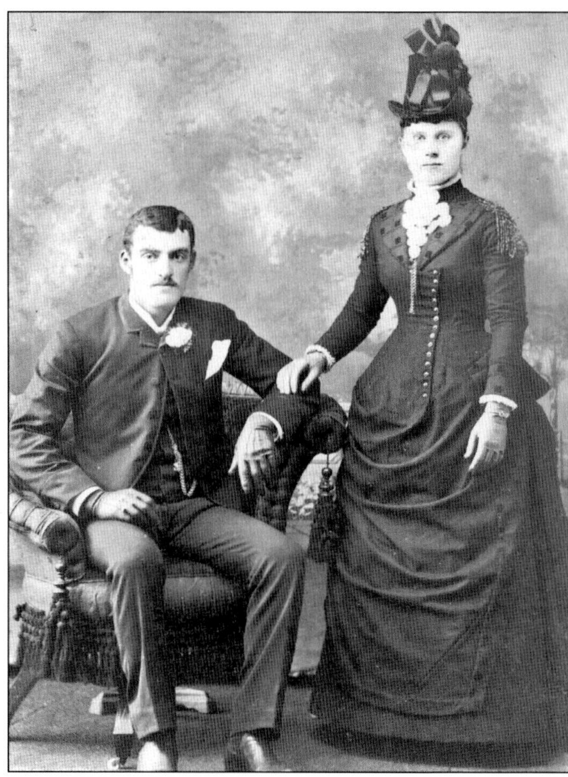

Robert Snyder and Blanche Rouse were married on November 16, 1887. They are seen here in their wedding portrait. They were to have four children, Isabel, Elizabeth, William, and Charles. After spending many years on their farm off Cayton Road near Florence, they purchased a house on Shelby Street. In the late 1990s, the house was demolished.

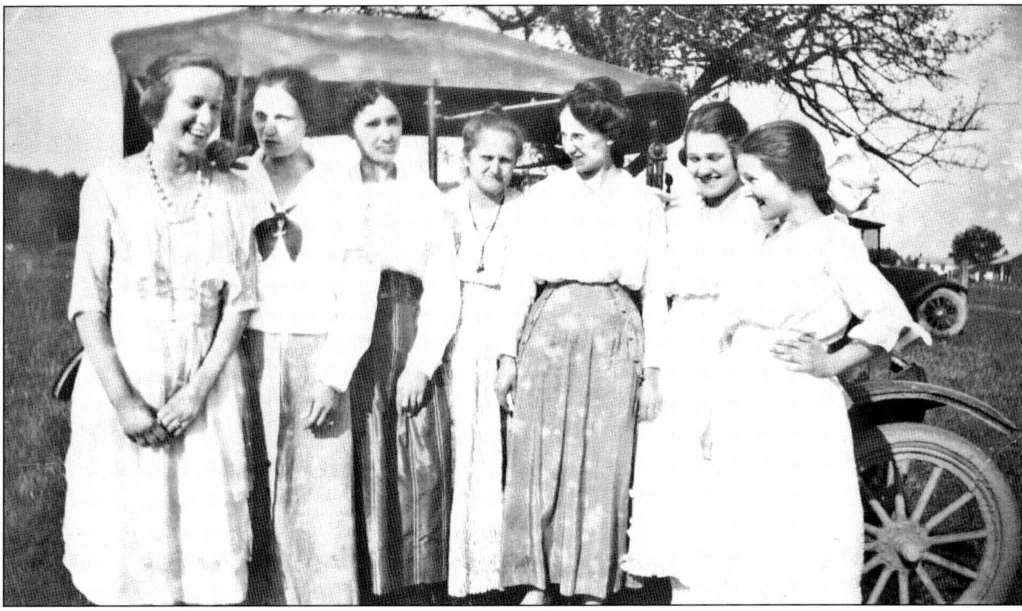

The daughters of Joel Angus and Mary Etta Tanner pose with their mother during a summer outing. Based on the family farm near Florence, Mr. Tanner had a dairy route throughout Boone and Kenton Counties. His wife churned all the butter by hand and assisted with the twice-daily milking. Pictured here, from left to right, are Geneva, Kitty, Agnes, Mary Etta (the girls' mother), Beulah, Eugenie, and Mabel.

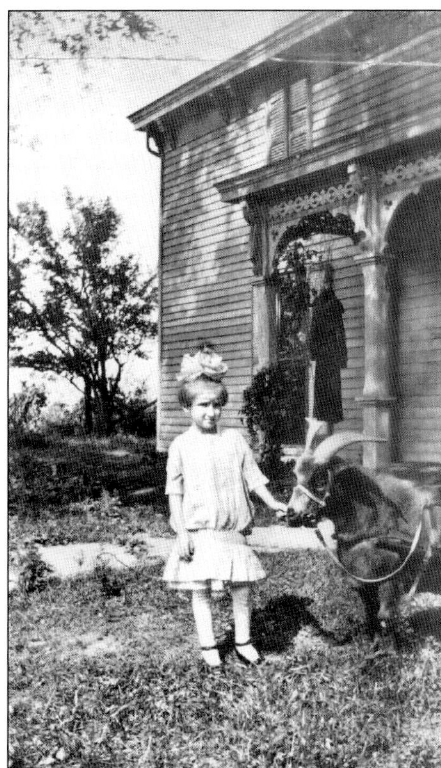

Family pets come in all shapes and sizes. Ruth Carpenter is seen here with her pet goat. Barely visible are the harness and the wagon shafts used to attach the goat to a small wagon.

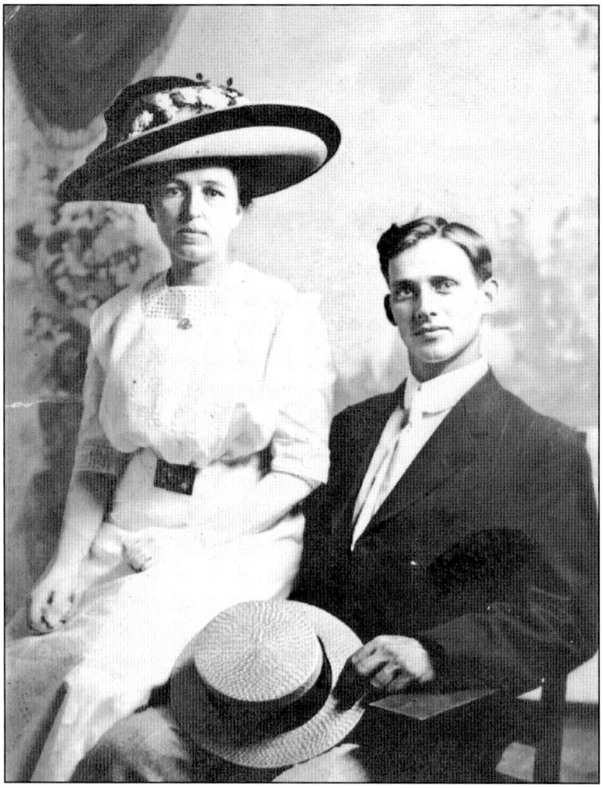

Shortly after their wedding, Lloyd Aylor and Emma Clutterbuck, daughter of Stonewall Jackson Clutterbuck, posed for the camera. The photograph captures the elegance of pre–World War I America and highlights the fashion of the era. The Aylors remained happily married for more than 50 years.

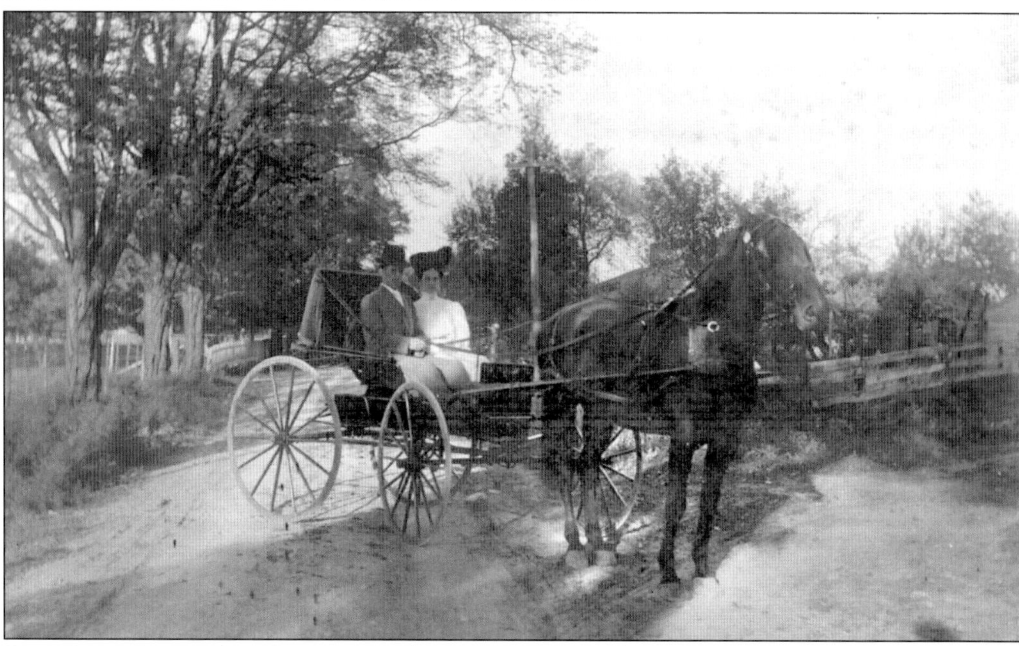

Seated together in their buggy are Ed Osborn and Eva Clutterbuck. The young couple, along with their horse, King, was on Price Pike when they stopped to have their picture taken. On November 2, 1910, they were married at the Lutheran parsonage on Burlington Pike. The well-known couple was a respected and vital part of the Florence community.

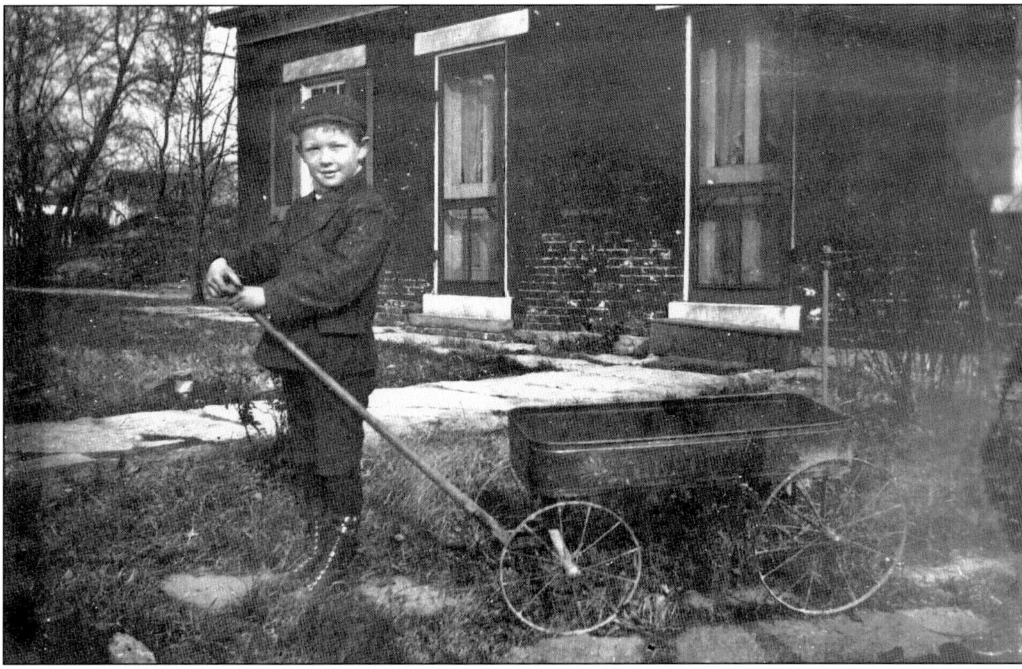

A young Russell House pauses with his wagon on Banklick Street. Typical of his time, he is seen in high laced boots. Wagons of this type were often used for both work and play. Russell later married Willa Yealey, the daughter of A. M. Yealey, and joined his father-in-law in developing the Wildwood Tourist Camp on U.S. 42.

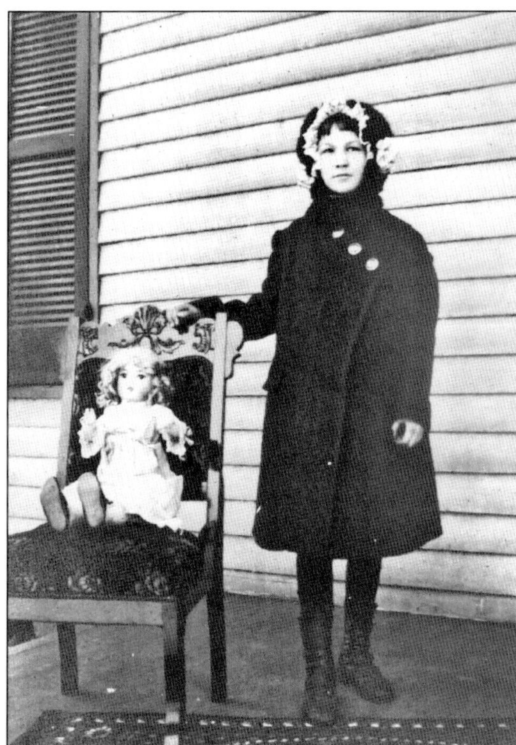

When Georgia Yealey posed with her favorite doll, childhood toys and entertainment were much simpler than today. Simple things such as dolls, tea sets, and books could be shared with childhood friends while growing up in Florence. Obviously this doll meant a lot to her, as she's caught posing for the camera outside on a cold winter day.

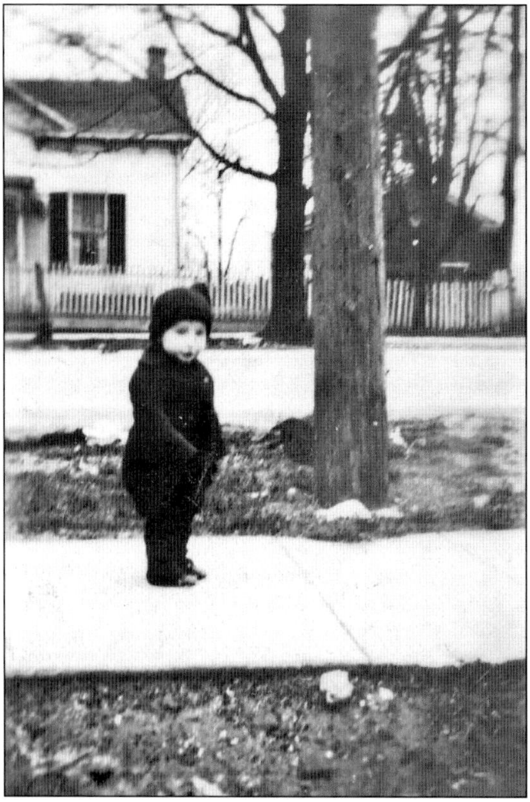

Bundled up for the cold winter weather, young Irvin Carpenter stands on the new concrete sidewalk along Shelby Street. Shelby Street, along with Main and Girard, was one of the first streets to sport sidewalks. As early as 1908, Mayor A. M. Yealey had overseen the construction of the original sidewalks.

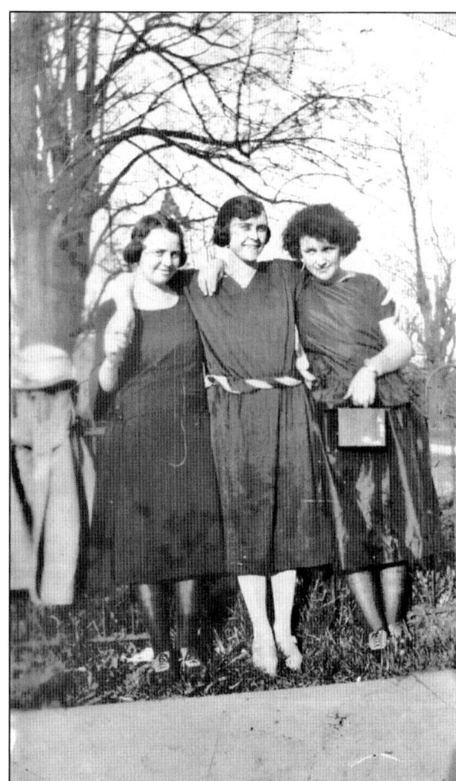

While growing up in a small town like Florence, life-long friendships easily developed. The town's population was much less transient than today. Seen here are Kathleen Laile (left), Pearl Markesbery (center), and Jenny Laile, friends and classmates at Florence High School. In another generation, their children would also be students there.

In the 1920s, traffic in Florence began to change from horse-drawn vehicles to automobiles. It was a time when Main Street was free of stoplights, there were no traffic jams, and no one needed to have a driver's license. Seated behind the wheel, young Jenny Laile seems ready for a drive through Florence.

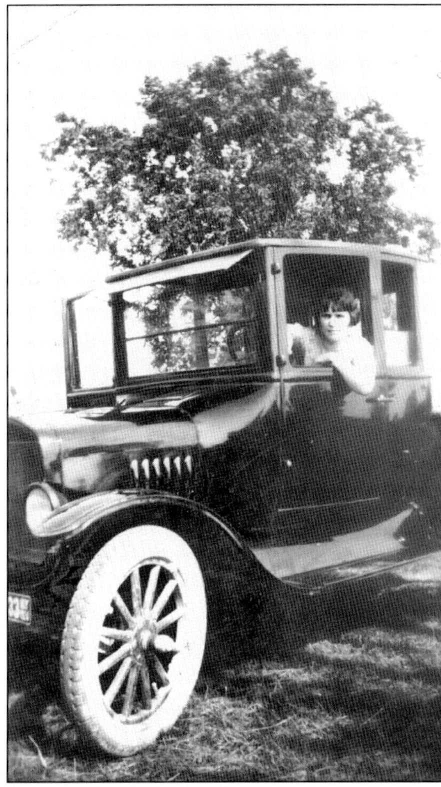

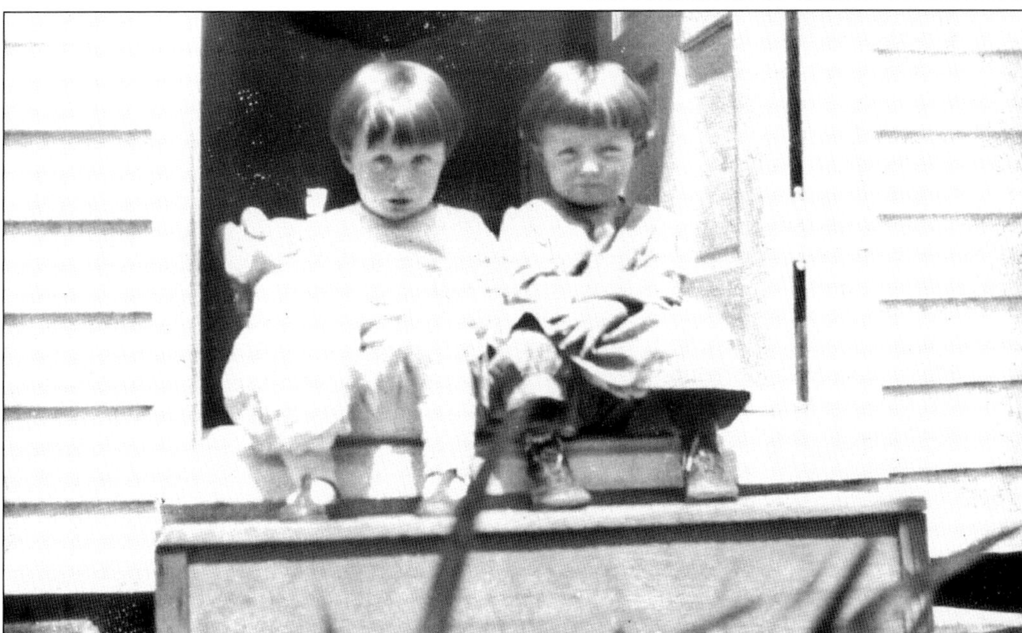

Seated on the steps of their grandparents' home on Shelby Street are Alice Fay Snyder (left) and Lula Robbins. When this picture was taken around 1922, Shelby Street was still an unpaved gravel street. Alice Fay and Lula were the granddaughters of Robert and Blanche Snyder.

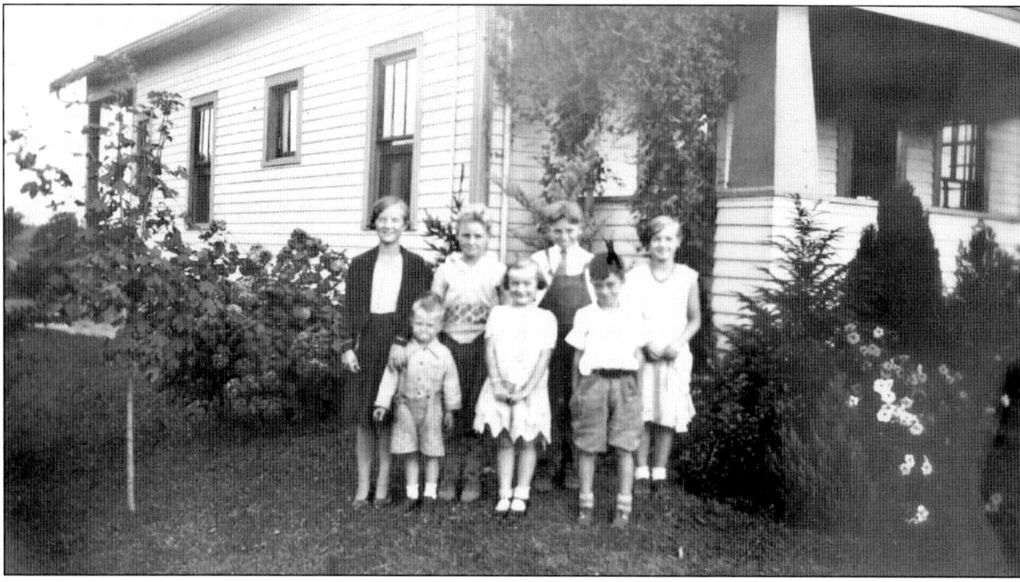

In the early 20th century, new streets appeared on the map of Florence. One of those was Dorotha Avenue. Typical of the new houses built there was the home of Willis and Ora Berkshire, pictured here in 1931. Gathered in the front yard are a group of young friends and relatives of the Berkshires. From left to right are (first row) John Robbins, Goldie Robbins, and Galen Berkshire; (second row) Lula Robbins, Leroy Bethel, Franklin Bauer, and Thelma Robbins.

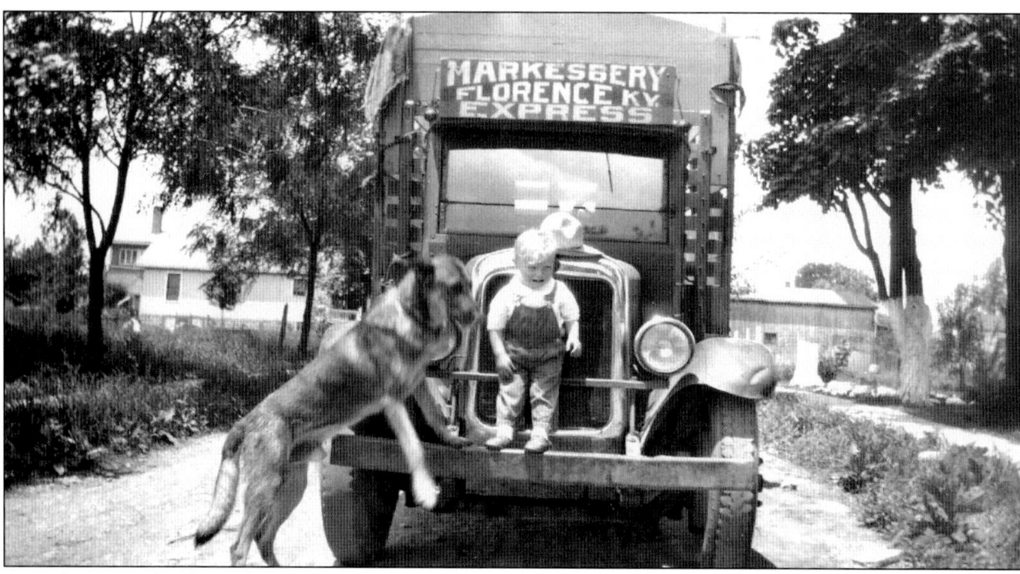

Standing on the front bumper of his father's truck in the early 1930s is young Don Markesbery. Not to be left out of the picture is the loyal family dog, Rex. The Markesberys have been prominent merchants in the Florence area for many years. Having graduated from Florence High School in 1948, today Don operates a successful construction company.

In the mid-1930s, Wanda Hue is seen here posing for the photographer on the back of a catalo. The catalo was a cross between a domestic cow and a bull bison. Breeders of the animal were crossing the country on a promotional tour when they stopped in Florence. Leaving the West Coast on July 3, 1936, they traveled at the rate of two to two and a half miles an hour. To finance the endeavor, the promoters charged 25¢ per person to have one's picture taken on the catalo. Standing to the left of the catalo is Charlotte Tobergte.

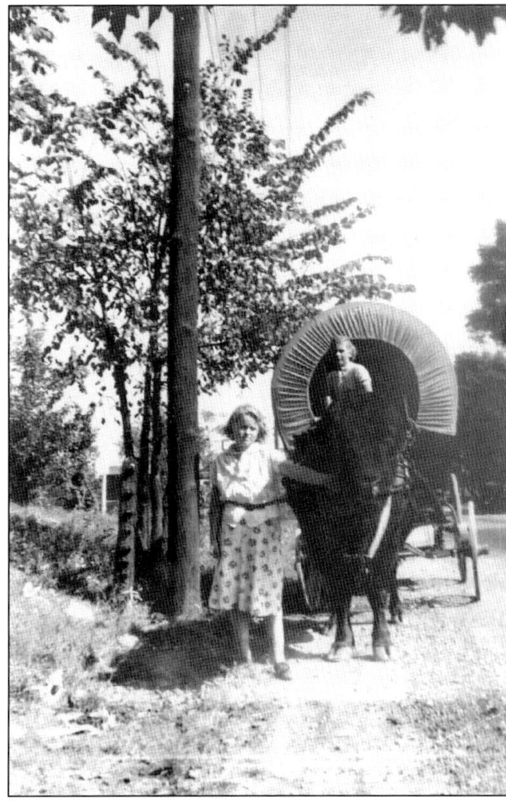

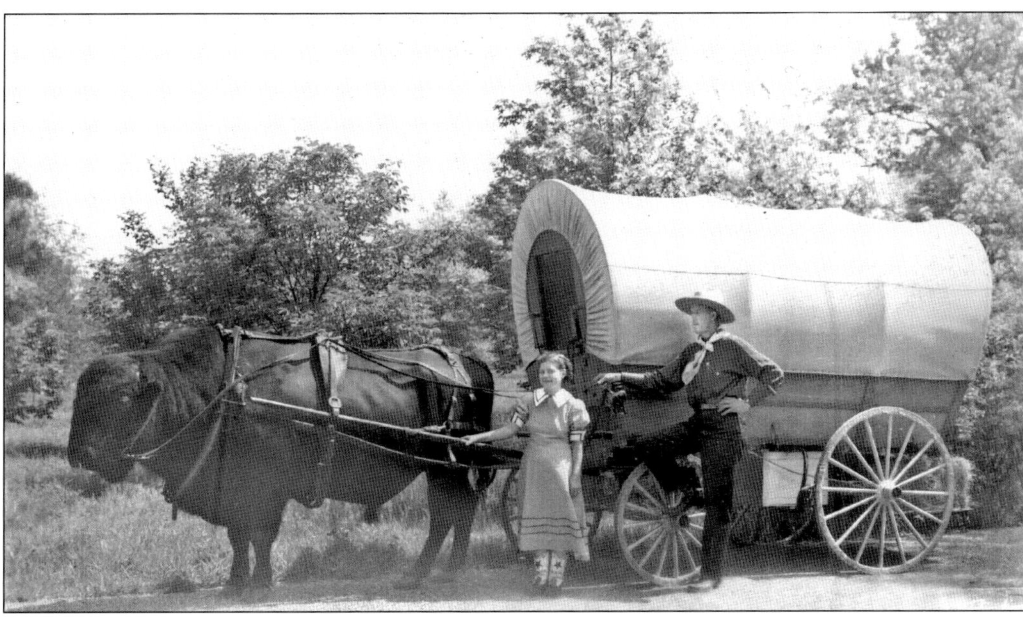

The advantages of the Catalo were reported to be "many and readily observed." Promoters claimed it had a longer lifespan, resisted tuberculosis and blackleg, dressed a greater percent of higher-priced cuts of beef, and bore valuable fur, and cows gave good rich milk and required no shelter in cold climates.

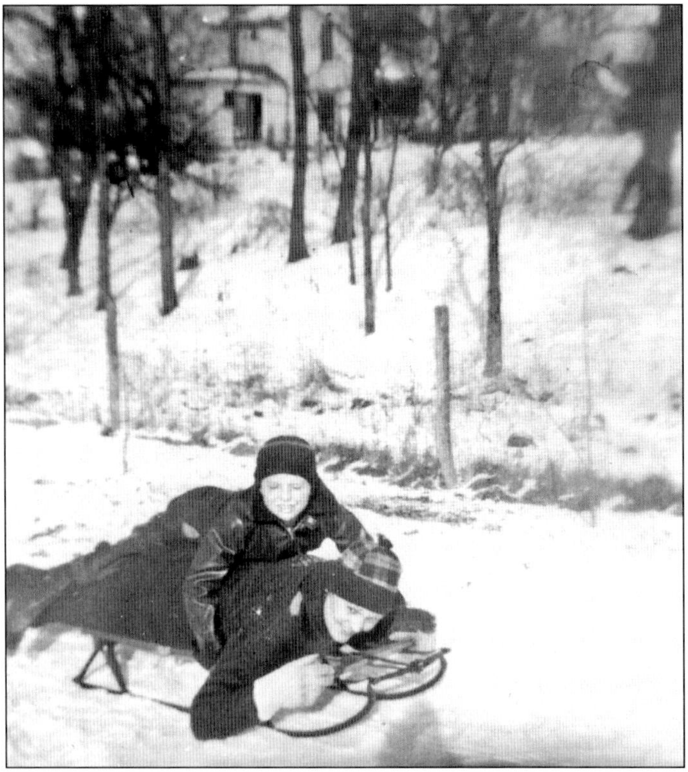

One of the joys of childhood is sledding after a winter snowfall. A popular parent who often joined the children of the neighborhood in their play was Emma Hue. In this picture, she is sledding with young Al Roberts. The house in the background was the home of Newt Long.

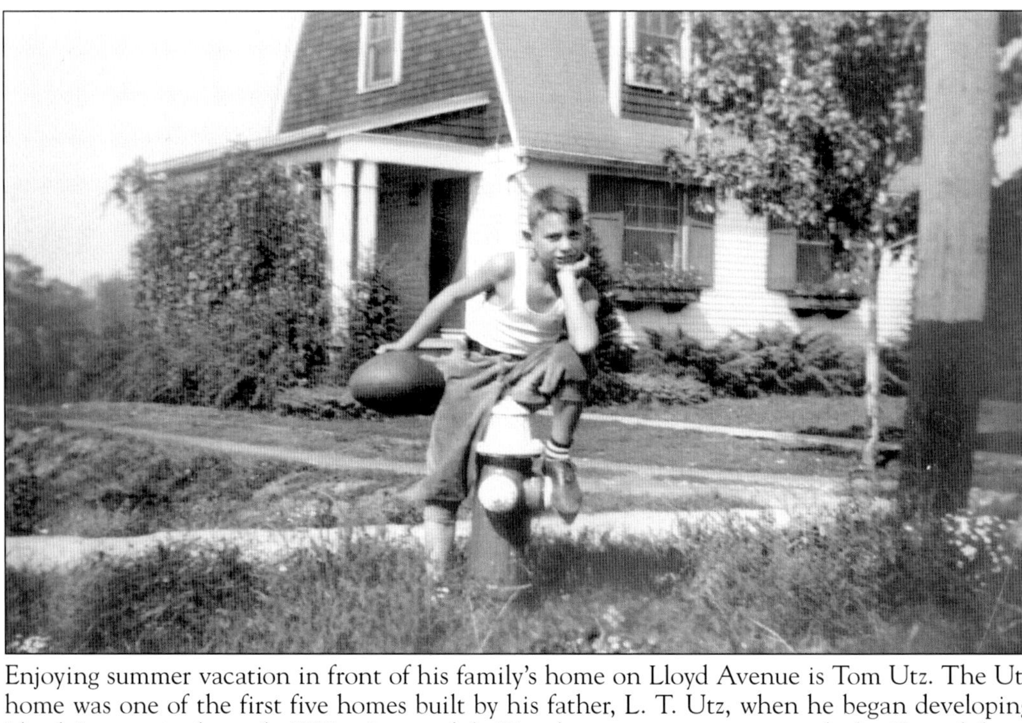

Enjoying summer vacation in front of his family's home on Lloyd Avenue is Tom Utz. The Utz home was one of the first five homes built by his father, L. T. Utz, when he began developing Lloyd Avenue in the early 1930s. As an adult, Tom became an executive with the Consolidated Telephone Company, continuing with Cincinnati Bell after the two systems merged in 1967.

Every young child dreams of having a pony. Here Albert Hue Jr. is seen on his pony in front of his family home on Dixie Highway. Like his father, Albert Sr., "Junior" was a longtime member of the Florence Volunteer Fire Department. He was also a familiar figure at the Florence Post Office, where he worked for many years. The Hue family's home, seen here in the background, was built in the 1920s by the Reverend George Royer.

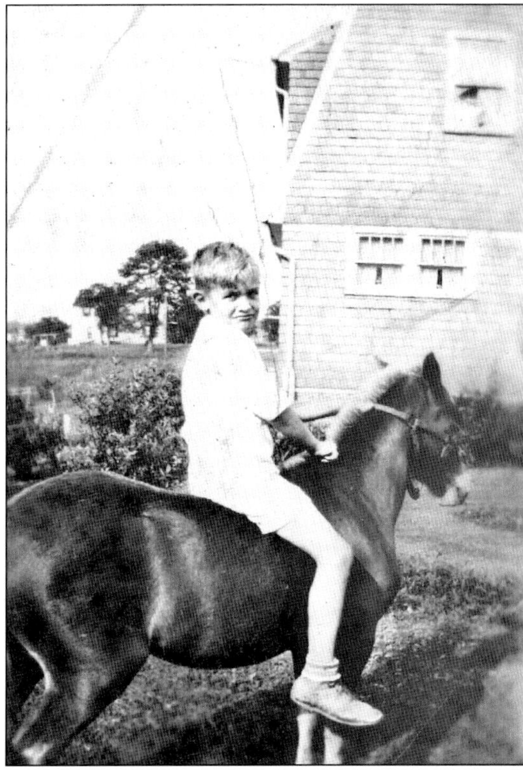

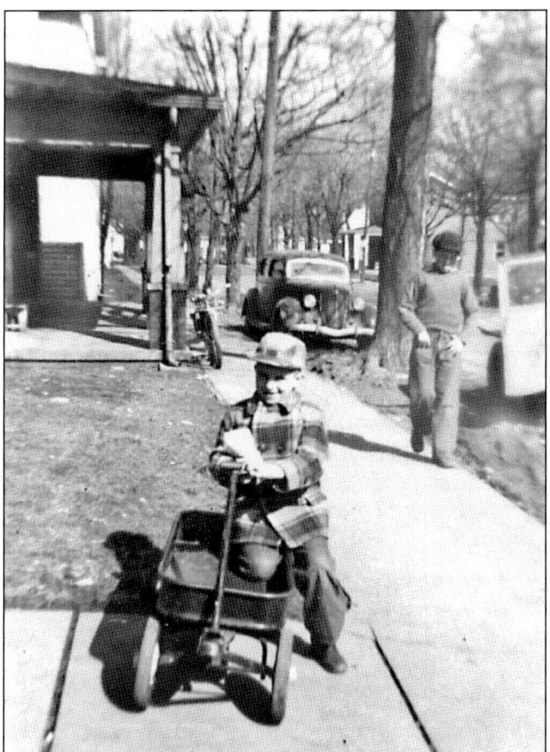

Young Robert Aylor pauses in front of his grandparents' house on Main Street to have his picture taken in his wagon. In the late 1940s, this section of Main Street was a combination of homes and businesses. Behind Bob can be seen the porch of neighbor Elmer Corbin's house. Across the street was the Florence Bank, the 10¢ store, and Jim Tanner's hardware.

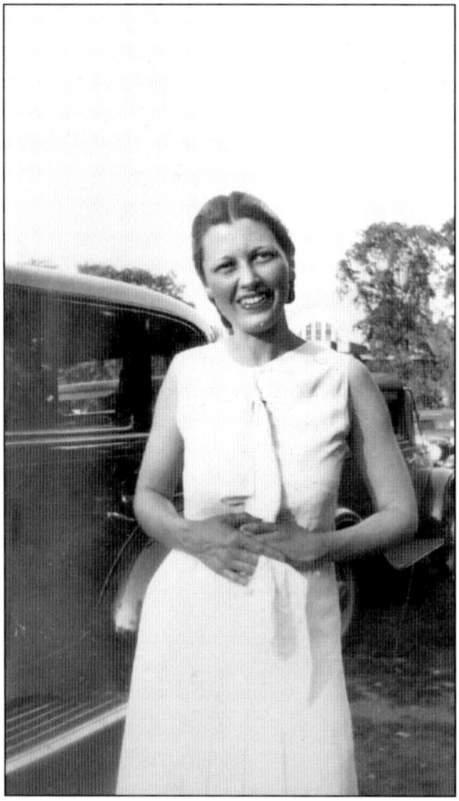

A life-long resident of Florence was Elizabeth Dell Goodridge Nestor. Mrs. Nestor attended Florence School prior to her graduation from Villa Madonna Academy. During World War II, she was a part of the American Red Cross's Nurses Training Program. Following the war, she was active in various historical groups such as the Daughters of the American Revolution and the Boone County Historical Society. Mrs. Nestor attended the Florence Christian Church.

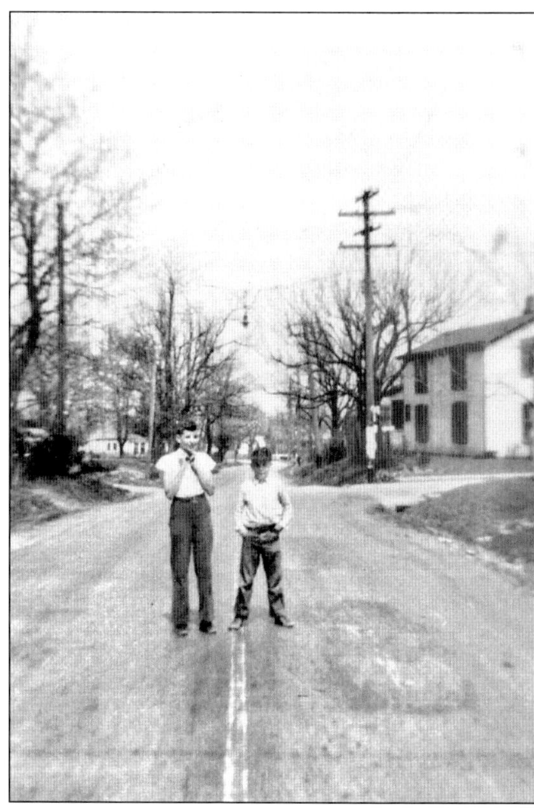

Doing what few would attempt today, Warren Neal (left) and Perry Renaker stand in the middle of Burlington Pike to have their picture taken in the early 1940s. The street in the background that turns off to the right is Shelby Street. The house on the corner was the home of Mrs. Fanny Utz and later the Donald Lipscomb family. Beyond the intersection of Burlington Pike and Shelby Street, the highway was called Locust Street.

In many ways, teenagers have changed very little since the 1940s. Caught hanging out after school are classmates Katherine Tanner (left), Margaret Odell (center), and Bobbie Smith. Bobbie Smith was a varsity cheerleader for all four years of her high school career.

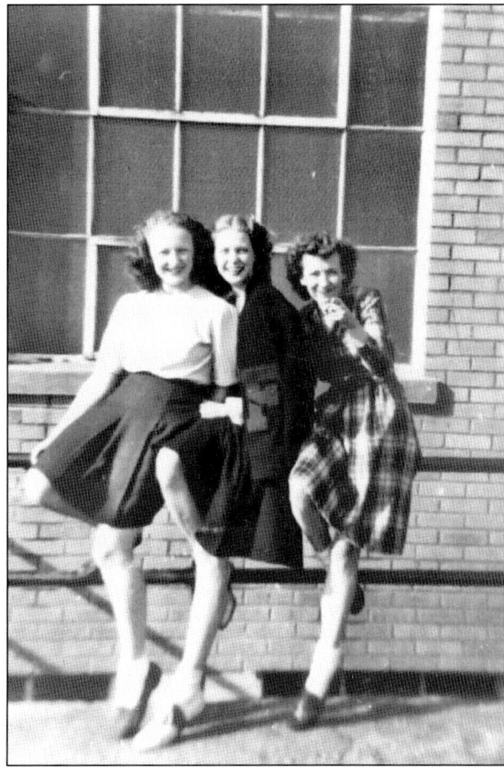

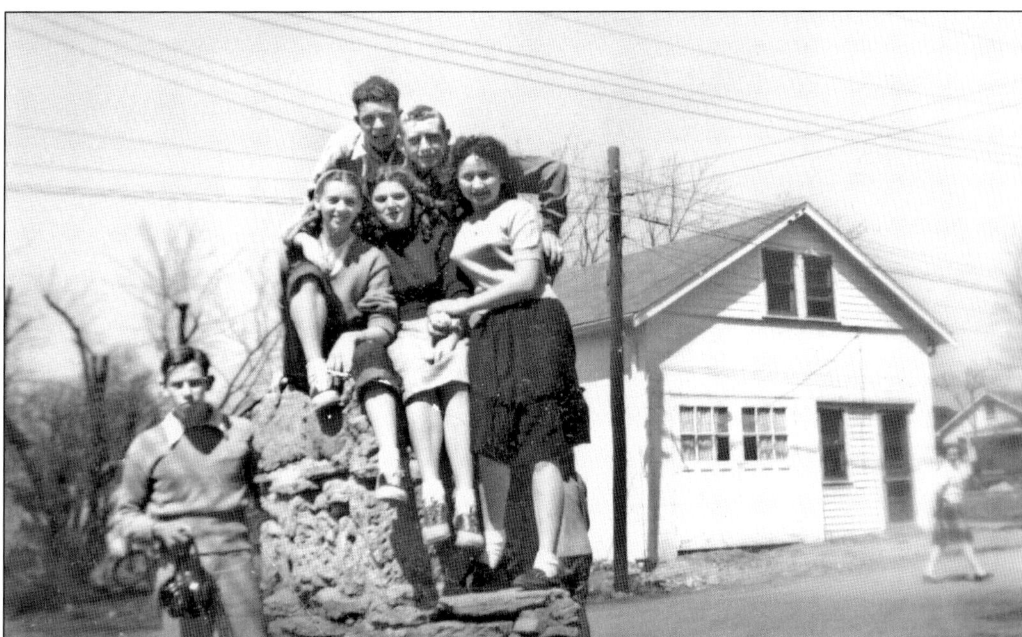

Gathered on one of the stone pillars that marked the entrance to the Florence High School driveway are, from left to right, classmates Robert Henneman, Roberta Markesbery, Bobby Martin, Gloria Hale, George Baker, and Mary Jane Yelton. Just behind the students, at the junction of Center and Oblique Streets (just out of camera range), stood the first house built in Florence.

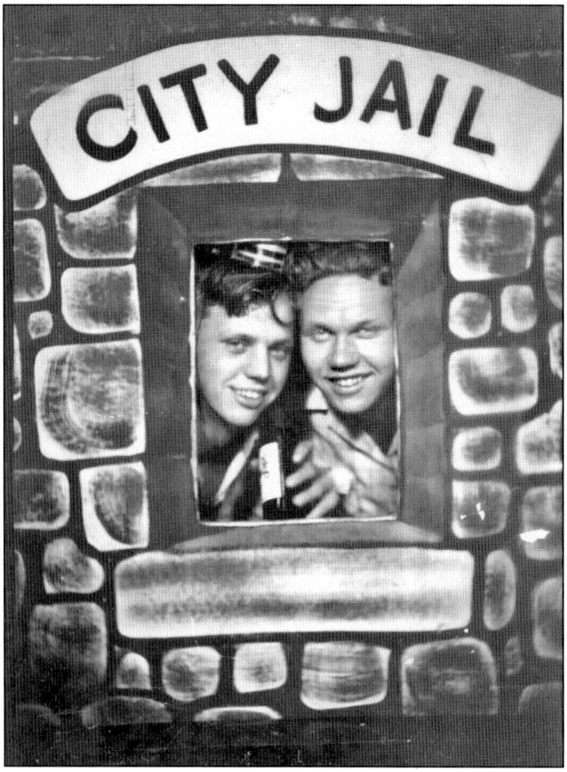

Good friends since their days in school, Al Roberts and Dan Houston share the joke of being photographed in "jail." The two became well-known and respected members of the Florence business community. Dan could be found at his Shell service station on Burlington Pike, Al at Roberts and Hudson Tires on Dixie Highway. Later both men worked together at Roberts and Hudson.

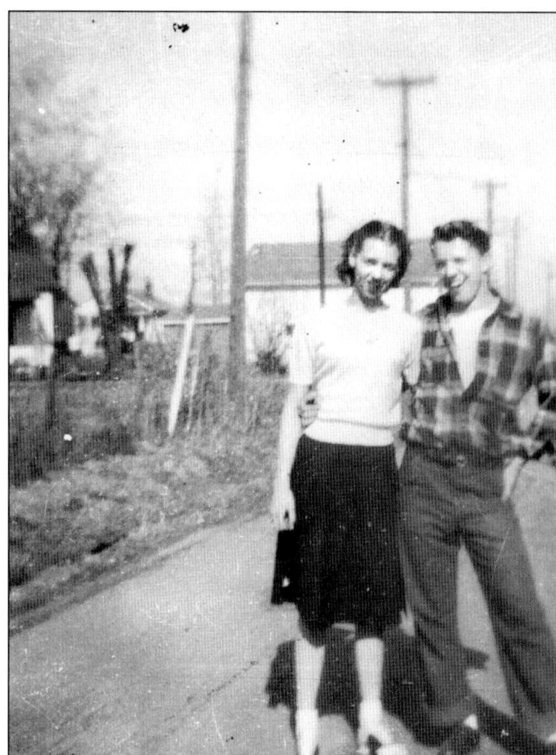

High school friendships often develop into romance. Standing together in front of Florence High School are Roberta Markesbery and Al Roberts. Popular coeds, they were active in many school activities. Al was a member of the varsity basketball and football teams, and they both appeared in their respective prom courts.

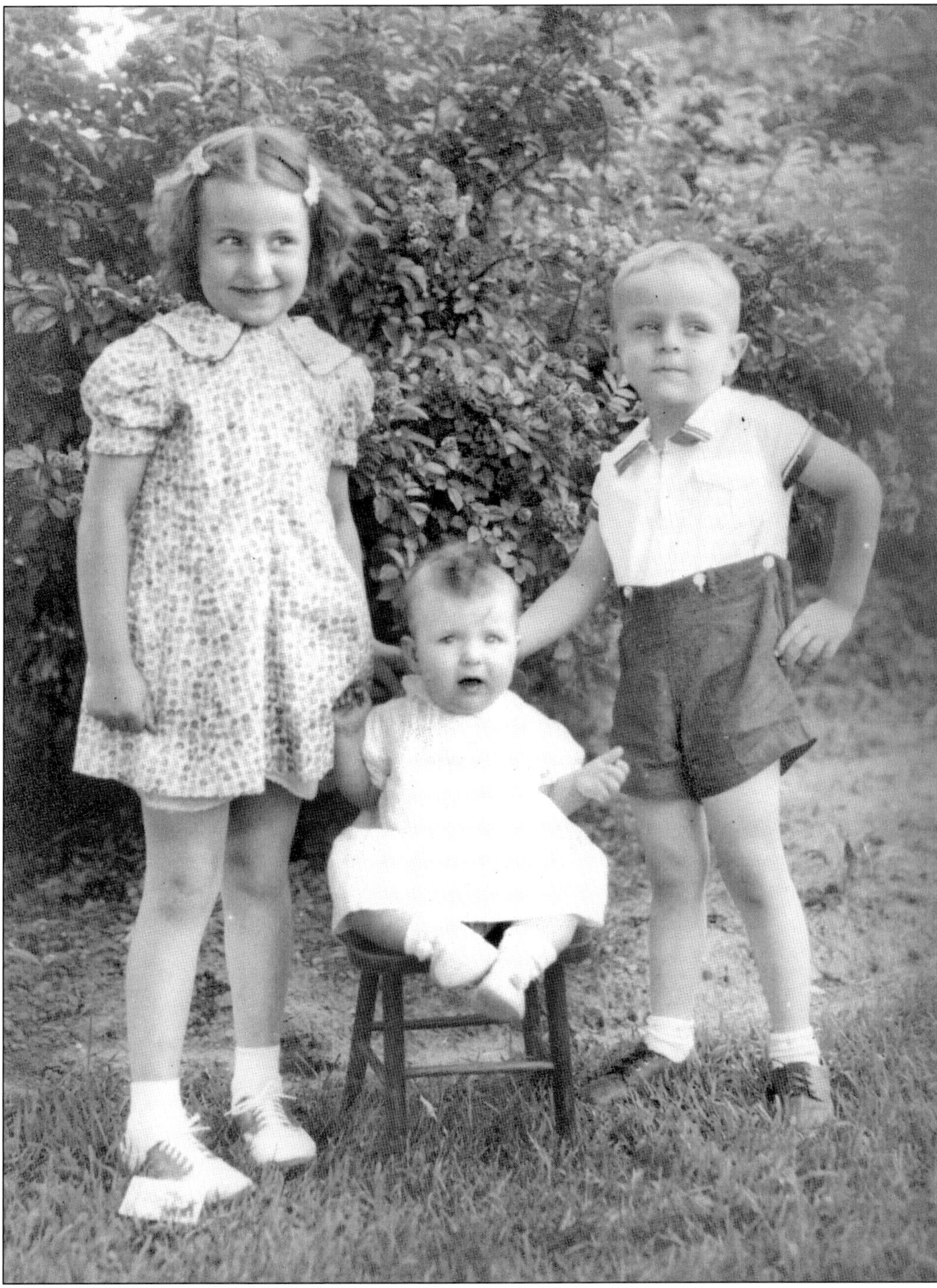

From their home on Main Street, the children of David and Selma Osborn witnessed many of the day-to-day events in Florence. Seen here are Virginia Lee (left), her sister Ella Mae, and their brother, David. Having a strong interest in history, Virginia Lee remembered the events she witnessed and those recounted to her by older citizens. Working hard to preserve and record the county's history, she has served two terms as president of the Boone County Historical Society.

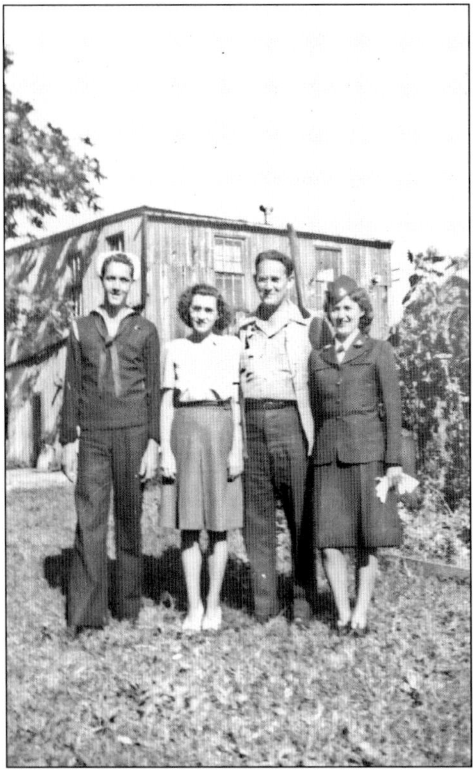

Among the residents of Florence who responded to the call of World War II were Gayle Rouse (left) and Jeanetta Rouse (right), seen here with their father, Franklin, and his wife, Bertie.

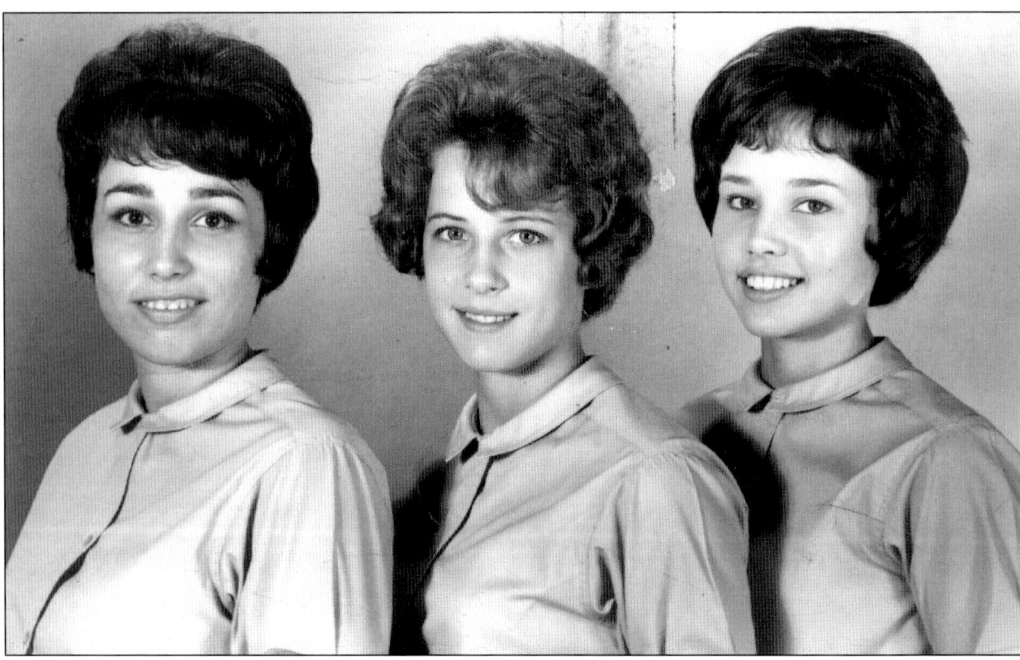

The Three Ks were a popular local singing group. The Three Ks were originally Karen, Kathy, and Kay Arnold. When Kathy got married, she was replaced by her cousin Debbie Arnold. The vocal group began with the encouragement of their grandmother Geneva Arnold. At the height of their career, they appeared regularly on WLW's *Midwestern Hayride*.

Five

School Days and Knights

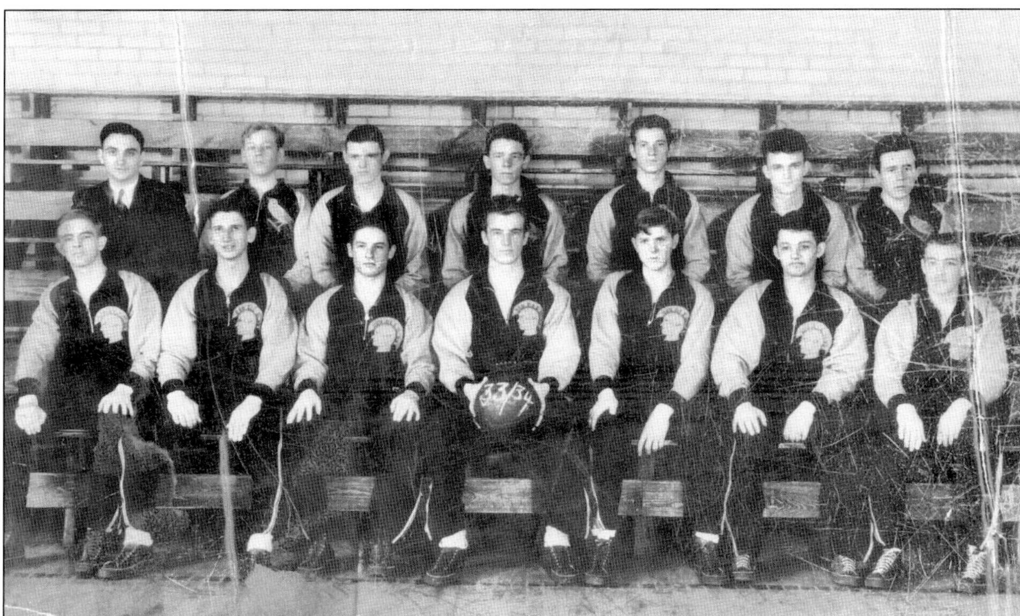

Members of the 1933–1934 boys' basketball team proudly display the school mascot on their team warm-up jerseys. Known as the Knights, the team's colors were orange and black. Their counterparts on the girls' squad were known as the Nightingales. Both squads played before large enthusiastic crowds in the school's new gymnasium.

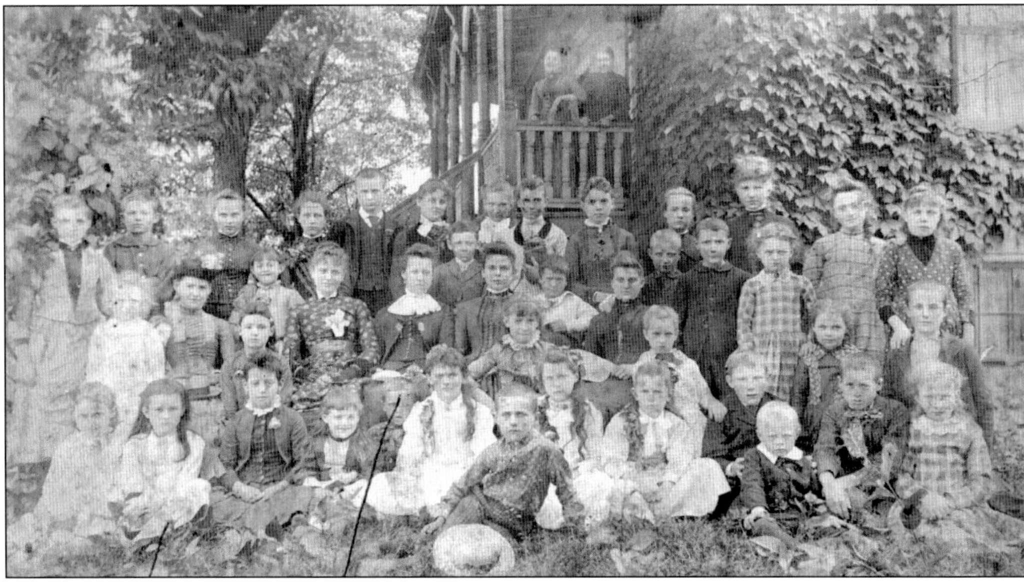

In the late 19th century, several private schools flourished in the Florence area. The school picture here was located at the end of Girard Street on Burlington Pike. Among the other private schools was one located in the town hall. Beginning in 1865, the right to teach in the town hall was sold to the highest bidder. The bids ranged from $1.50 to $3 per month.

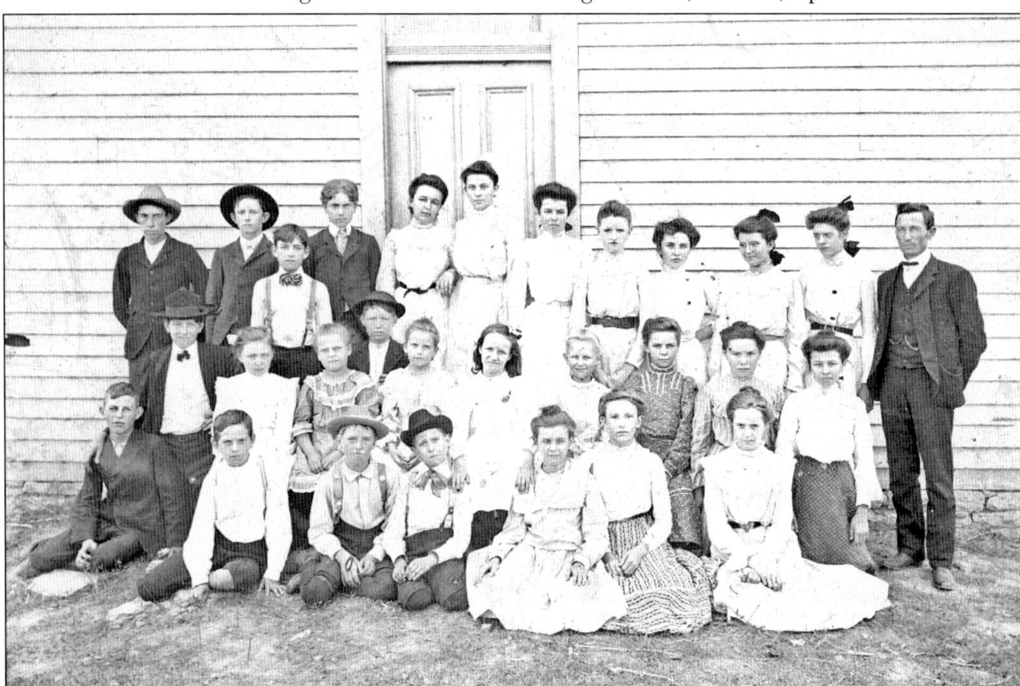

In 1888, an acre of land was purchased from Ned Galway for the construction of a two-room public school on Shelby Street at the junction of Montgomery Street. The school pictured here was the first public school in Florence to separate the primary and advanced grades. Twenty-three years later, the Commonwealth of Kentucky would finally approve the course of studies needed in order to obtain a high-school diploma.

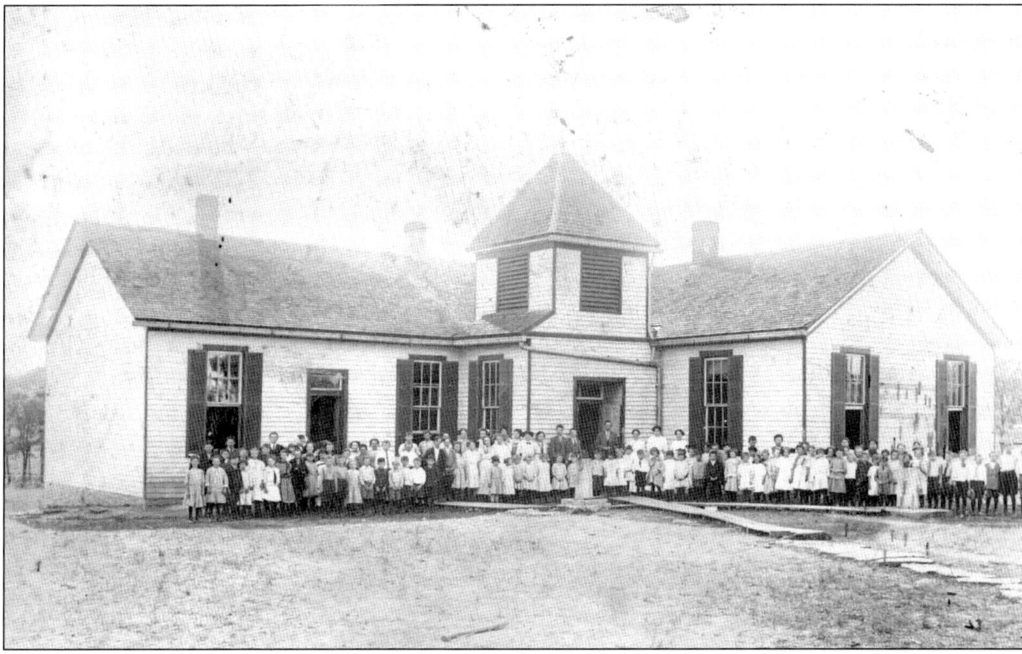

In this pre-1925 picture of Florence School, both elementary and high school students are clearly visible. Shortly after this picture was taken, a second wing was added to accommodate a growing student population. With the addition of the second wing, the building acquired a *U* shape and the teaching staff expanded to seven to handle the increased enrollment.

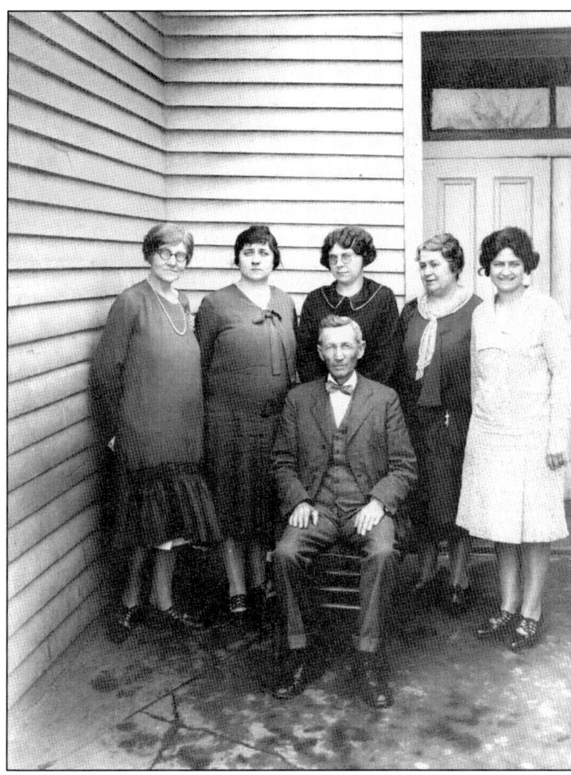

The faculty of Florence High School for the year 1928–1929 is pictured here before the front doors of the school. Standing from left to right are Mrs. Laubish, Mrs. Flossie C. Martin, Mrs. Eunice Pettit, Mrs. Alice Wolfe, and Mrs. Sarah Huey. Seated is Principal A. M. Yealey. From a two-member faculty at the beginning of the 20th century, the Florence School faculty had grown to six members.

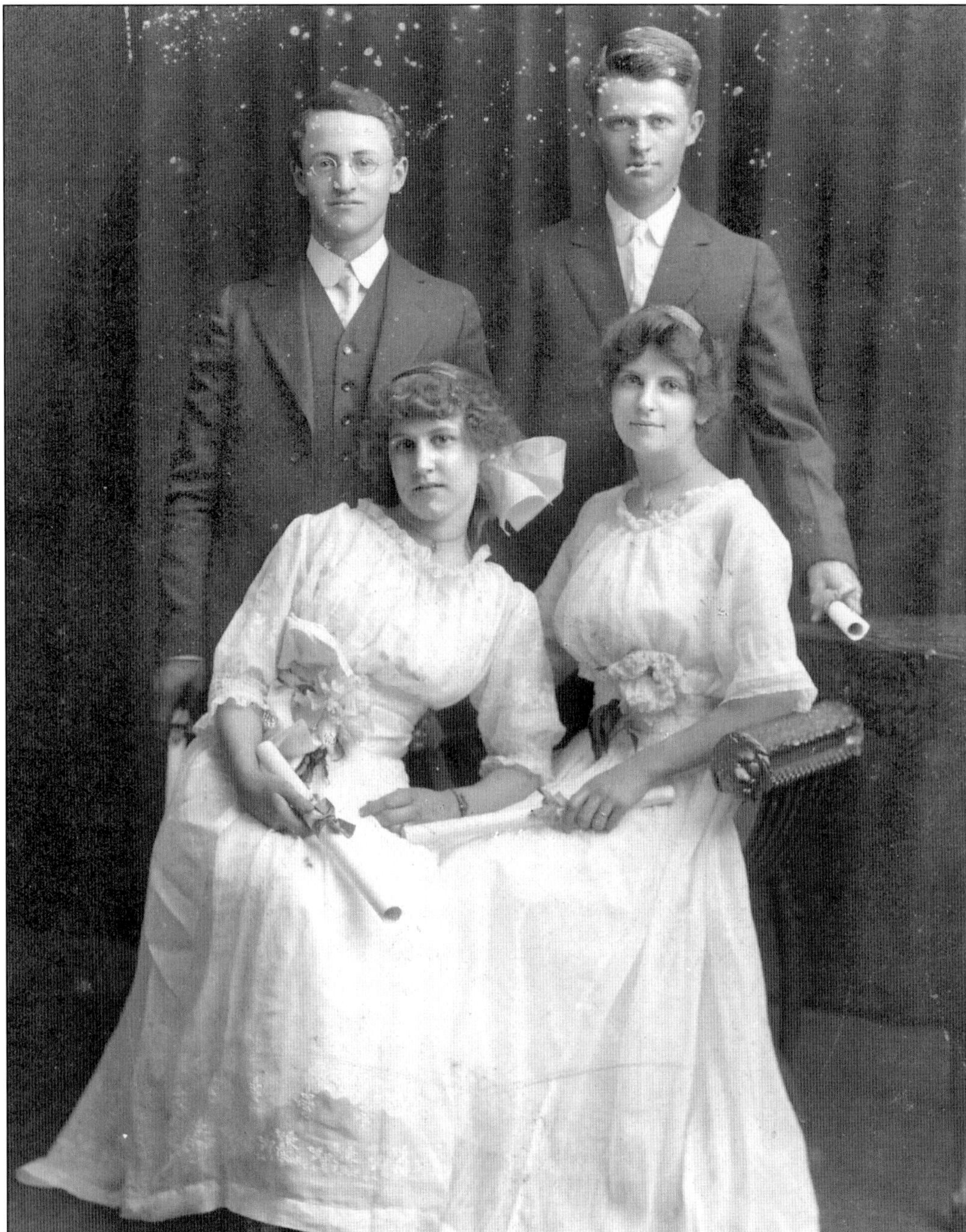

In 1915, Florence High School granted diplomas to its first graduating class. In 1911, state high-school inspectors had approved the course of study and courses to be taught at a graded high school in Florence and granted the right of each student graduating from the schools to enter any college without an examination. From left to right, members of the class were (seated) Mabel V. Tanner and Ruby Corbin; (standing) Harry Tanner and Robert Robbins. Their class sermon was delivered by Reverend Wallace on May 5 at the Baptist church. The class address followed on May 13, given by Reverend Harris at the Christian church.

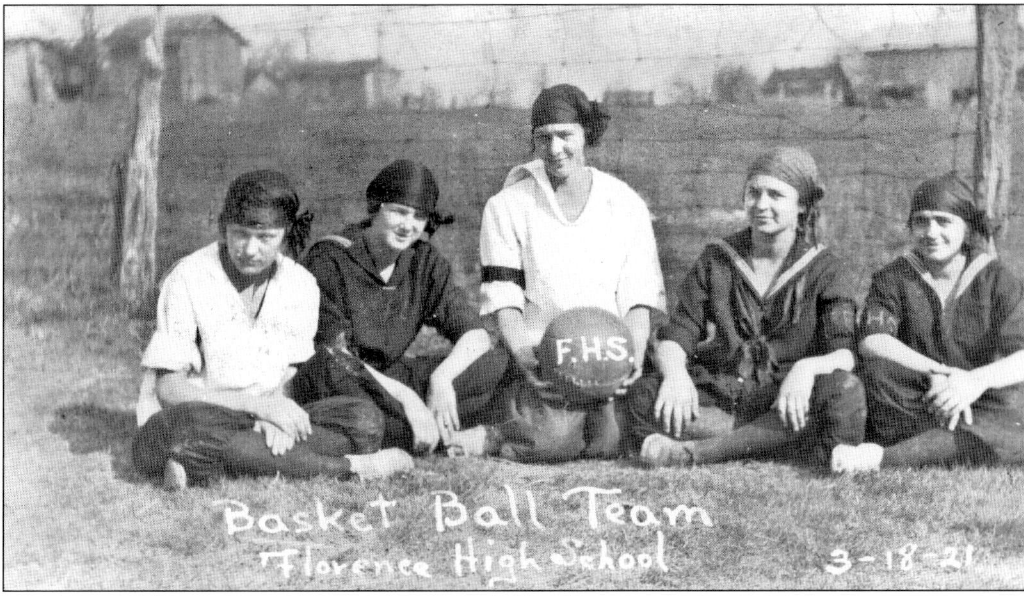

Girls' basketball was a popular sport at Florence High School in the 1920s. Since the old school building had no gymnasium, basketball games were played on an outdoor court. Members of the team posed for the photographer on March 18, 1921. From left to right are Geneva Tanner, unidentified player, Iva Tanner, Imogene Miller, and Mary Whitson.

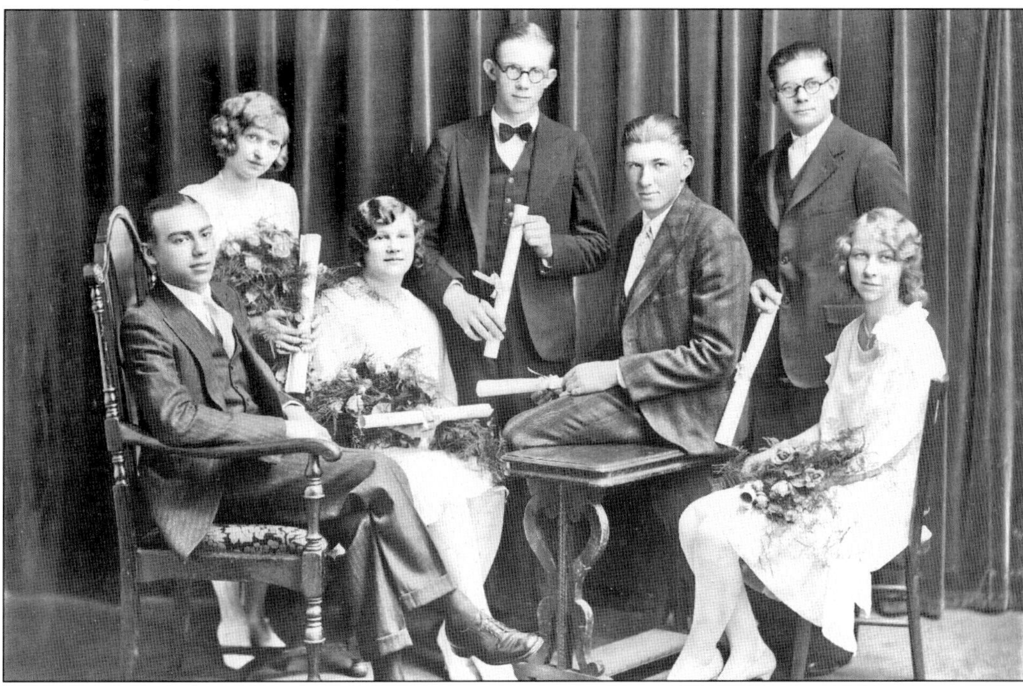

The motto of the class of 1929 was, "The past forever gone, the future still our own." Commencement exercises were held on May 23, 1929, at the Rho-Albee Theater. The commencement speaker was John Uri Lloyd. Members of the class seen here include Cora C. Wesler, Zelma R. Ogden, Lucille E. Taylor, Robert W. Tanner, John G. Laubisch, Mason G. Schadler, and Alvin H. Dringenburg.

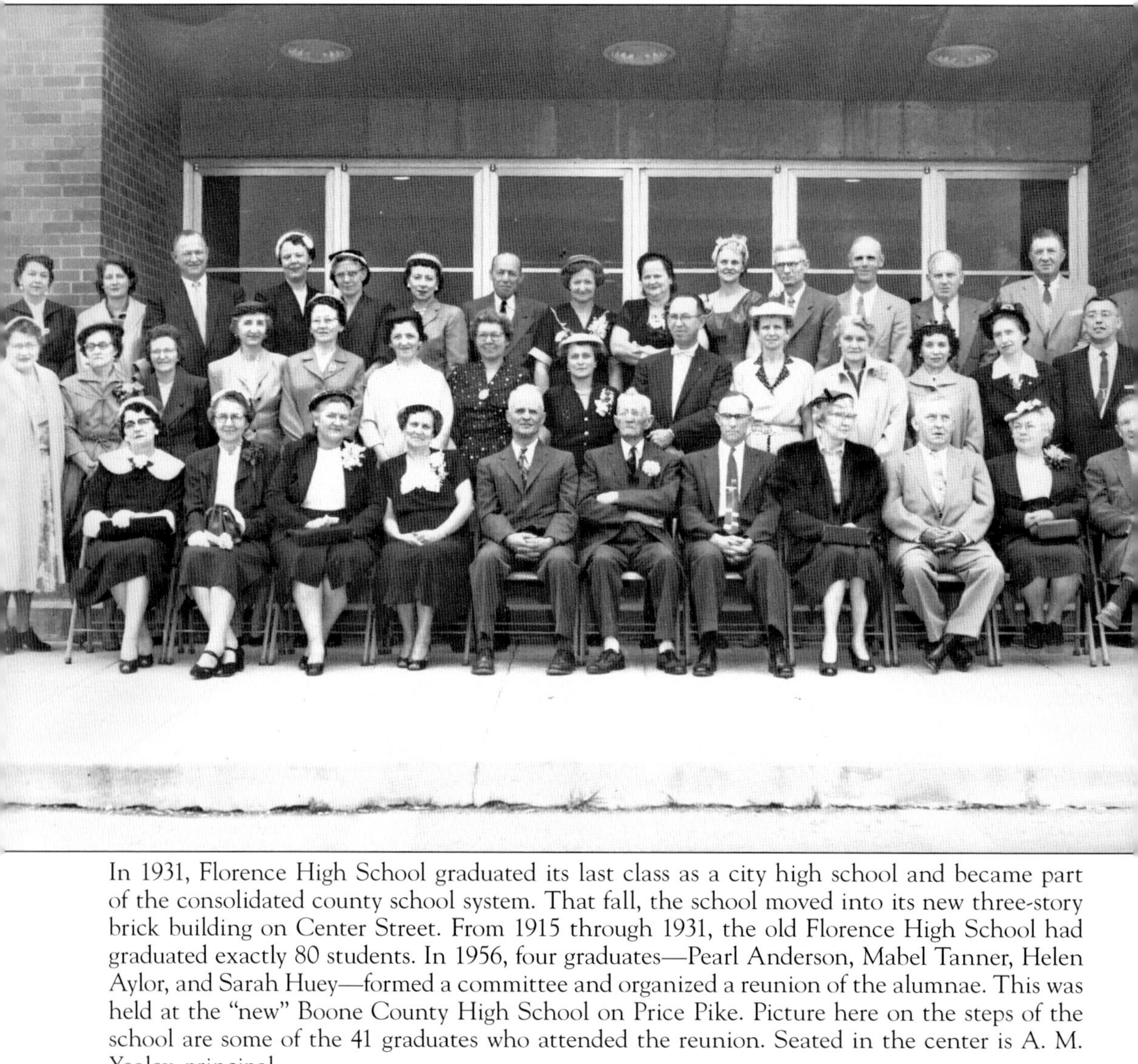

In 1931, Florence High School graduated its last class as a city high school and became part of the consolidated county school system. That fall, the school moved into its new three-story brick building on Center Street. From 1915 through 1931, the old Florence High School had graduated exactly 80 students. In 1956, four graduates—Pearl Anderson, Mabel Tanner, Helen Aylor, and Sarah Huey—formed a committee and organized a reunion of the alumnae. This was held at the "new" Boone County High School on Price Pike. Picture here on the steps of the school are some of the 41 graduates who attended the reunion. Seated in the center is A. M. Yealey, principal.

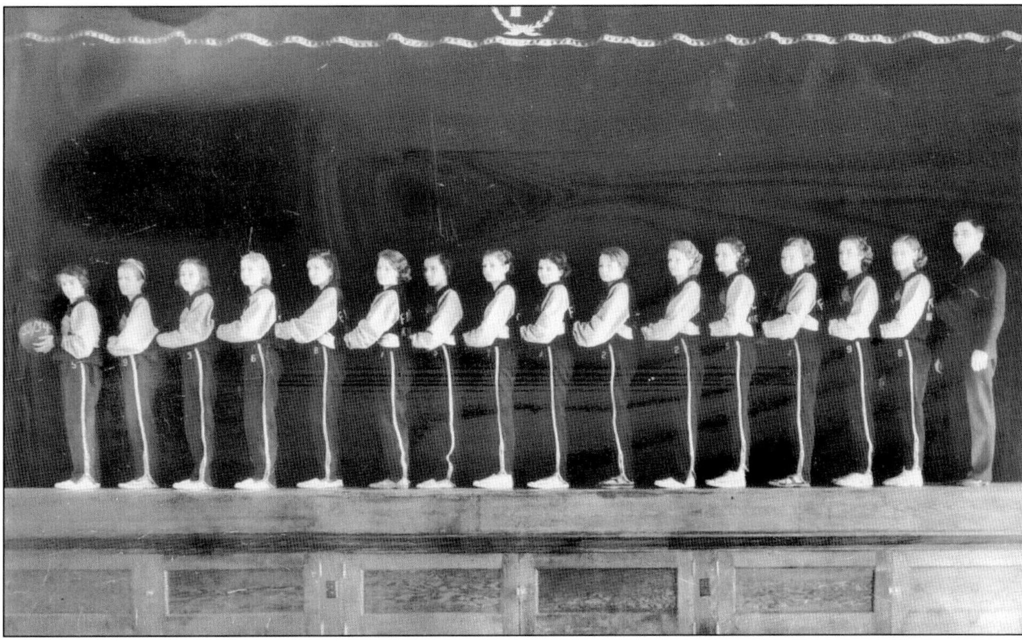

Standing across the stage in the school's gym are the members of the girls' basketball team of 1932–1933. In 1931, the school moved to its new building, which included a gymnasium. The teams no longer had to play on an outdoor court. Starters on the squad were Mary Laubish, Mary Markesbery, Virginia Miller (captain), Elva Smith, Marian Sullivan, Marjorie Bell, Helen Miller, and Helen Taylor. Charles Alphin was the coach.

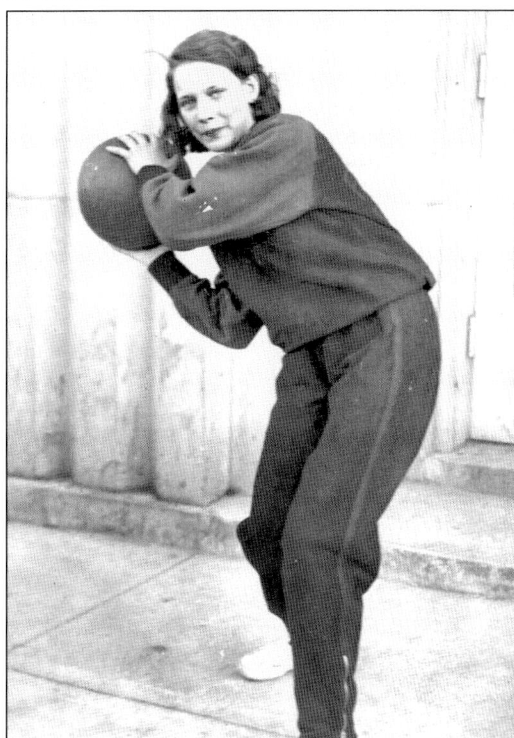

Girls' basketball was a popular sport at Florence High School in the 1930s. The team's nickname was the Nightingales. One of the outstanding players on the 1932–1933 team was senior Marjorie Virginia Bell, pictured here. Wearing the number seven on her jersey, she played center on the team.

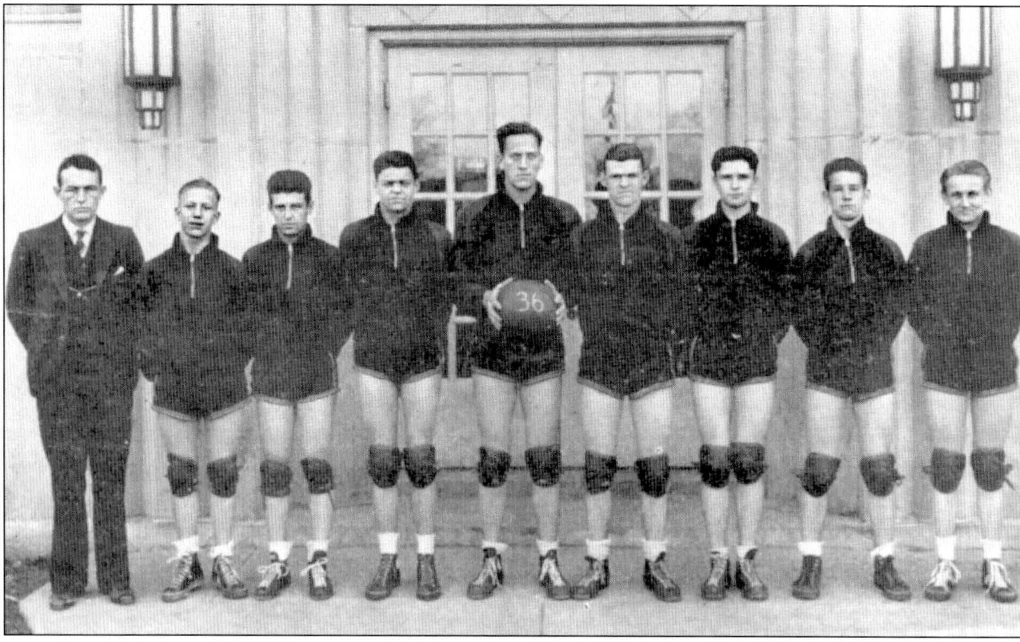

"We love the orange and we love the black, and on our school we'll never turn our back. We'll always keep her on the right track, right track, Florence High School." These lines from the school's fight song no doubt rang out many times as the student body supported this boys' basketball team during the 1936 season.

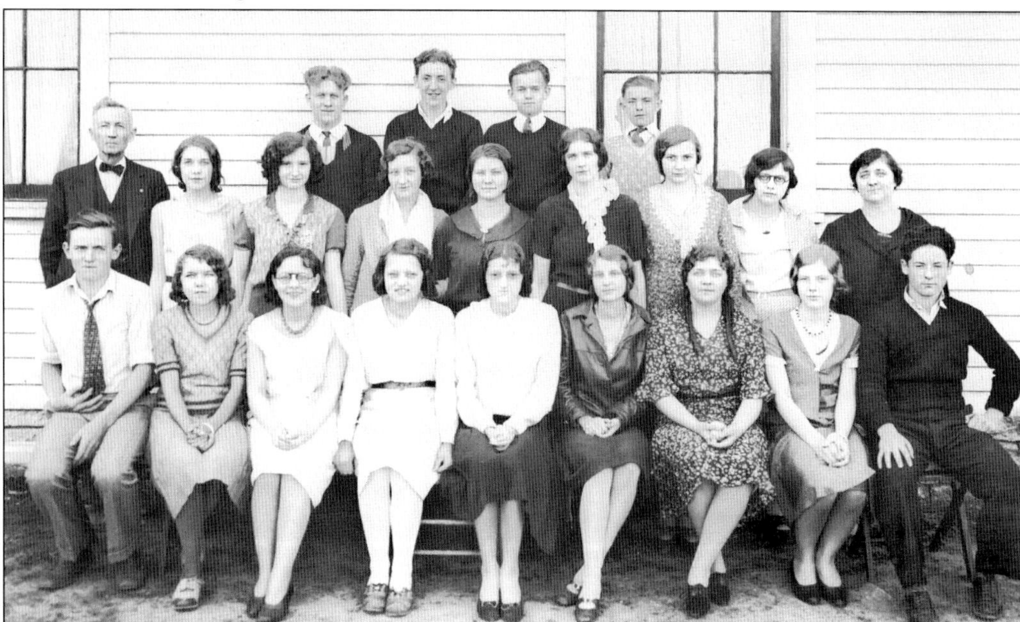

The students pictured here were members of the first classes to graduate from the new Florence High School. They are seen here in front of the old school building, where they spent the majority of their formative years. Standing at the left is Principal A. M. Yealey, who retired at the end of the 1931 school year. Seated in the lower right-hand corner is Cornelius "Connie" Reagan, Florence's World War II hero.

The *Stringtonian* was the yearbook of Florence High School. From the early 1930s through the school's final graduating class in 1954, the *Stringtonian* recorded the history and memories of the school. During the years of its publication, the cover designs ranged from images of the Florence knight (the school's mascot) to Felix Moses in his peddler's wagon.

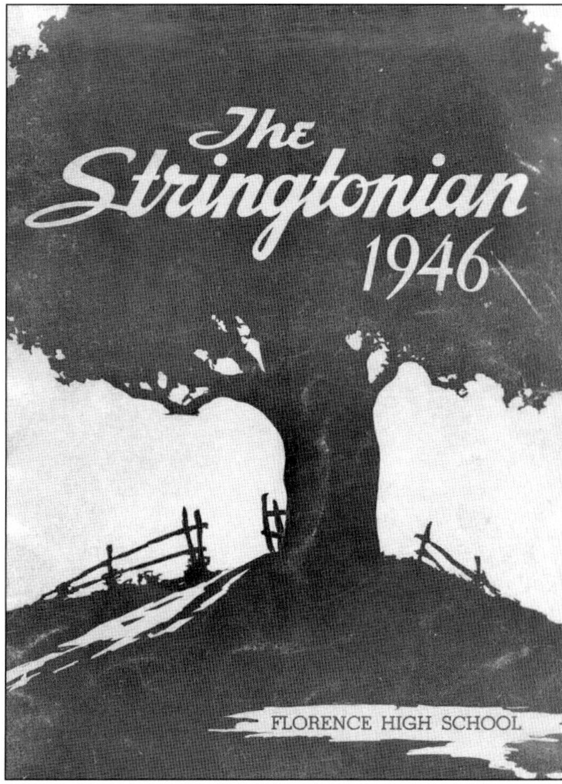

Caught on film are members of the Florence High School boys' basketball team and cheerleaders for 1946–1947. Shown are, from left to right, (first row) cheerleaders Bobbie Smith, Margaret Odell, and Beverly Markesbery; (second row) John Miller, George Baker, Perry Renaker, Tommy Doyle, and Jerry Rouse; (third row) Coach Rector Jones, Billy Ray Markesbery, Billy Woods, Bobby Martin, Dan Houston, Roy Woods, and Harold Zimmerman; (fourth row) Marvin Zimmerman, Walter Arnold, Ralph Quinn, Al Roberts, and C. A. England.

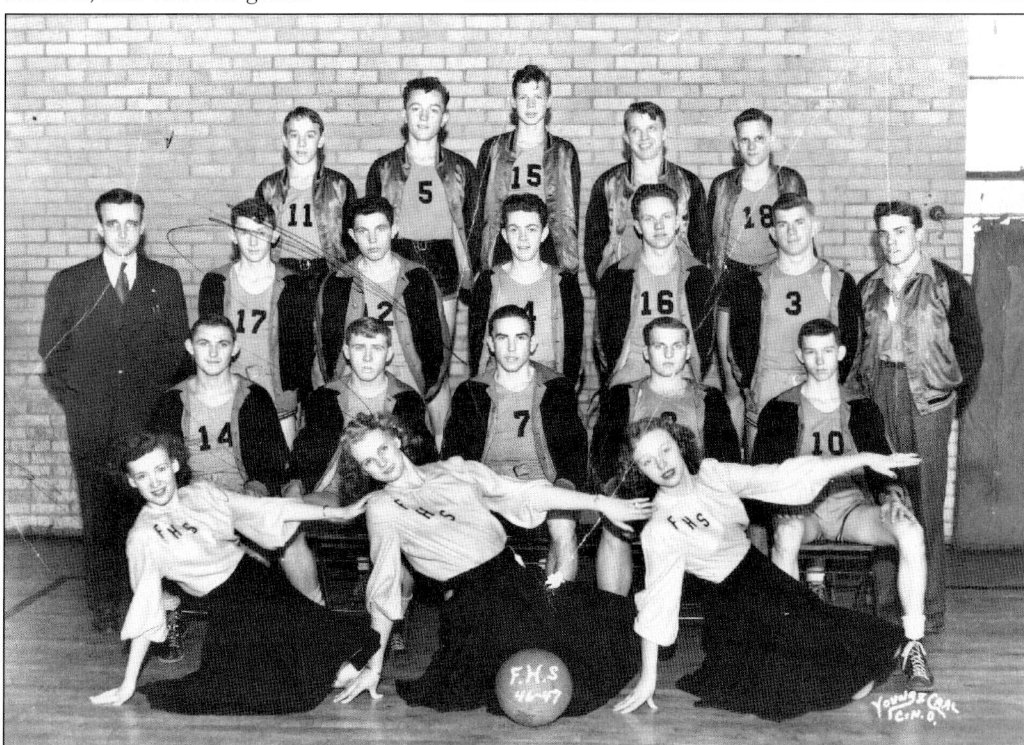

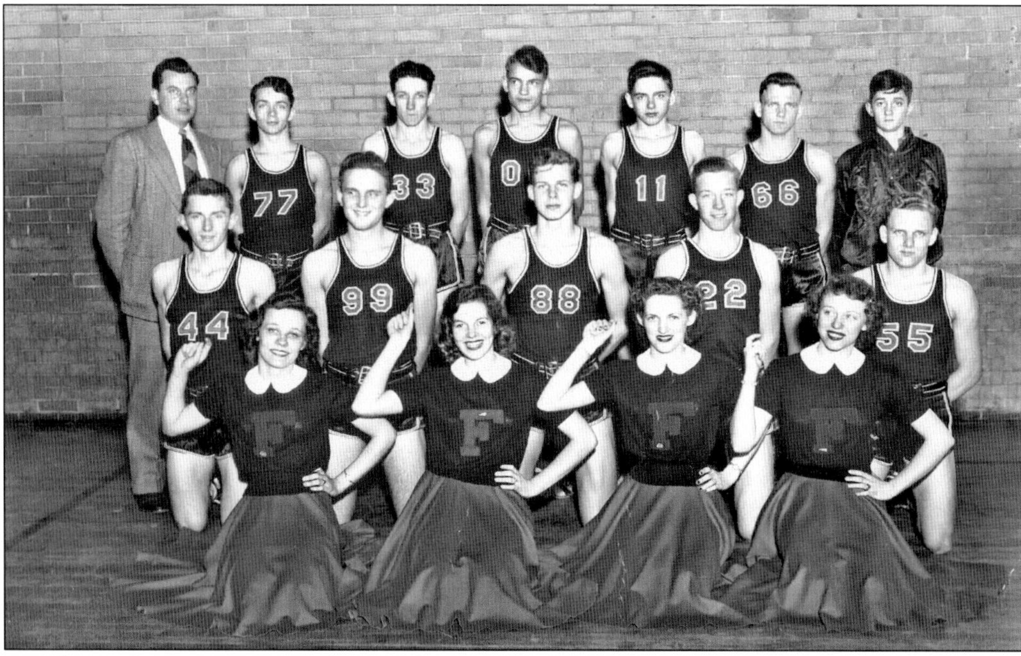

Members of the 1948–1949 Florence basketball team included, from left to right, (kneeling) Billy Ray Markesbery, Donald Lipscomb, Ralph Quinn, Bobby Rowland, and C. A. England; (standing) Coach Victor Bruner, Roy Martin, Wendell Cooper, Charlie Dinn, Billy McKibben, Jesse England, and Irvin Luck. Cheerleaders from left to right are Faye Arnold, Roberta Reynolds, Betty Benton, and Beverly Markesbery.

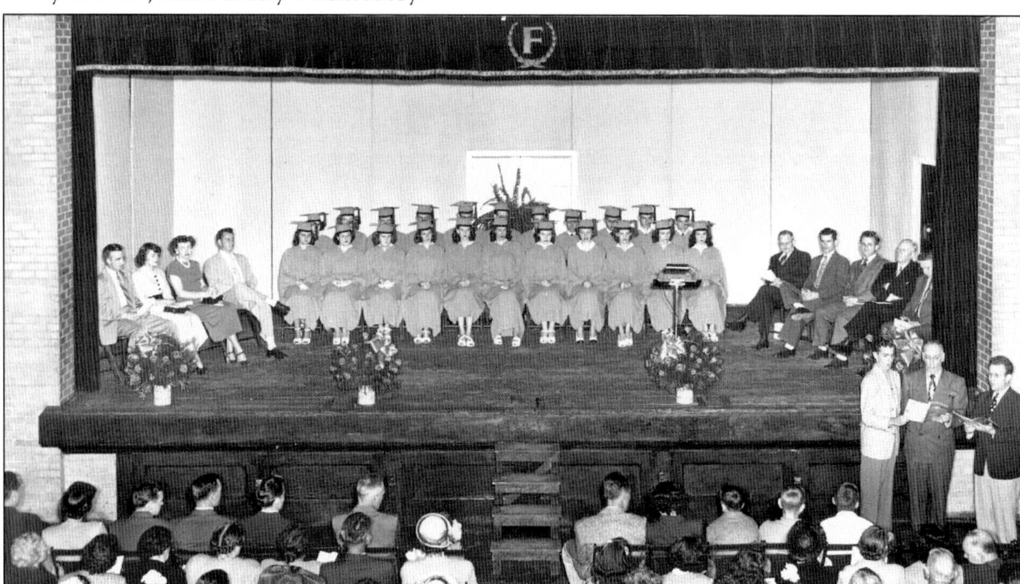

The dream of every high school student is . . . graduation! Traditionally the commencement exercises at Florence High School were held on the stage in the school gymnasium. At center stage are the members of the class of 1949. Seated to the left and right are the members of the faculty. The trio seen on the bottom right of the picture is performing for the audience. Well-known Florence musician Lawrence Aylor can be seen on the right of the group.

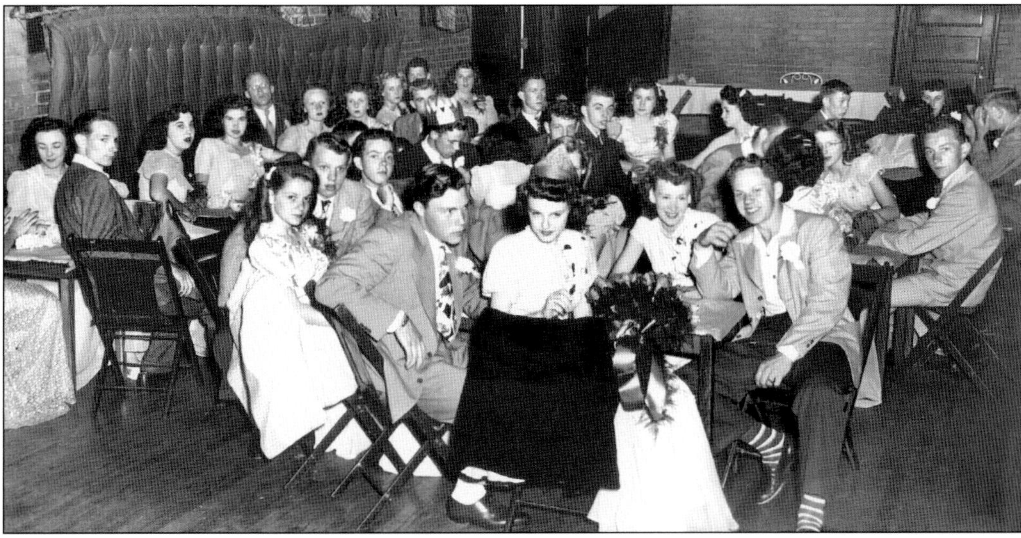

Taking a break from dancing, the students at the 1947 prom seem to be enjoying themselves. Members of the prom court that year were King Harold Zimmerman and Queen Wanda Dinn. Attendants were Jean Rose Baker, Perry Renaker, Bobbie Smith, and Bobby Martin. Making a fashion statement with his striped socks is Dan Houston.

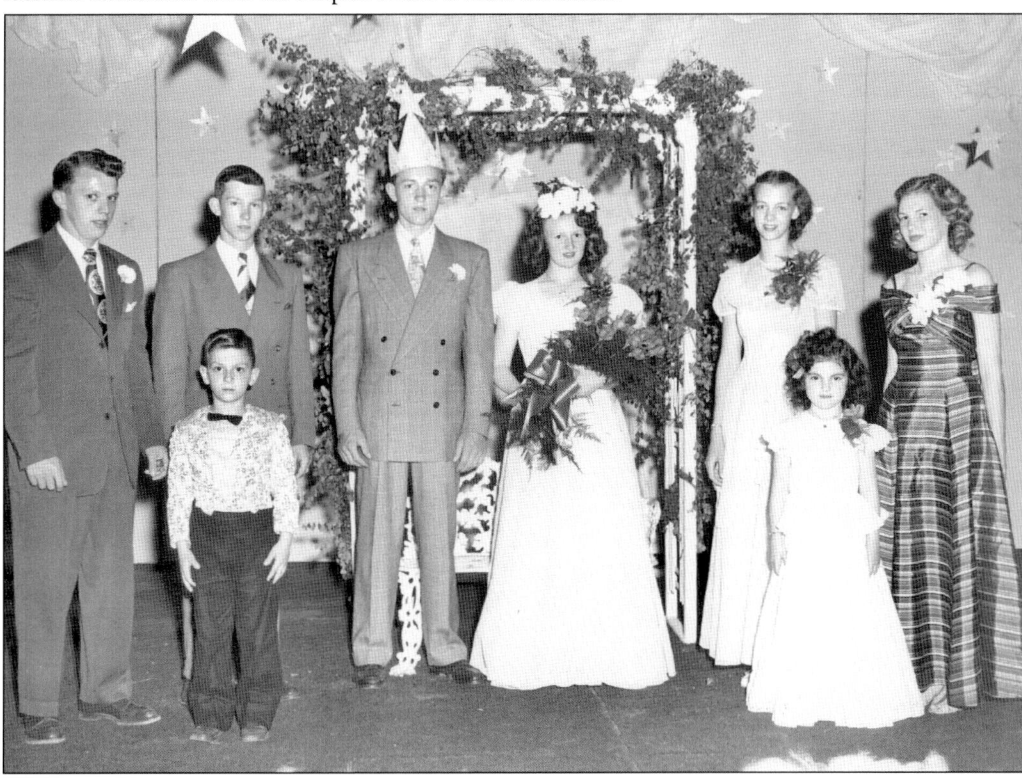

In May 1948, members of the junior and senior classes gathered in the school's gymnasium for the prom. Pictured here is the prom court for the year. From left to right are (first row) Roy Hoffman and Linda Blackburn; (second row) Al Roberts, Jerry Rouse, Walter Arnold, Katherine Tanner, Roberta Markesbery, and Roberta Reynolds.

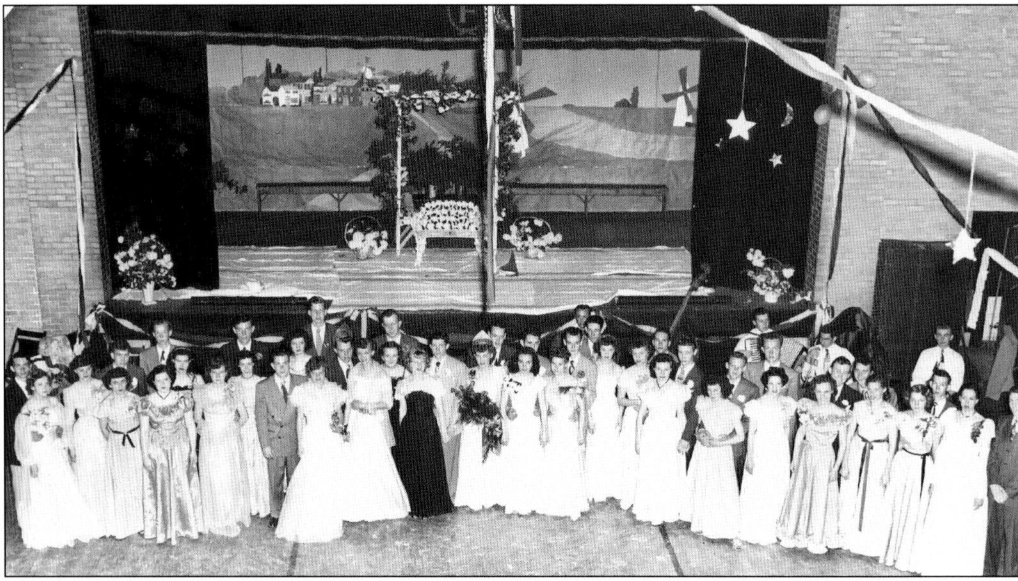

Unlike today, high school proms were usually held in the school gymnasium. Seen here following the coronation are members of the 1949 junior and senior classes of Florence High School. Among the students pausing for the photographer are prom queen Betty Benton and prom king Al Roberts.

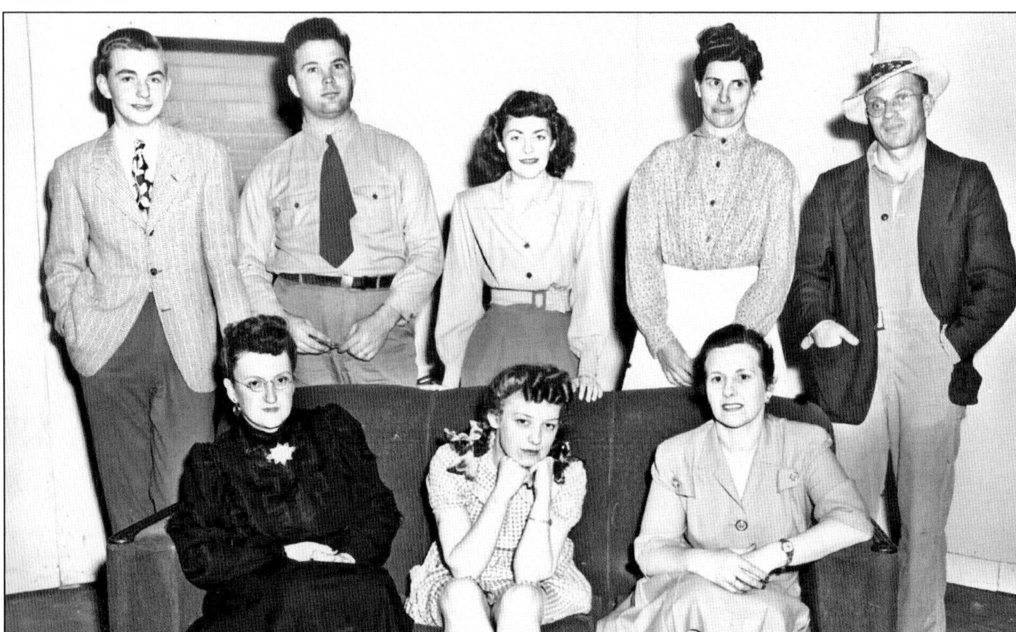

In the 1940s, Florence High School had an active PTA. To help support the school, members of the faculty, the student body, and parents presented plays in the school's gymnasium. Pictured here are several members of the cast of *Billy's Goat*. Shown from left to right are (seated) Ruth Cooper, Margaret Hopper, and Sarah Lusher; (standing) Charles Popham, J. Paul Rimmer, Byar Worthington, Ethel Tanner, and Charles Tanner. Local Lutheran pastor J. Paul Rimmer was serving as interim school principal while principal Rector Jones was serving in World War II.

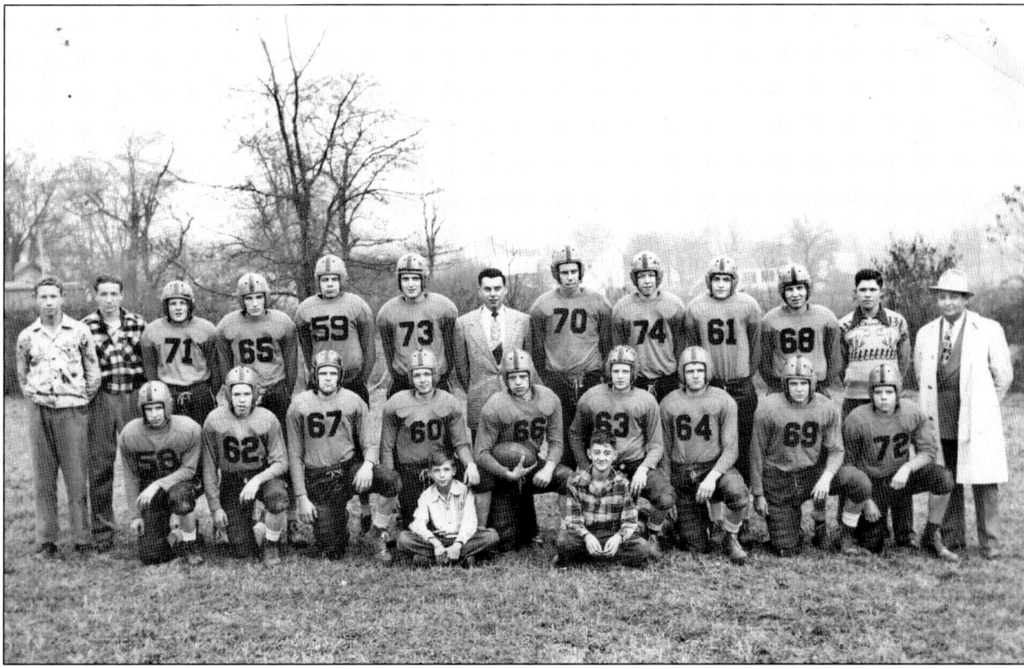

Pictured here are members of the 1948–1949 Florence High School six-man football team. From left to right are (seated) unidentified and Russell Luck; (kneeling) Jackie Renaker, Marvin Laile, C. A. England, Roy Martin, Alfred Roberts, Sunny Stansel, Jesse England, Bruce Brown, and Paul Quinn; (standing) Robert Henneman, Wendell Cooper, Owen R. Bethel Jr., Billy Ray Markesbery, Jan Fields, Don Lipscomb, Mr. Brunner (coach), Robert Hennemann, Bobby Rowland, Charles Dinn, Bud Abbott, Don Martin (manager), and Bill McEvoy (coach).

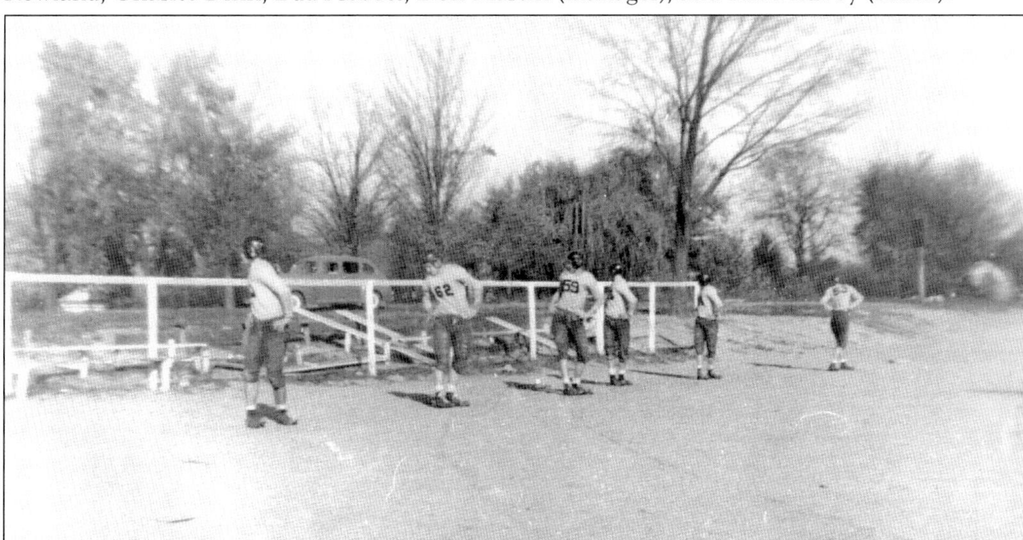

Prior to the consolidation of the county system that resulted in the formation of Boone County High School, there were four high schools in Boone County—New Haven, Hebron, Burlington, and Florence. Due to their small enrollment, none of the schools could field a full 11-man football team. As a result, the high schools played a state-sanctioned six-man schedule. Seen here practicing behind the school are members of the Florence six-man football squad.

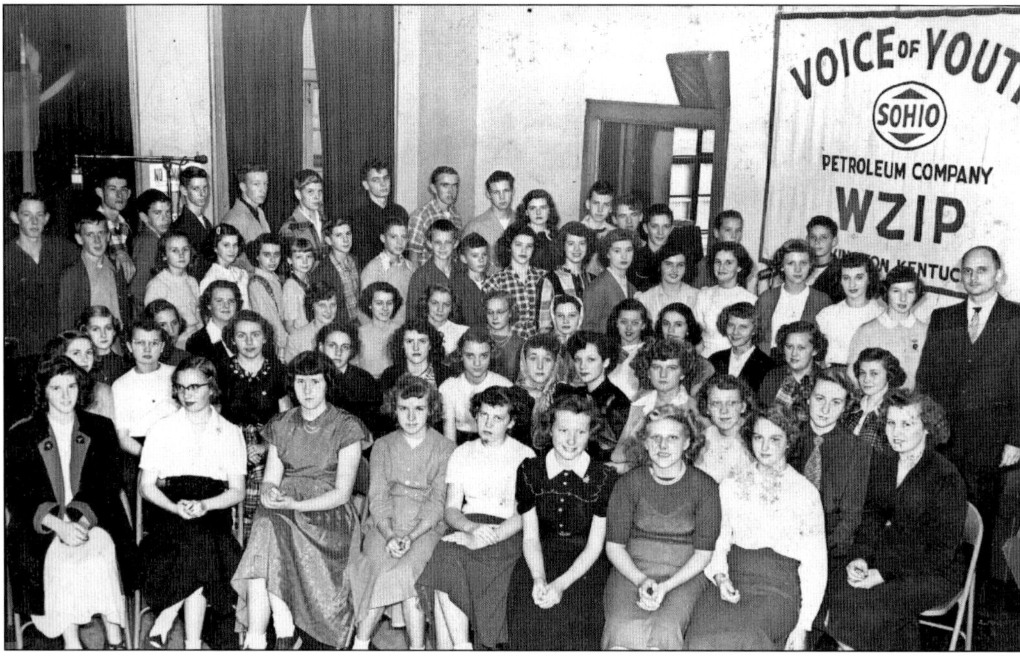

In the early 1950s, members of the Florence High School Glee Club traveled to Covington to record a performance for radio station WZIP. The *Voice of Youth* program was sponsored by the SOHIO Petroleum Company. The size of the group reflects the popularity of the choral program at Florence. To the right stands director Dean Bloss.

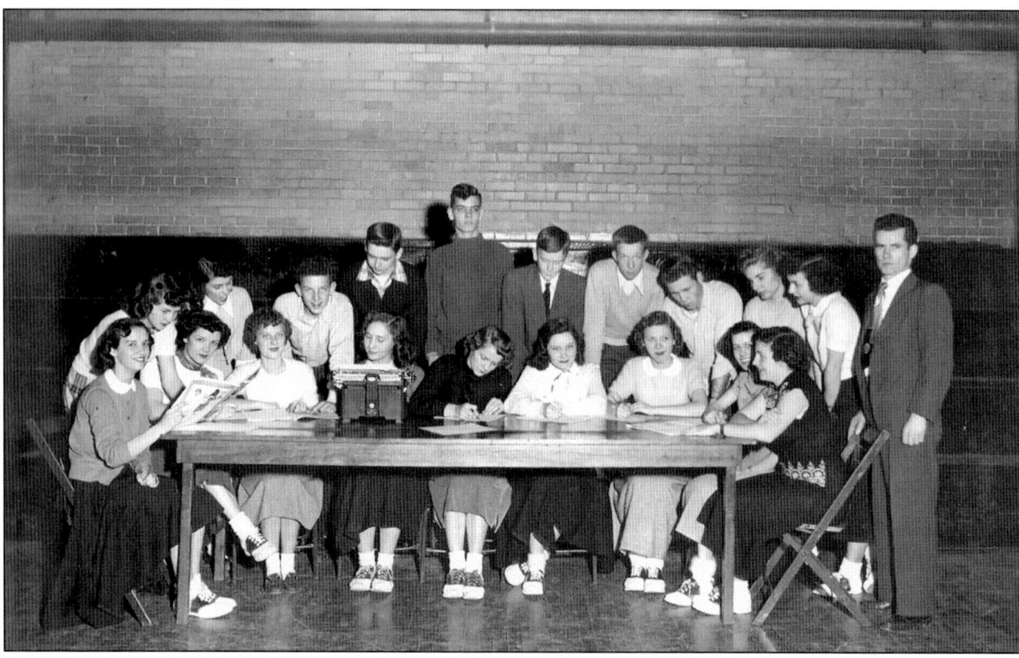

Gathered around the typewriter are the members of the journalism class of 1950 at Florence High School. During that time, the *Boone County Recorder* published special editions called *Boone County School News*. Each of the four county high schools contributed to the paper. The journalism students are seen here trying to meet their deadline for the next edition.

Six

A. M. Yealey

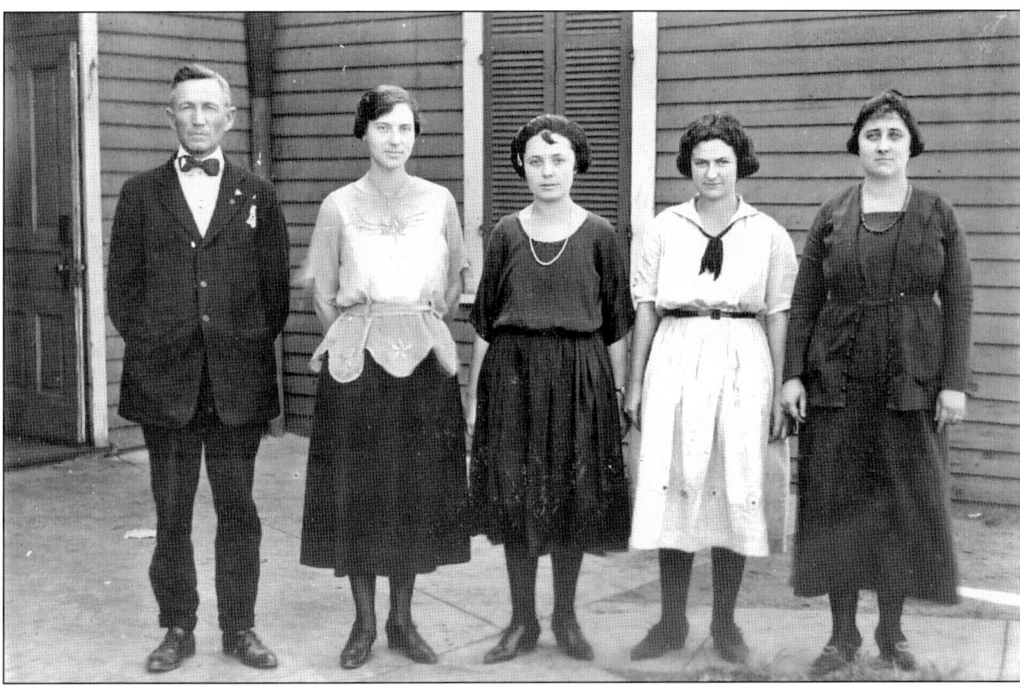

From 1900 through 1931, A. M. Yealey was principal of the Florence School. Under his guidance, Florence went from a two-room frame school to a six-room schoolhouse and a faculty of seven. In that time, it progressed from an ungraded school to an accredited high school, and the campus expanded from one to six acres. Teaching salaries exceeded those of any school in the county. In 1931, the school had a surplus of $14,000 in the Florence Deposit Bank.

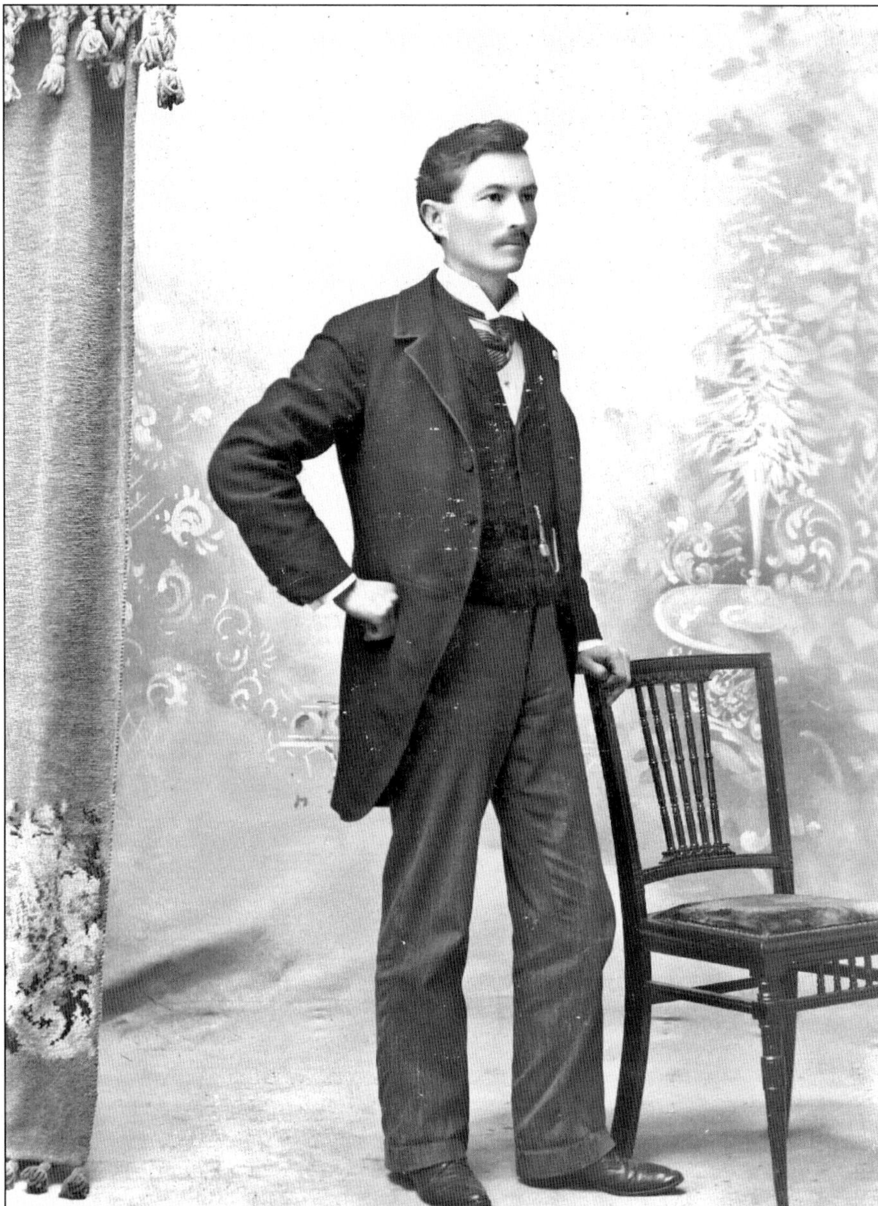

Descended from German immigrants who settled in the area of Union County, Ohio, A. M. Yealey attended the National Normal University in Lebanon, Ohio, Wilmington College in Wilmington, Ohio, and the University of Cincinnati. After teaching in Union County for five years, Mr. Yealey temporarily left the teaching profession for a career in business. Following his marriage to Lucy Ann Rouse in 1898, he became a farmer and a teacher in rural Boone County schools. In 1901, he became the principal of Florence School. He established the first high school in Florence in 1911 to be accredited by the Southern Association of Colleges and Schools. After 29 years of dedicated service to the students of Florence, Mr. Yealey retired. Following the death of his wife during World War II, he returned to teaching, spending two years at Florence and three years at New Haven. His children were Willa Yealey House, Russell Yealey, and Georgia Yealey Tanner.

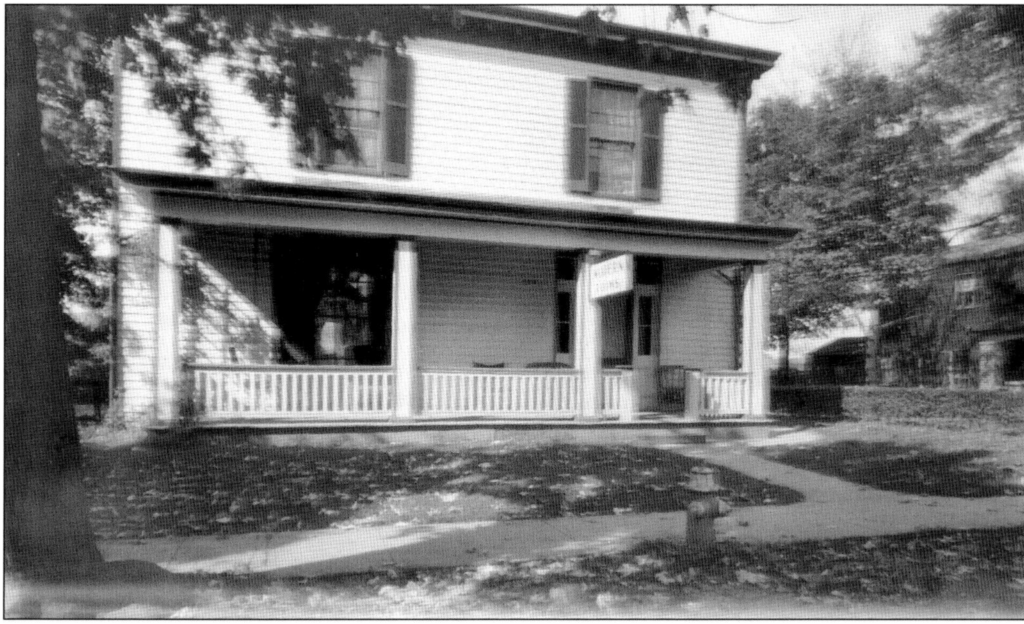

This house at 268 Main Street was home to A. M. Yealey and his wife, Lucy. Clearly visible is a sign advertising "Modern Rooms." Before motels dotted the landscape, several families opened their homes to tourist and boarders. Mr. Yealey eventually added two rooms to the front of the house that became an ice-cream parlor. The house with the addition remains on Main Street today.

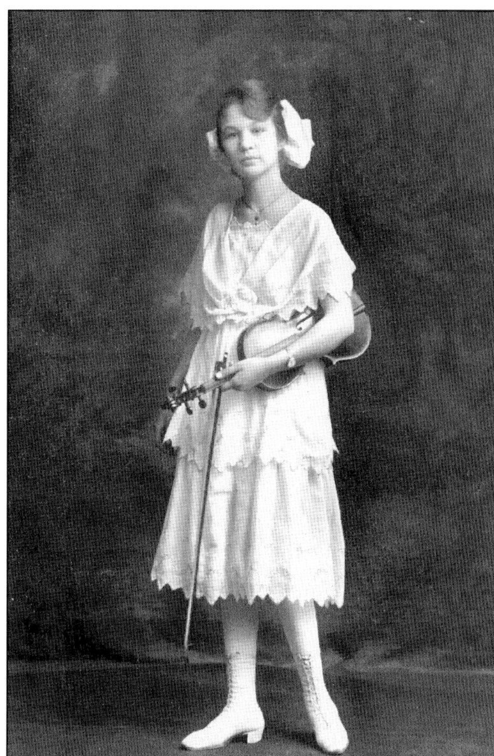

Reflecting a simple classical elegance, Georgia Yealey, daughter of A. M. Yealey, poses here with her violin. Georgia was the niece of Albert and Nellie Rouse Metzger, two talented local musicians. A 1920 graduate of Florence High School, she eventually took both violin and piano lessons. Following graduation, she worked at the Florence Deposit Bank.

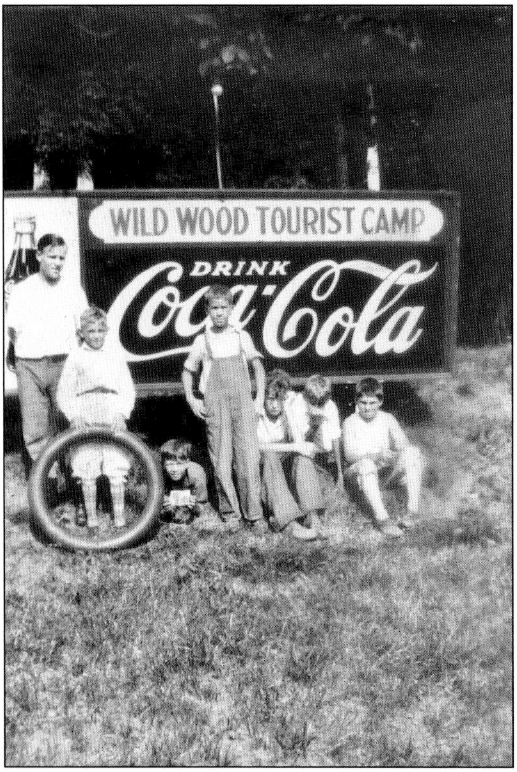

In 1931, in partnership with his son-in-law Russell House, Mr. Yealey built the Wild Wood Tourist Camp, the forerunner of the eventual Wildwood Motel. The motel derived its name from the impressive grove of trees on the site, many of which were well over 100 years old. The property was originally a part of the farm of Rev. William Carpenter, who arrived from Virginia in 1813 during the settlement of the county.

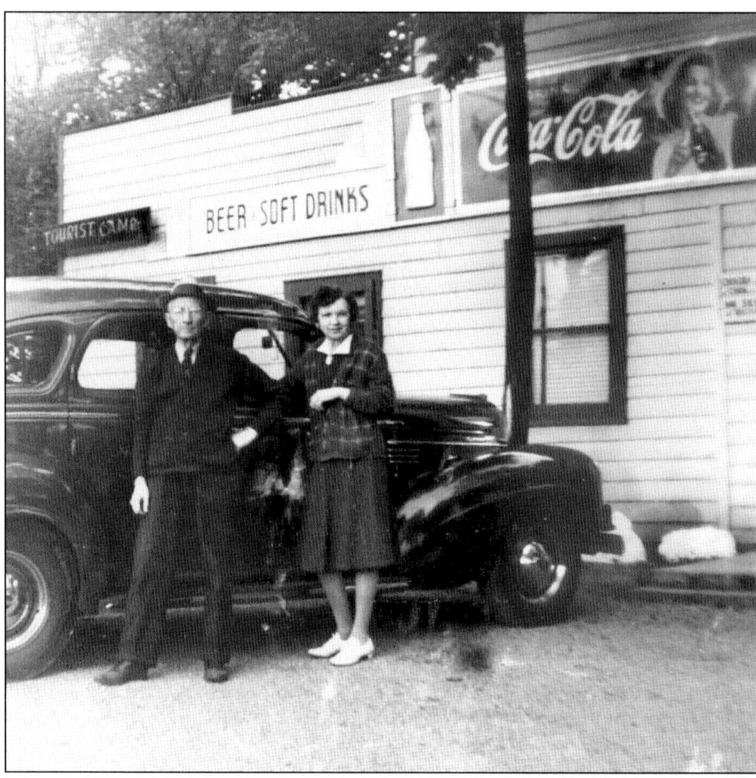

Before the days of the Wildwood Motel, Mr. Yealey operated the Wild Wood Tourist Camp. Unlike the motel, the tourist camp put travelers up in small cabins dispersed among the trees. Offering tourists both lodging and refreshments, it was a tranquil stop along U.S. 42. Mr. Yealey is seen here with his daughter Willa.

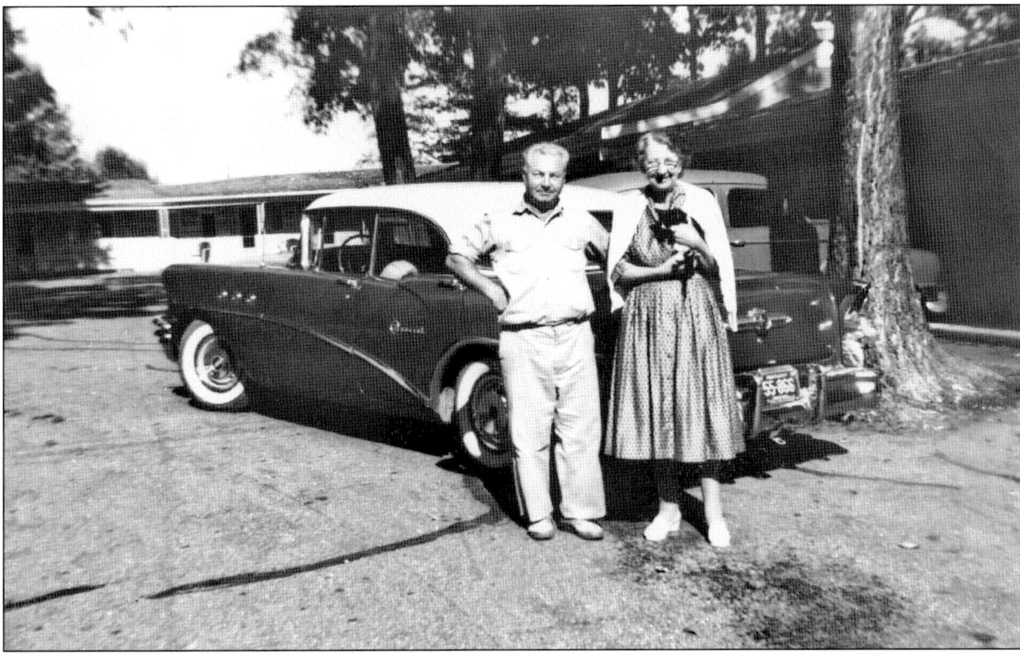

By the early 1950s, the Wildwood Motel had expanded and shed the label of Tourist Camp. When this picture was taken, U.S. 42 was still the major route between Cincinnati, Ohio, and Louisville. Seen here are Russell and Willa House. In an attempt to develop tourism, Russell, along with co-owner A. M. Yealey, was among numerous Boone County motel owners who petitioned Frankfort to develop Big Bone State Park.

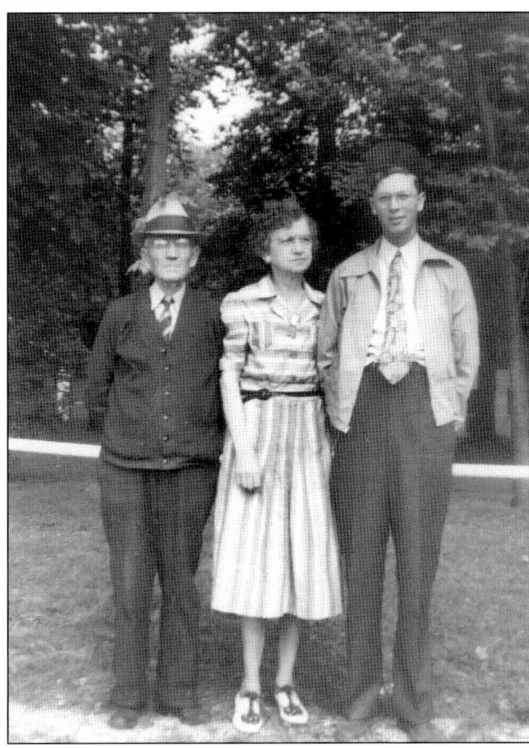

Mr. and Mrs. Yealey had two grandchildren, George Robert Tanner and Mary Russala Yealey Demoisey. Seen here with his grandparents is Bob Tanner. He was a well-known pitcher for the local baseball team. Bob would later go on to study medicine and become a doctor.

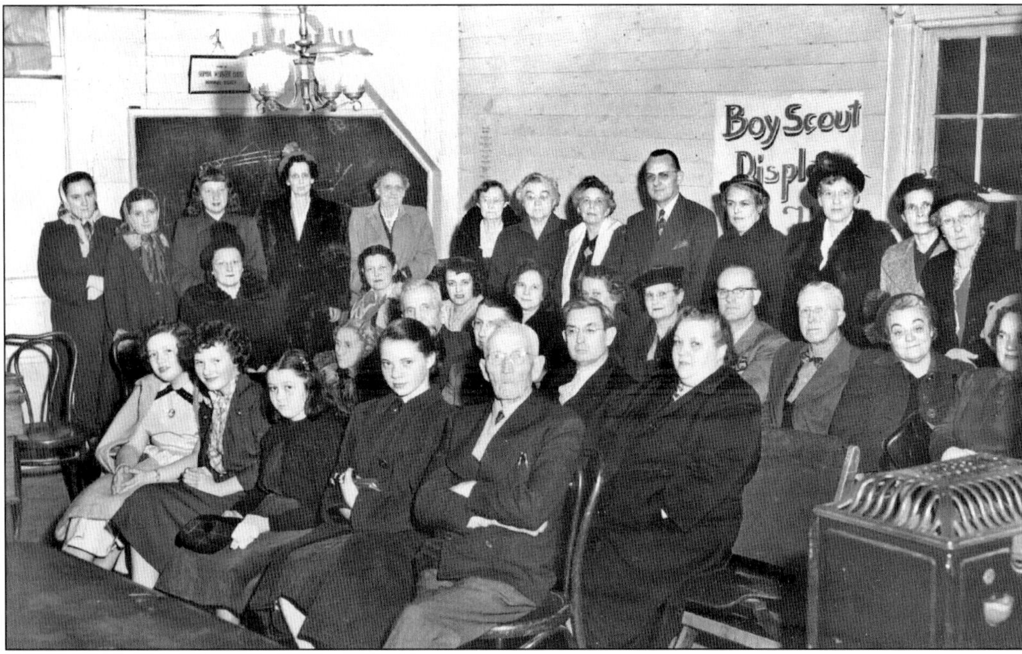

One of A. M. Yealey's great interests was the study of history. He is seen here (seated front row, left) at an early meeting of the Boone County Historical Society. Meetings were held on the second floor of the old town hall. At a time when local history was not always appreciated, Mr. Yealey collected local documents and memorabilia for the reference of future generations of Boone Countians.

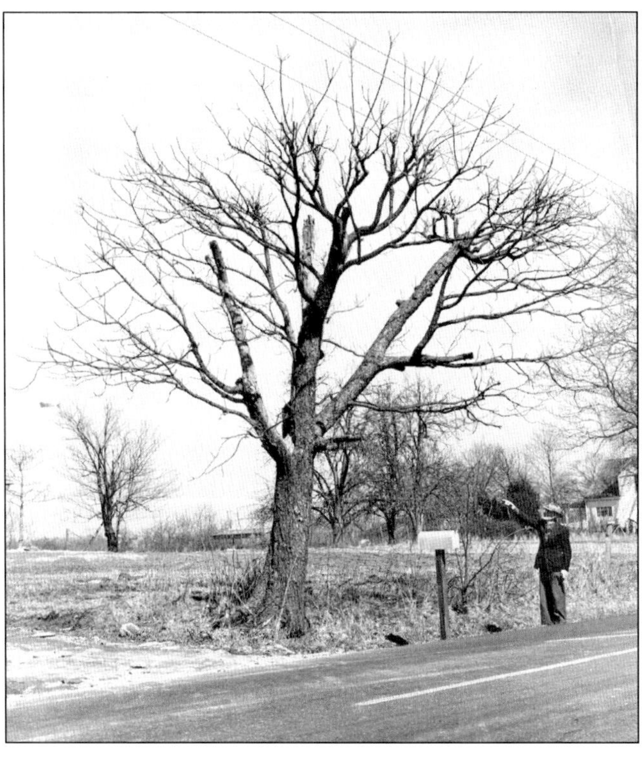

In the 1950s, Mr. Yealey began to write articles for the *Boone Recorder* and the *Walton Advertiser* under the title of "Early History of Boone County." Mr. Yearly is seen here pointing toward the "Hanging Tree" near Camp Earnest Road along Burlington Pike. The story of the tree was featured in one of his articles. In 1960, his articles were collected and published as the *History of Boone County Kentucky*.

Seven

CHURCHES

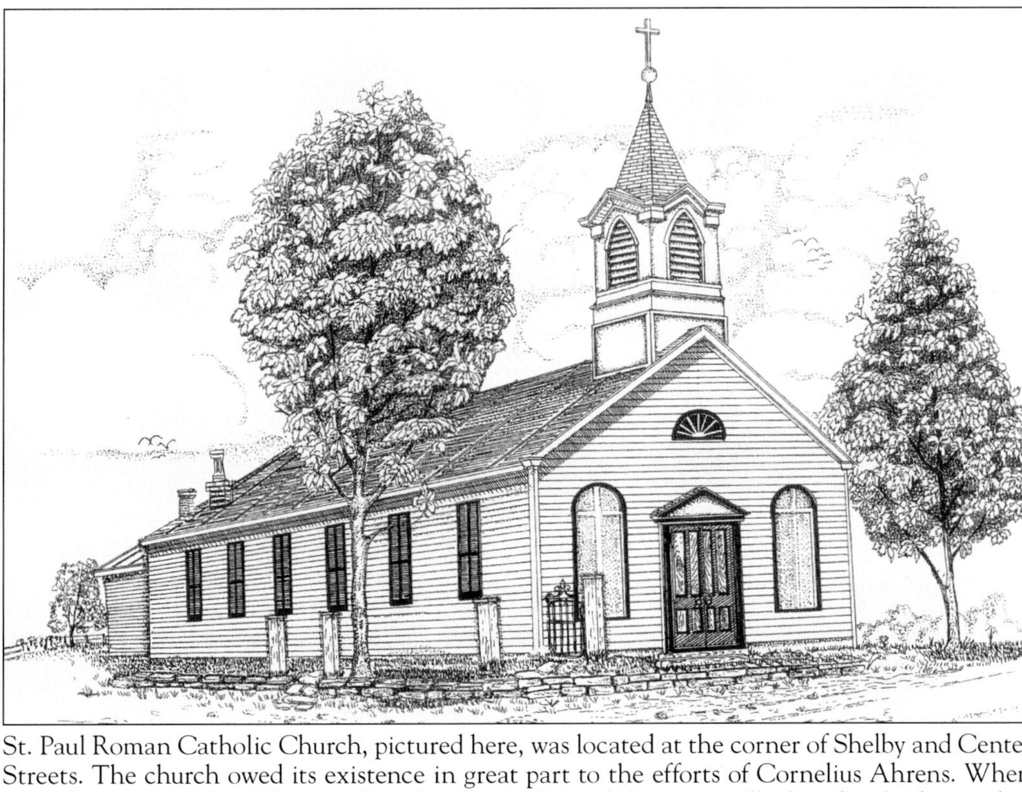

St. Paul Roman Catholic Church, pictured here, was located at the corner of Shelby and Center Streets. The church owed its existence in great part to the efforts of Cornelius Ahrens. When Mr. Ahrens arrived in Florence from his native Ireland, he reportedly found only three other Catholics in town. Mr. Ahrens invited the Reverend Thomas Butler of Covington to say mass in his home and suggested establishing a parish in Florence. Land for the church was donated by Ezra Fish, and the men of the parish soon built the 25-by-40-foot building. The church's steeple stood 30 feet high. This church building served the parish until it relocated to its present site of Dixie Highway. Today's church building is the second at that location.

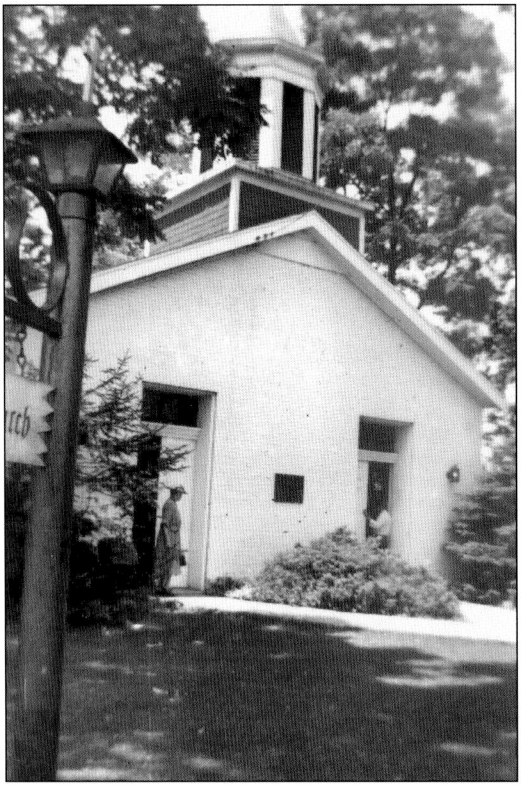

The Florence Christian Church was founded around 1830, when members gathered in area homes to worship. In 1831, the congregation erected their first house of worship at the corner of Main Street and U.S. 42, where it has remained to this day. In 1862, the wounded and dying soldiers who participated in the skirmish at Florence were laid out on the grounds of the church.

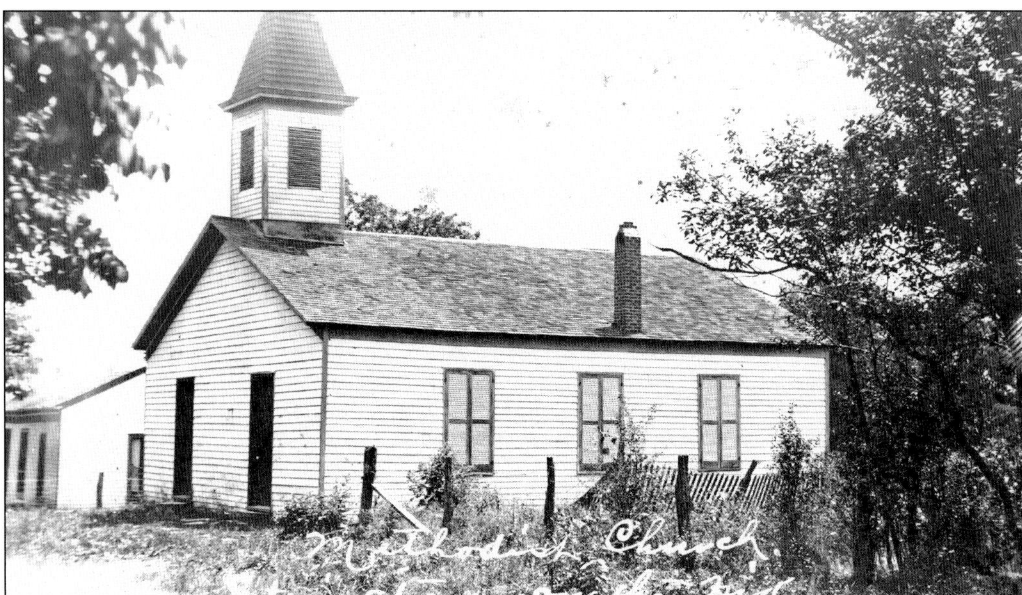

For over 80 years, this small church on Banklick Street was home to the Florence Methodist community. The church was organized in 1841, and the frame building was completed the following year. Typical of many churches in the county at that time, it had two front doors. The lot on which the church was built had been purchased from Samuel Craig for $80. In the early 1930s, the church relocated to Main Street.

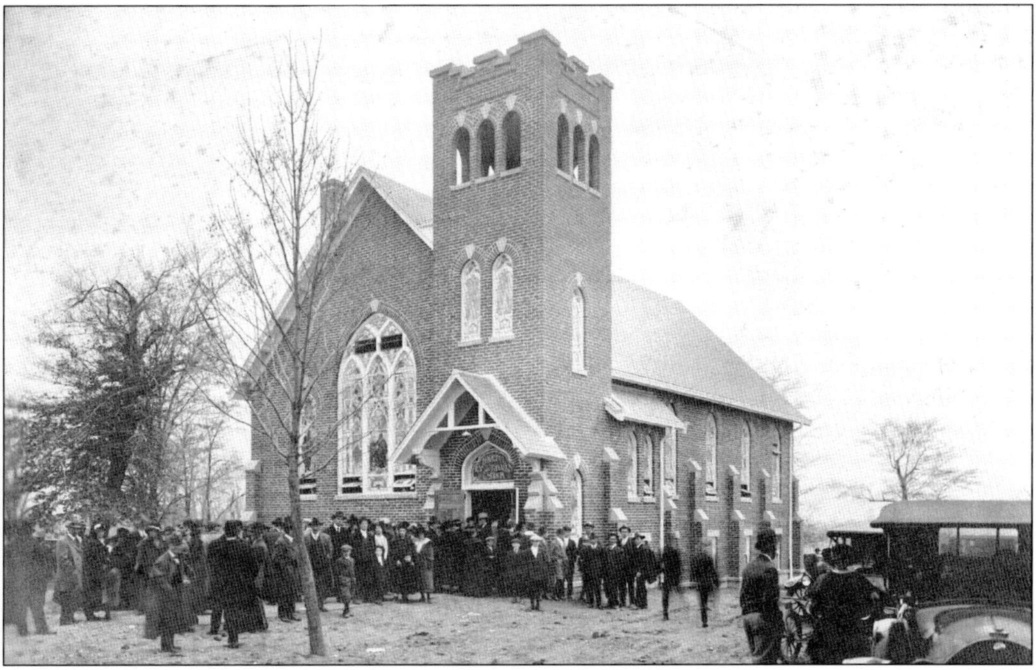

Located just outside the city of Florence is Hopeful Lutheran Church. Founded in 1806 by Lutheran families emigrating from Madison County, Virginia, the church has been a prominent part of the Florence community for nearly 200 years. The dedication of the present sanctuary is seen here on November 11, 1917. To commemorate the occasion, Pastor George A. Royer composed an original hymn titled "Tressler."

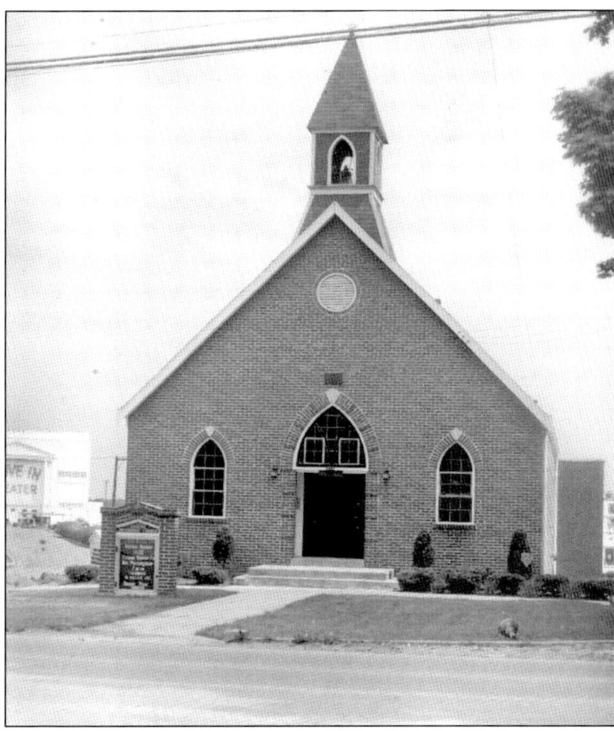

By 1931, the Florence Methodist Church had outgrown the original small frame church on Banklick Street. Church members purchased a lot on Main Street for the purpose of erecting a new church. The church, seen here in the late 1950s, saw several additions as membership grew. Today the building is home to the Main Street Baptist Church. Florence United Methodist Church is now located off Pleasant Valley Road.

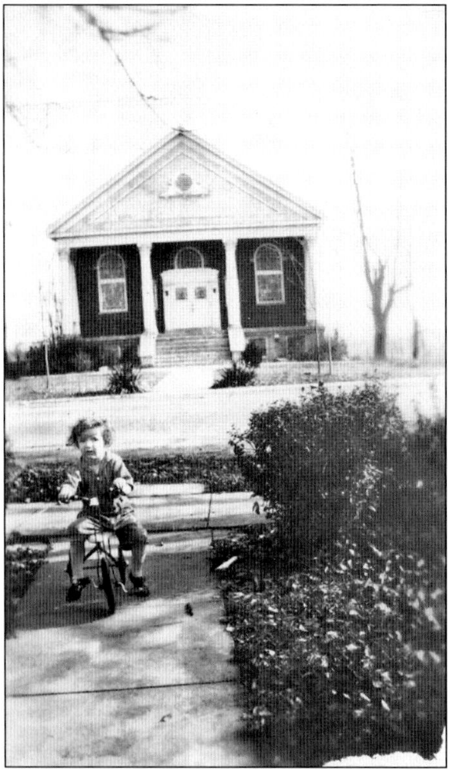

In 1930, the members of the Florence Baptist Church dedicated their second church sanctuary. This building replaced the original church building erected on this same lot, which had been purchased from the Wilhoit family. Today this building still stands as a part of the expanding church complex. Pictured here on his tricycle is Wendell Cooper, who lived across the street from the church.

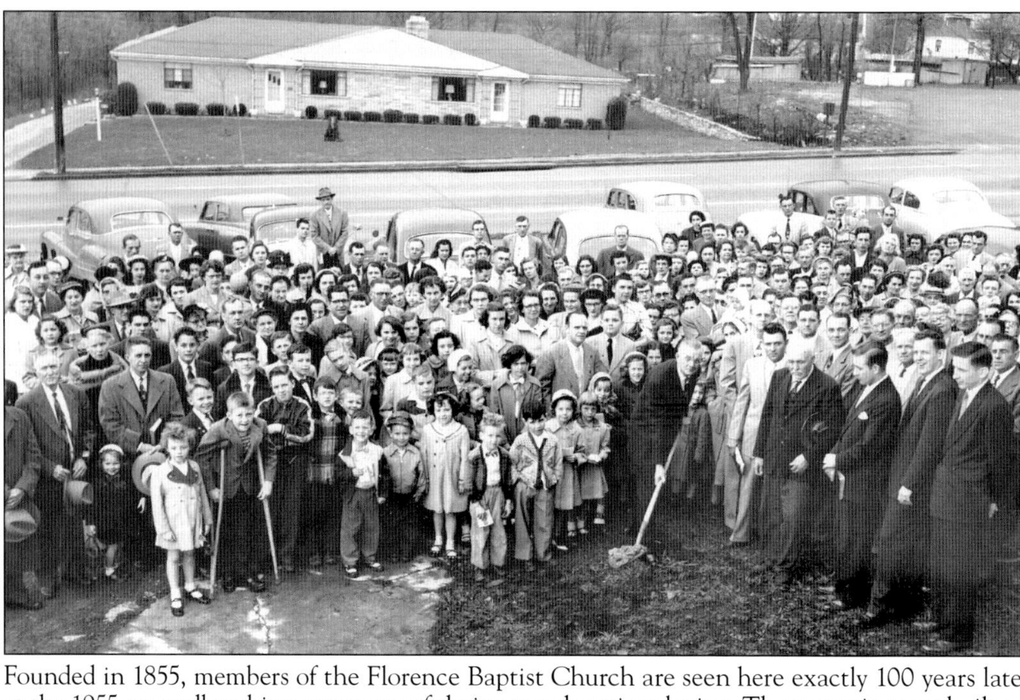

Founded in 1855, members of the Florence Baptist Church are seen here exactly 100 years later at the 1955 groundbreaking ceremony of their new educational wing. The new wing was built on the site of the original church building. The congregation gathered here has grown considerably from the original seven members who founded the church.

The First Baptist Church on Girard Street served the members of the African American community in the Florence area. Built in 1870, the building was home to the church members for almost 100 years. Members of the Fisher family were prominent members of the congregation. The building still stands on Girard Street, but it is no longer home to the Baptist church.

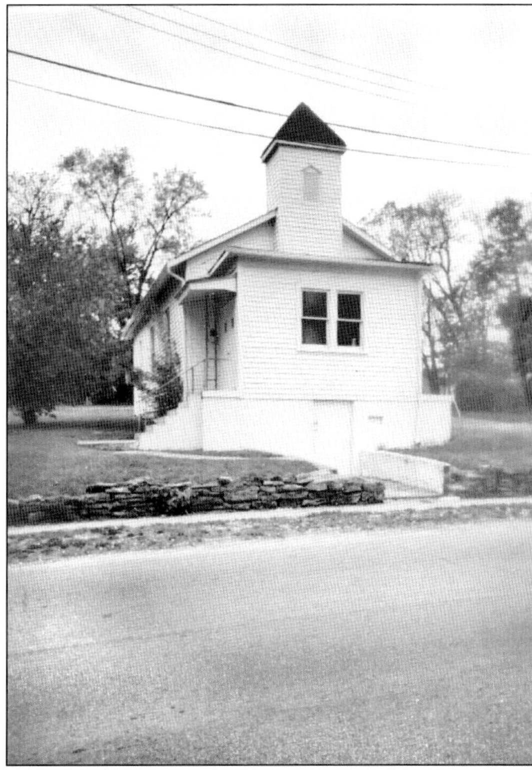

Kentaboo Baptist Church was organized as a mission of the Garvey Avenue Baptist Church in 1947. Then and now, the congregation is located at the junction of Kentaboo, Highridge, and Curtis. The mission became a full-status church in 1950. Seen here in front of the building are members of the Sunday school. At left is Mrs. Nellie Roland, one of the teachers.

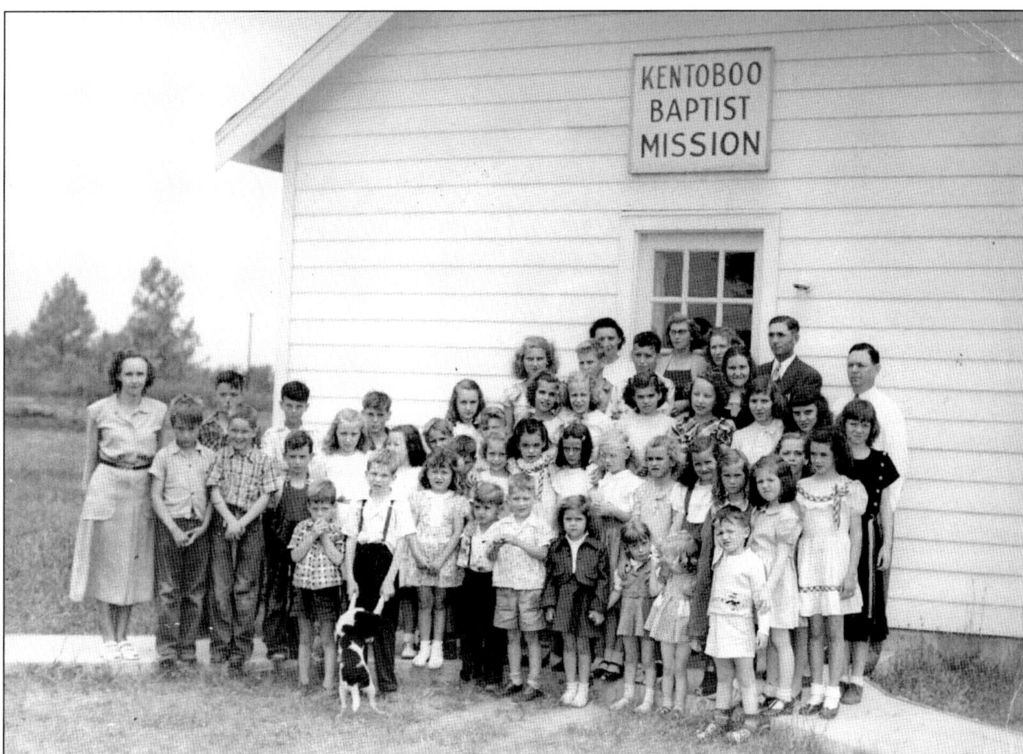

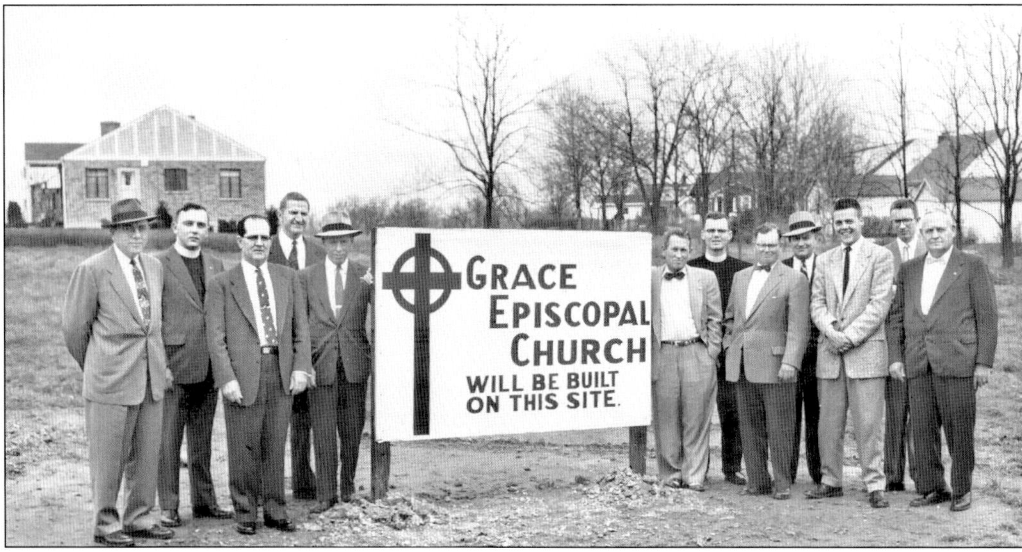

Grace Episcopal Church began as a mission of Trinity Church, Covington, in 1954. On August of that year, 51 people met in the Florence firehouse for the first worship service, morning prayer. In July of the following year, the groundbreaking ceremony for the future church building was held. Pictured here at the site on Price Pike are, from left to right, unidentified, the Reverend Bruce Weatherly, Mr. Wasson, "Doc" Rusk, Fred Macklin, Bud Foscue, the Reverend F. W. Kephart Jr., Bob Ellis, Bill Ware, Newell Grahm, Arthur Willis, and Elbert Bohon.

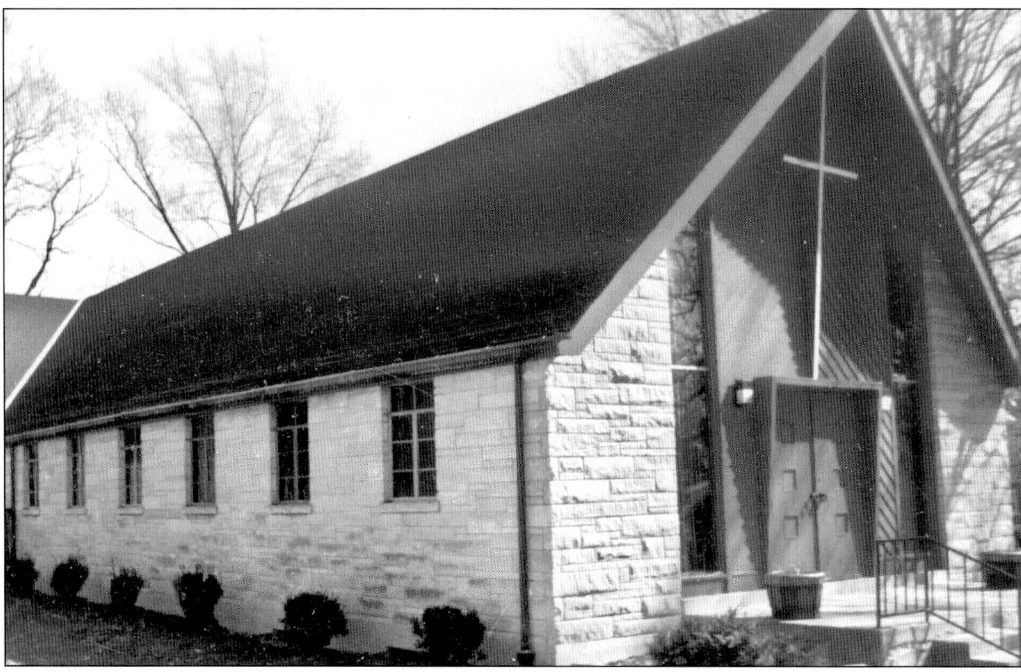

In October 1955, Bishop Moody of the Diocese of Lexington officiated at the cornerstone-laying ceremony of Grace Episcopal Church. The building was designed by George Roth. He, along with general contractor Cyle Nicholson, was present for the ceremony. The first service in the new building was celebrated in April 1956. In May 1957, Grace, which had begun as a mission of Trinity Church, Covington, was granted parish standing.

Eight

COMMUNITY

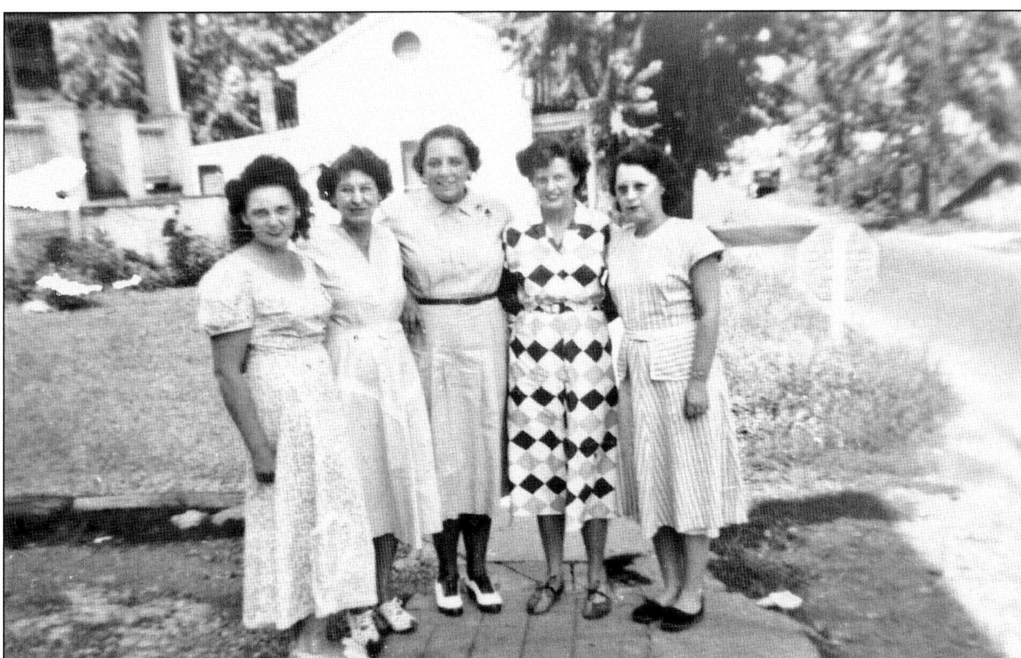

Friendships developed at work often carry over into the community. Seen here are several of the switchboard operators for the Consolidated Telephone Company. Originally located in the Meyer's Building on Main Street, the company eventually moved their operations to Girard Street, where this picture was taken.

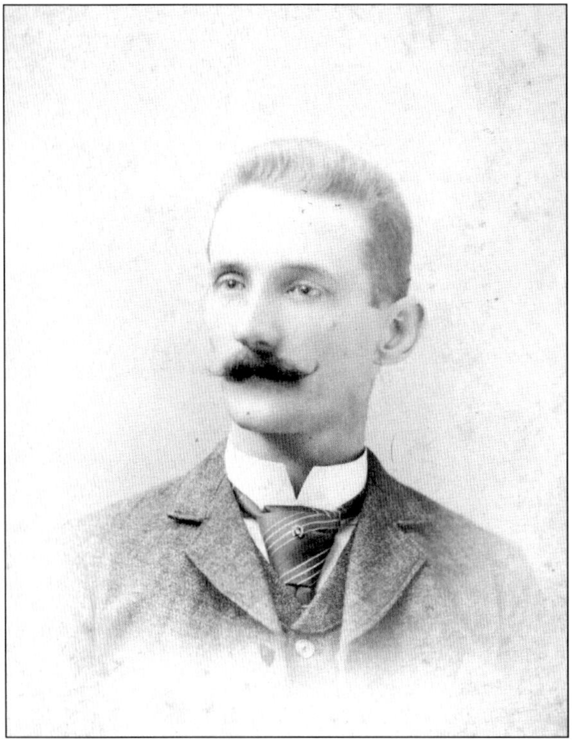

Florence native Dr. Frank Sayre graduated from Miami Medical College in Cincinnati in March 1893. He is seen here at the beginning of his medical career. His father, Adolphus, was also a physician, with a practice in Florence. Dr. Frank Sayre began his practice in Hebron but returned to Florence in 1916, where he had his home and office on Main Street until his death in 1928.

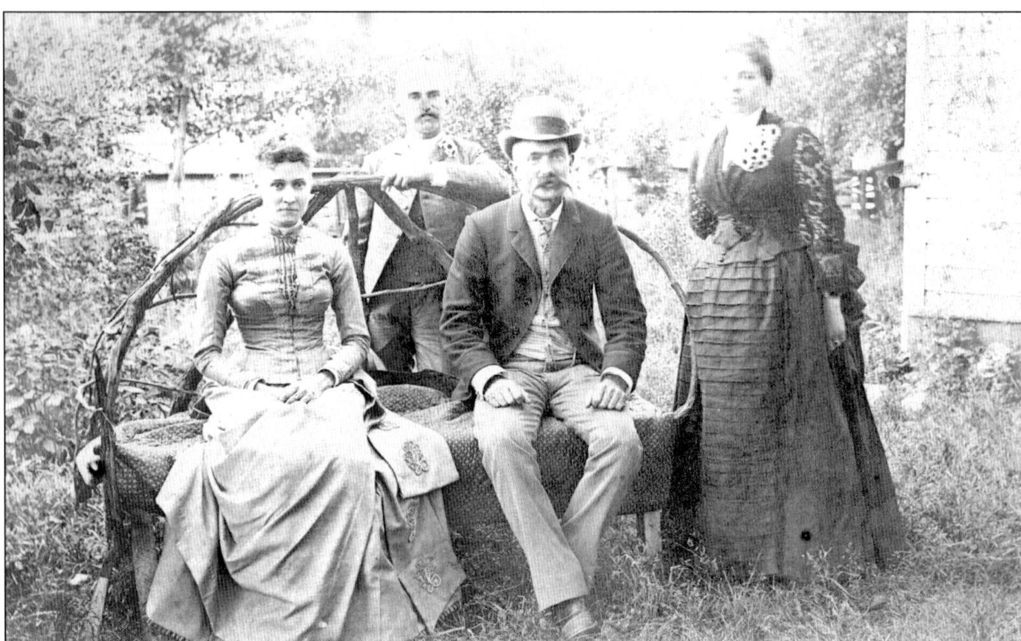

Seated together on this rustic settee are John and Carrie Tanner Goodridge. The elegantly dressed couple is perhaps entertaining friends on a Sunday afternoon. Both the Goodridge and Tanner families had come from Virginia early in the county's history and were well known in the Florence area. Sadly the couple's marriage was not a long one, as Carrie died in 1899, soon after this picture was taken.

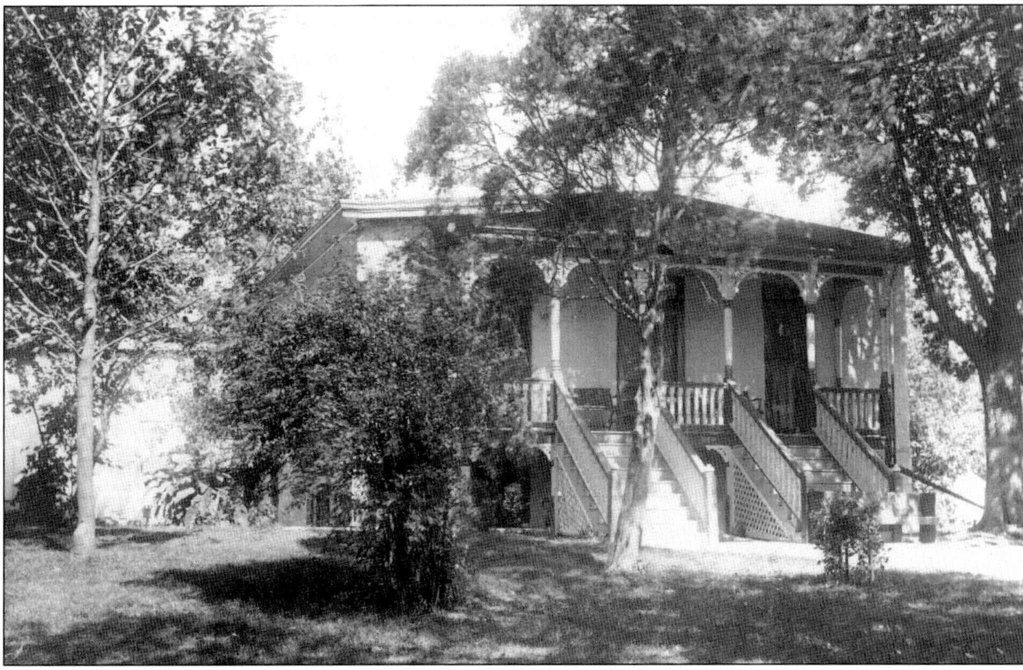

Reminiscent of the Louisiana bayous, this elegant antebellum home stood at the end of Girard Street. In 1883, it was the home of Florence physician S. S. Scott. In the late 19th century, the building housed a private school. When this picture was taken, it was the home of George Rouse. Mr. Rouse had been a prosperous farmer on Burlington Pike near Florence before retiring to this home.

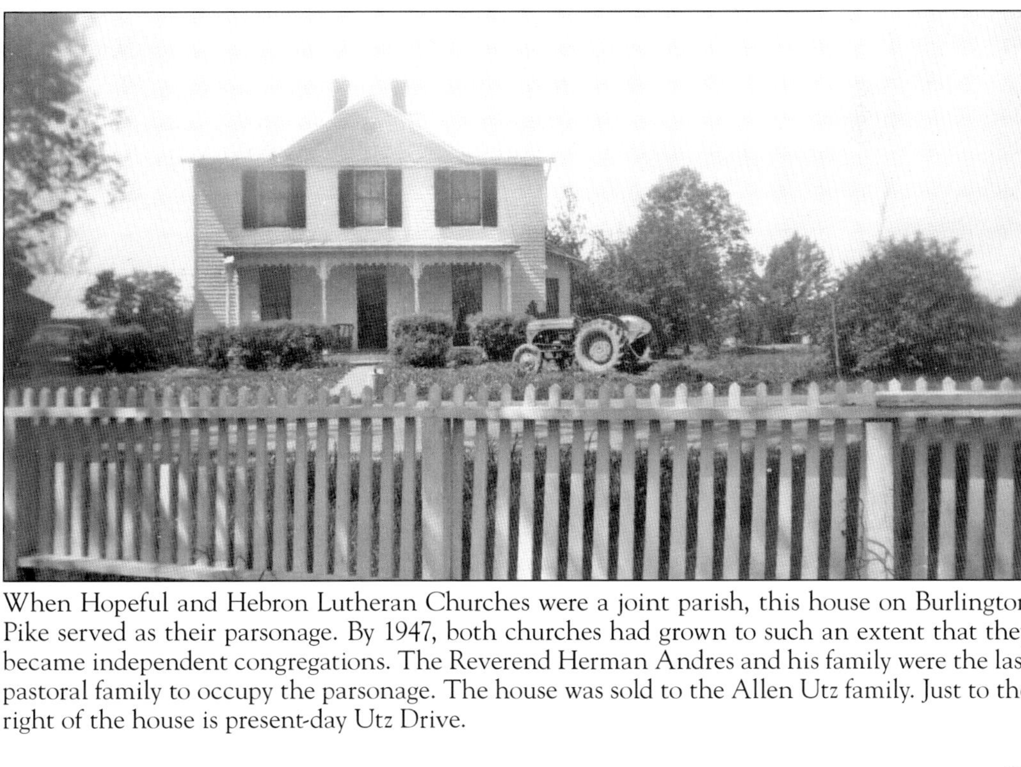

When Hopeful and Hebron Lutheran Churches were a joint parish, this house on Burlington Pike served as their parsonage. By 1947, both churches had grown to such an extent that they became independent congregations. The Reverend Herman Andres and his family were the last pastoral family to occupy the parsonage. The house was sold to the Allen Utz family. Just to the right of the house is present-day Utz Drive.

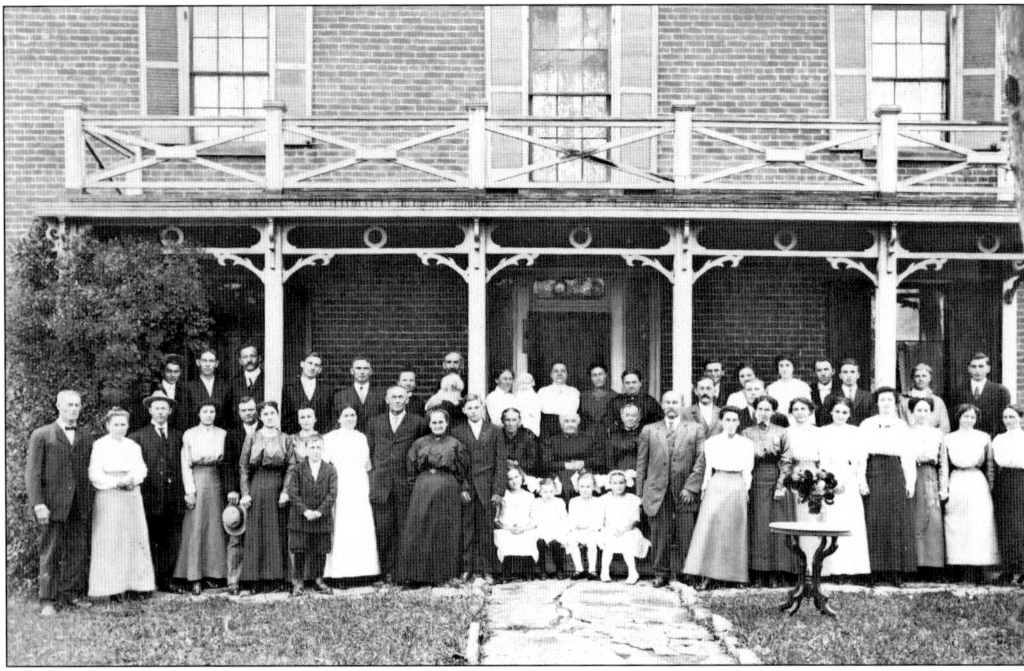

Around 1910, the family of Joshua Z. and Frances Tanner gathered to have their picture taken in front of the family home on Burlington Pike. Frances Tanner is seated in the center surrounded by her children and grandchildren. The home stood on the sight of today's Stringtown Park on Burlington Pike.

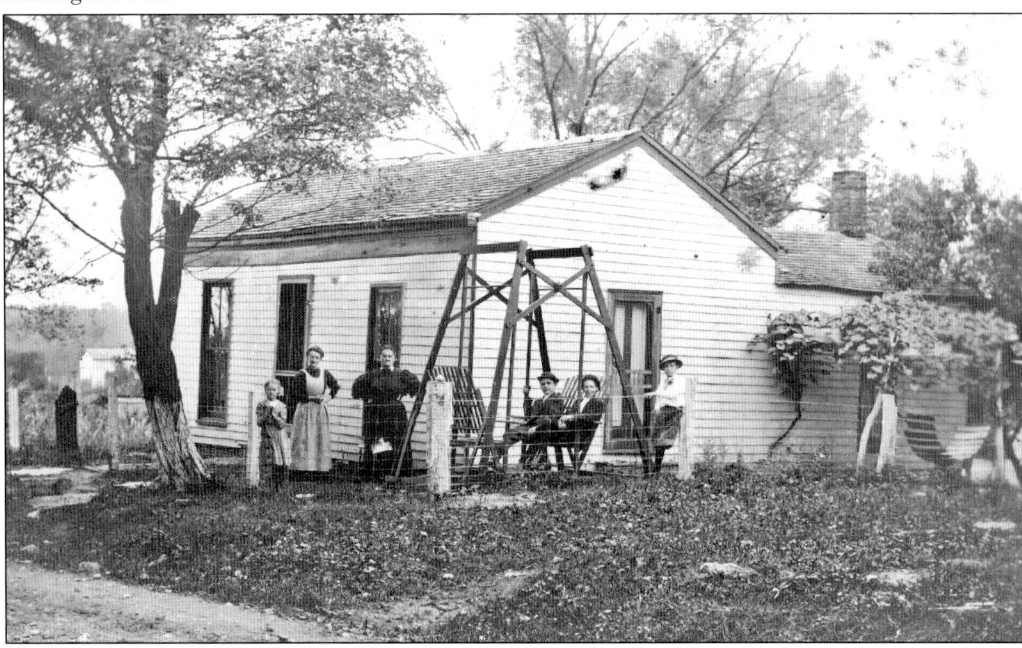

This small house on Banklick Street sat next to the old Methodist church. Note the barn seen in the background; today Dixie Highway runs through the once-productive farm that surrounded this barn. In the 1940s, this was the home of Fanny Clarkson. Today the Social Security Building sits on this site.

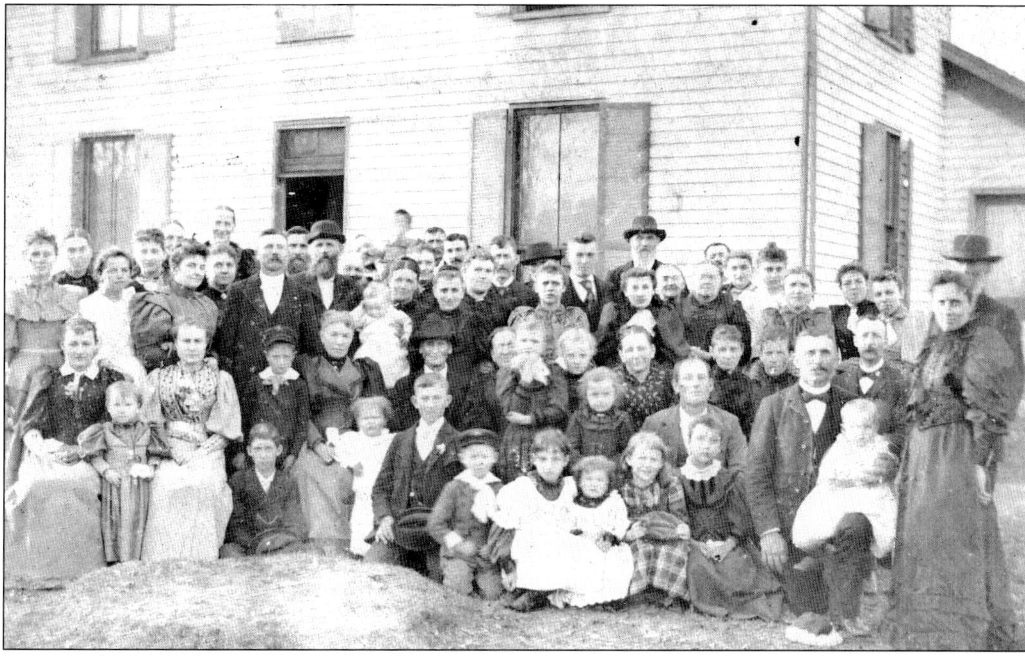

Pictured here are the Reverend H. Max Lentz and members of the Hopeful Lutheran congregation. While serving the church as pastor, Reverend Lentz also published a local newspaper, the *Boone County Banner*. During his 10-year pastorate, he also completed a history of the first 100 years of Hopeful Lutheran Church.

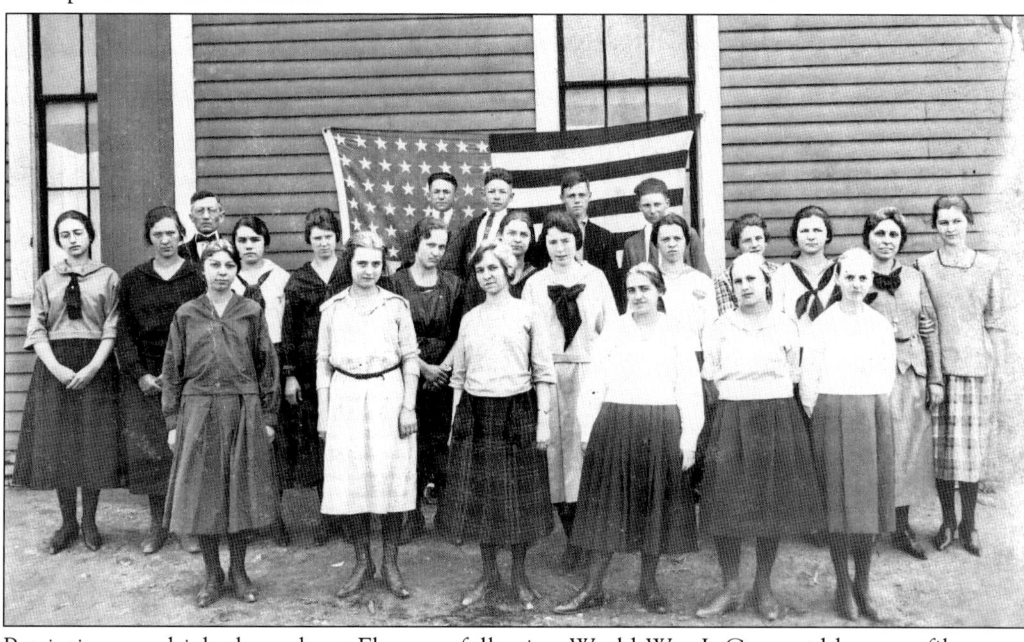

Patriotism ran high throughout Florence following World War I. Captured here on film are a group of students celebrating Armistice Day. Armistice Day (November 11) was designated a federal holiday to commemorate the service and sacrifice of the men and women who served during World War I. The name was changed to Veterans' Day by an act of Congress on May 24, 1954, to include the veterans from both world wars and Korea.

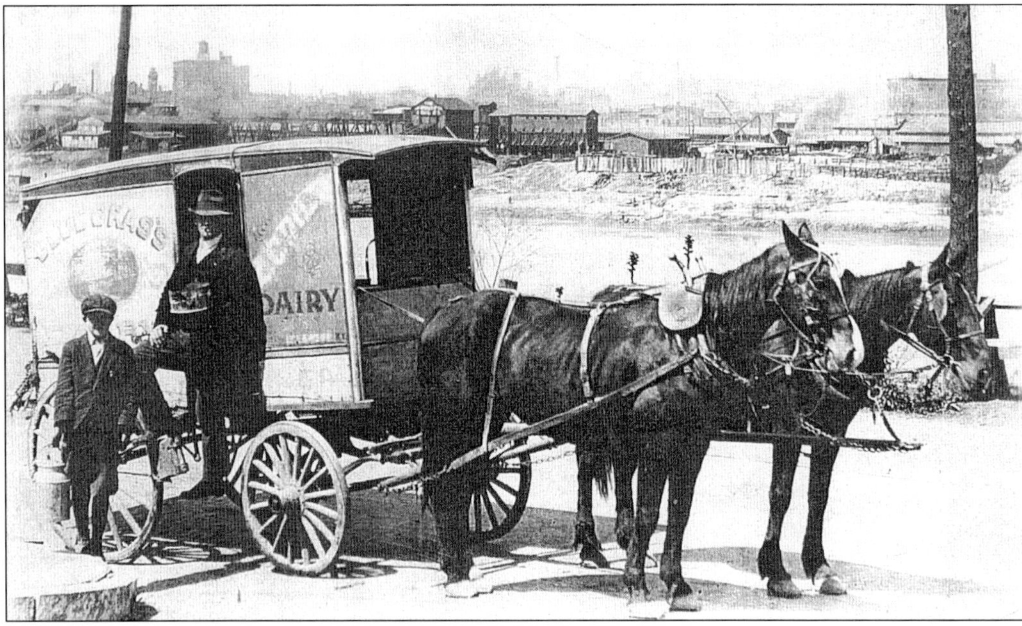

Joel Angus Tanner ran a prosperous dairy farm just outside of Florence. At the turn of the century, milk was a household staple like today, but in the days before supermarkets and convenience stores, milk was often delivered by a horse-drawn wagon. Mr. Tanner is seen here along with his son Walter delivering milk to some of his customers in Ludlow. The Ohio River is clearly visible in the background.

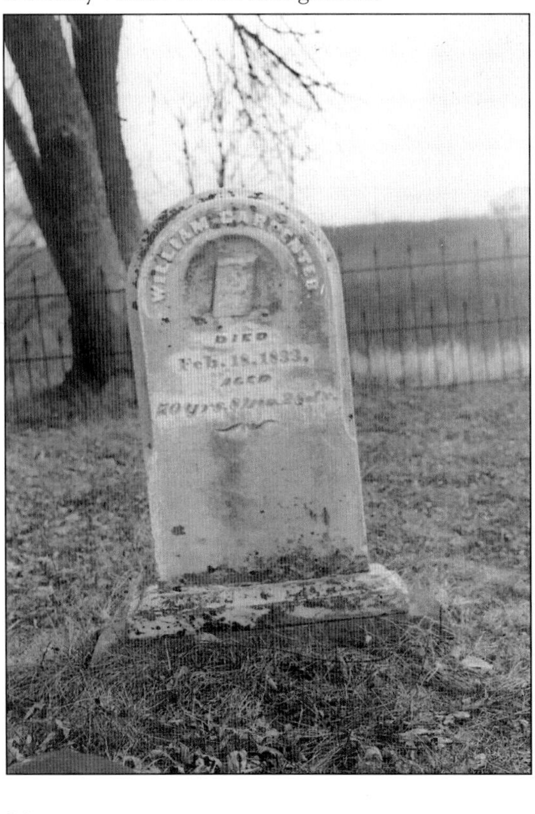

Seen here is the gravestone of the Reverend William Carpenter Jr., who immigrated to Boone County from Virginia in 1813. Reverend Carpenter was one of the largest landowners in the Florence area and a proud veteran of the American Revolution. He served under Gen. George Washington and was present at the surrender of Lord Cornwallis at the Battle of Yorktown.

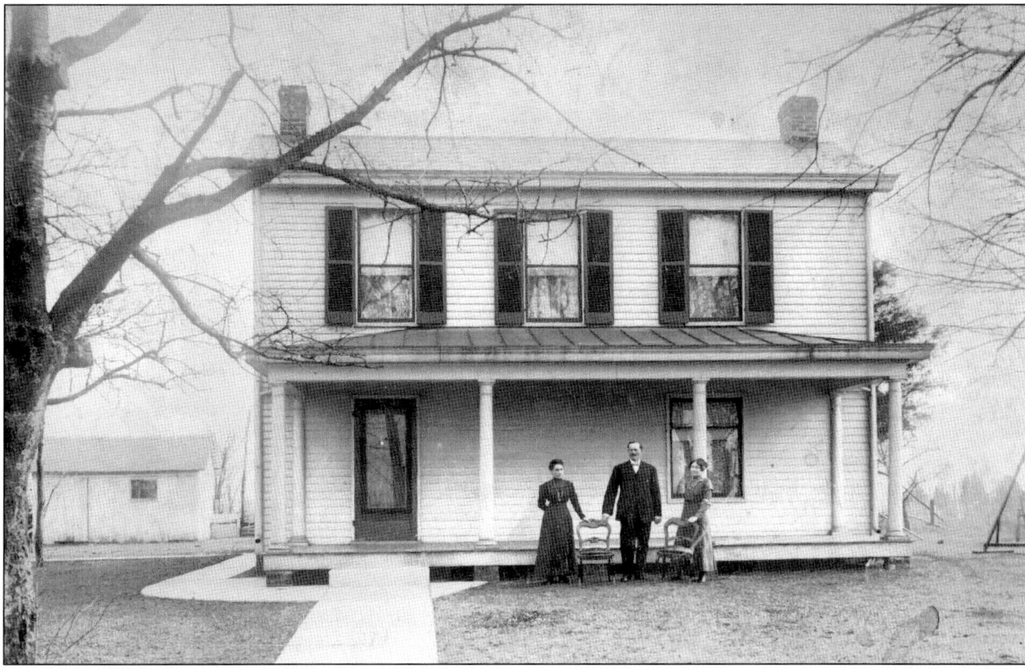

Seen here in front of their home at the corner of Burlington Pike and Oblique Street are, from left to right, Clara and Jim Tanner and their daughter, Lena. Mr. Tanner operated a hardware store on Main Street as well as serving as postmaster. When rural free mail service began, he became one of the first rural carriers in the county. This picture was sent as a Christmas greeting to friends and relatives in the early 20th century.

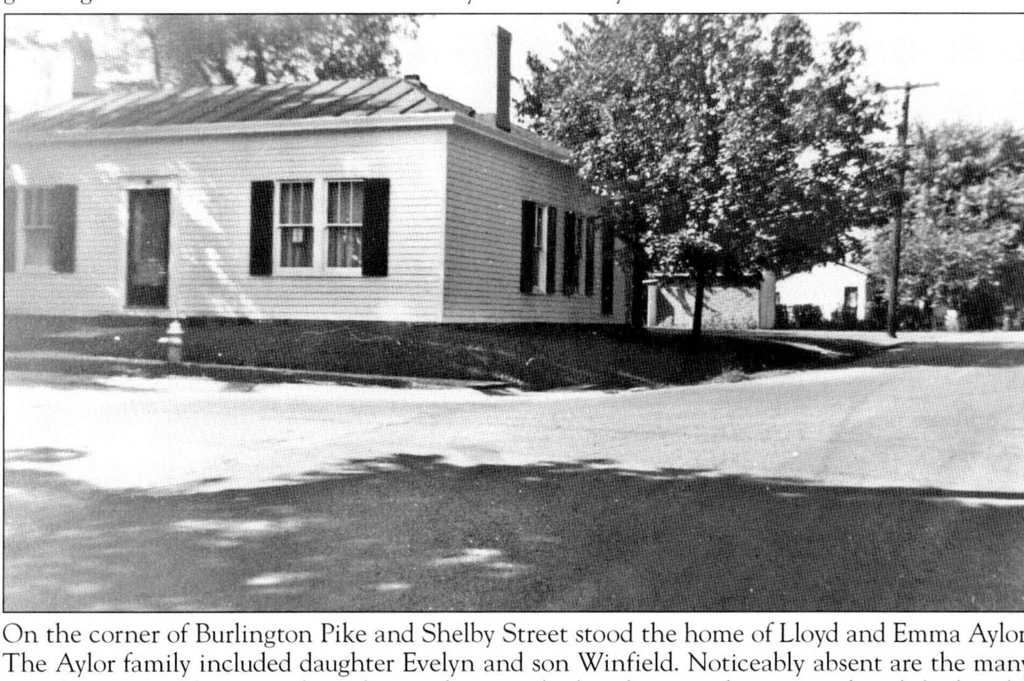

On the corner of Burlington Pike and Shelby Street stood the home of Lloyd and Emma Aylor. The Aylor family included daughter Evelyn and son Winfield. Noticeably absent are the many cars that clog Burlington Pike today. Unfortunately this charming house was demolished in the late 1960s along with the Donald Lipscomb home across the street.

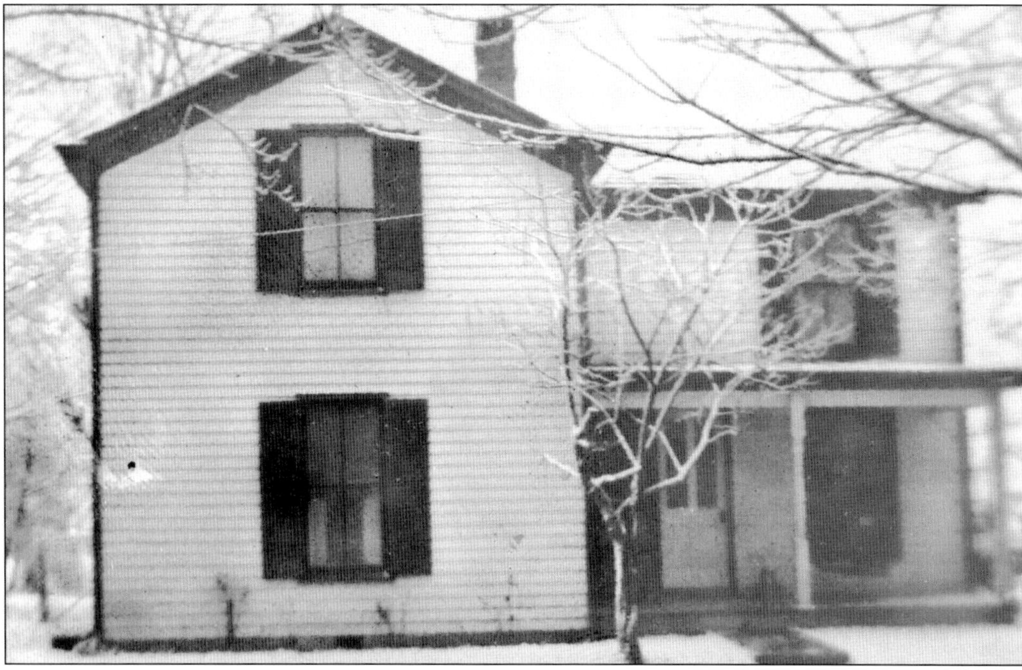

This home, located on the northeast corner of Burlington Pike and Shelby Street, was the home of Willie and Fannie Utz when this photograph was taken in the early 20th century. The house was then sold to the Donald Lipscomb family. During the late 1960s, the house was demolished so that planned improvements on the end of Shelby Street could begin. The work was never done, and the lot sits empty today.

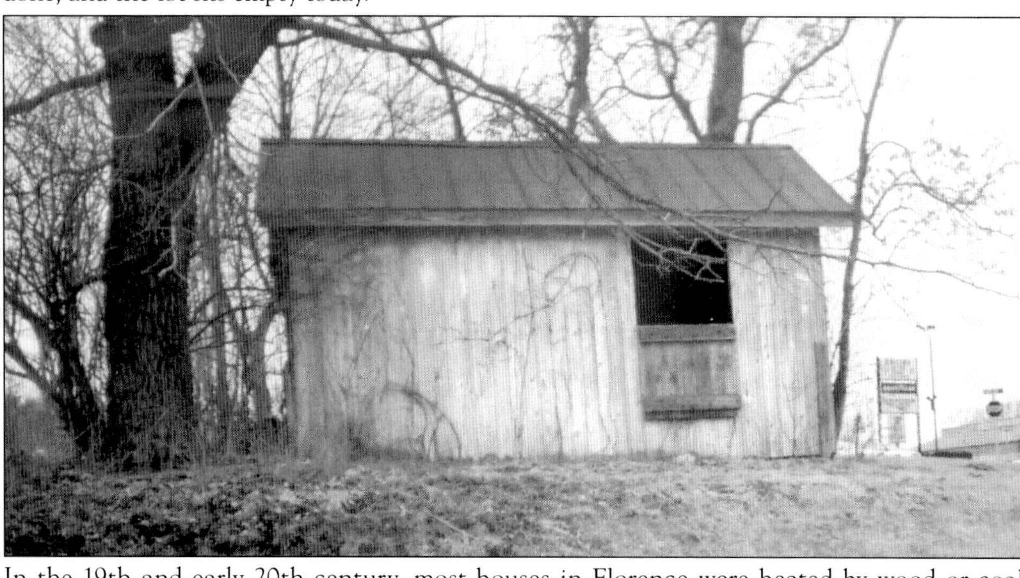

In the 19th and early 20th century, most houses in Florence were heated by wood or coal. Coal houses such as the one seen here were built to store the fuel. This structure was located off an eight-foot alley that ran between the lots on Shelby and Girard Streets. By locating these necessary building along the alley, delivery wagons could make their deliveries without driving through residents' yards. This small piece of Florence history was demolished in the early 21st century.

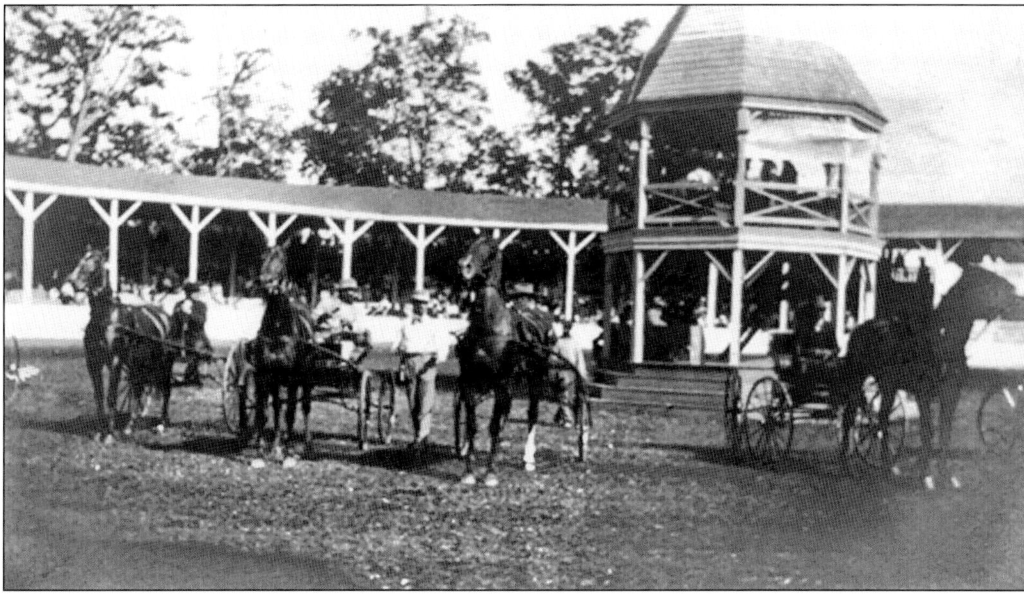

From its opening in 1896 through 1932, the Florence Fair was one of the premier fairs of the area. The amphitheater area, seen here, was 160 feet in diameter. Ten rows of seats were topped by a covered promenade. The fairgrounds were located along the Union Pike (U.S. 42) across from the Christian church in a wooded area known as Carpenter's Woods. (Courtesy of Lloyd Library and Museum, Special Collections 106, Box 2, Folder 2.)

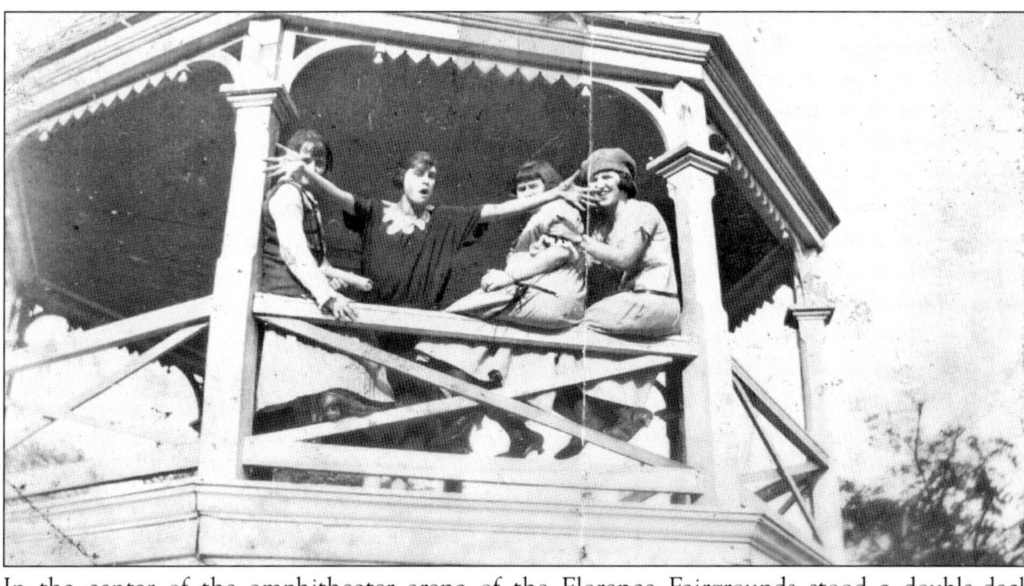

In the center of the amphitheater arena of the Florence Fairgrounds stood a double-deck octagonal bandstand. For over 35 years, the fair was a popular annual event. Greeting fairgoers from the top deck of the bandstand are Jennie Laile (left), Pearl Markesbery (with outstretched arms), and two unidentified friends.

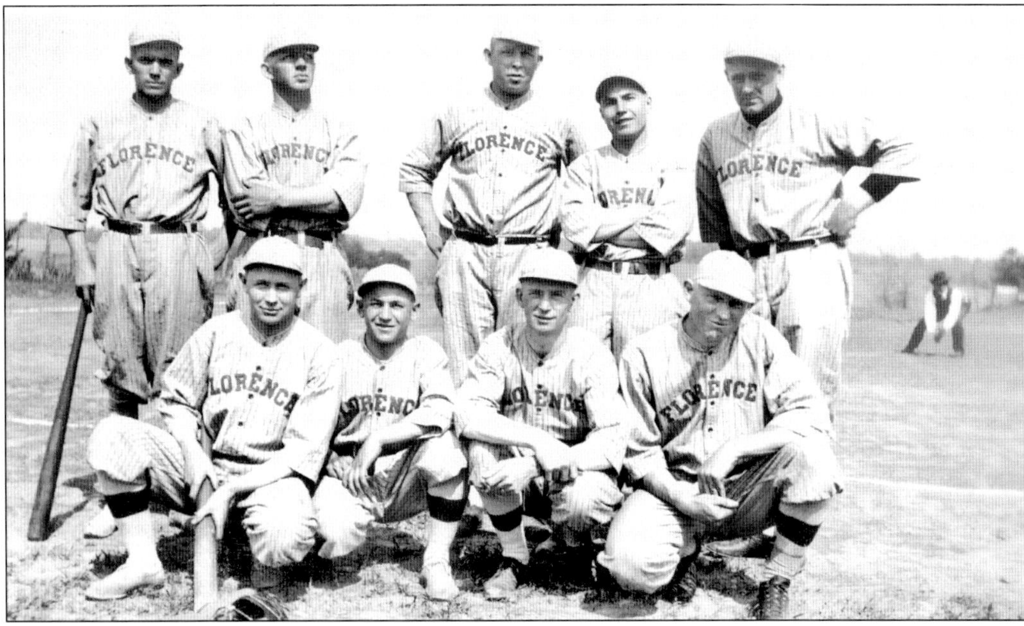

Taking time out before the game, members of the 1921 Florence baseball team pose for the photographer. During that decade, Florence was one of the semi-professional teams in the Boone County League with a loyal following of fans. The four players in the front row include, in no particular order, Russell House, Charlie Carpenter, Frank Sayre, and L. T. Utz.

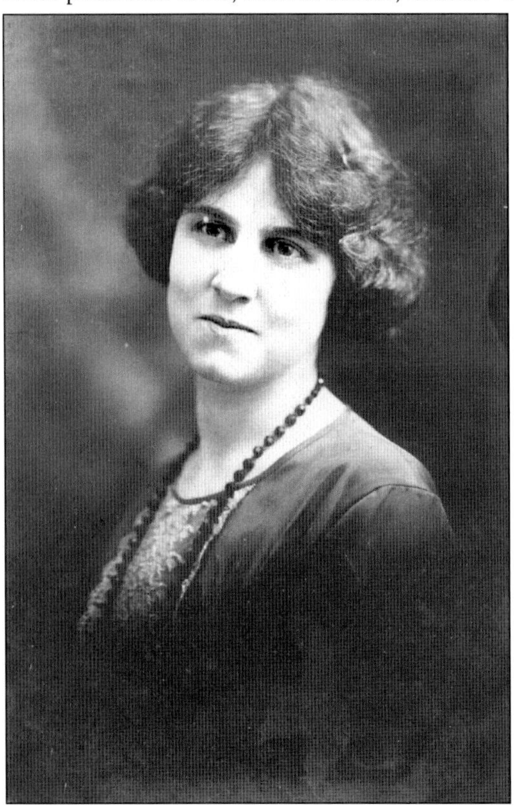

A familiar face at the Florence Post Office in the late 1920s was postmistress Mabel Tanner. A member of Florence High School's first graduating class in 1915, she was appointed to the post during the presidency of Herbert Hoover. This picture appeared in the local papers to announce her appointment. With the change of administrations in 1932, the position was reassigned. After leaving the post office, Miss Tanner was a clerk at Martin's Grocery.

Lloyd Avenue was the site of one of Florence's first subdivisions. The developer, L. T. Utz, is pictured here. Mr. Utz, a Boone County native, was a well-known and respected member of the Florence community. After the first homes were completed in the early 1930s, the Utz family themselves became residents of one of the new homes. Mr. Utz also served as the sheriff of Boone County.

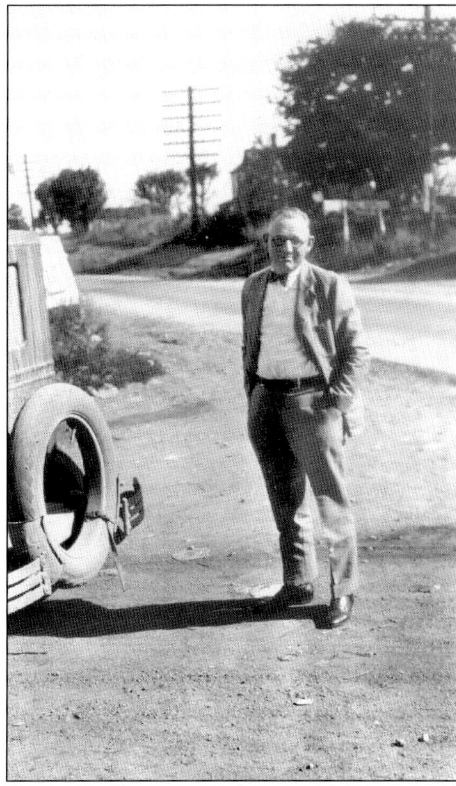

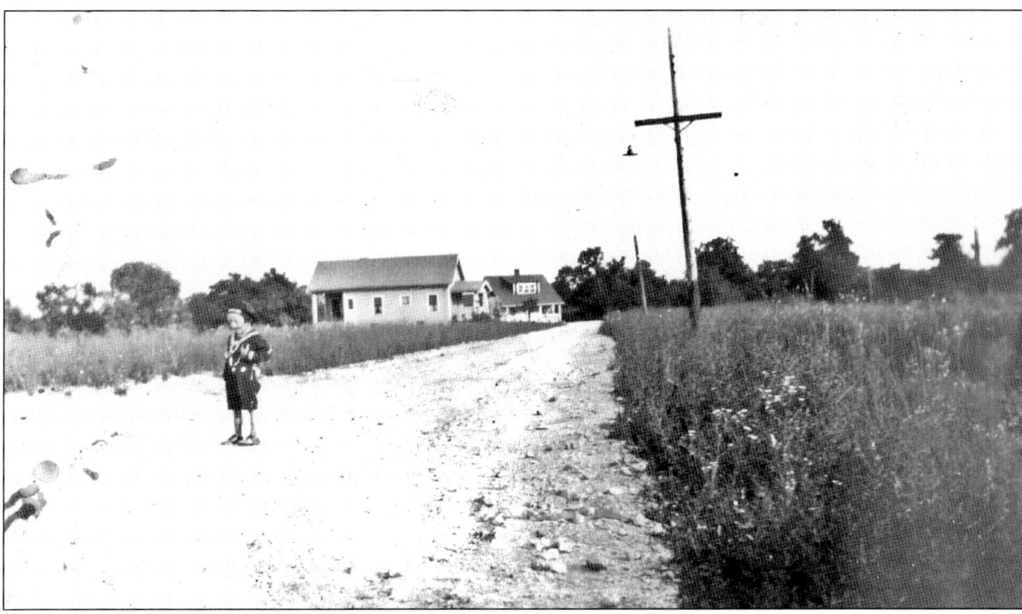

When this picture on Dortha Avenue was taken around 1930, the street was unpaved and an early streetlight can just be seen to the right of the street. The young boy in the picture is Irvin Carpenter. The house at the far end of the picture was for many years the home of William and Anne Fitzgerald. In today's Florence, Irvin would be standing in the intersection of Dixie Highway and Dortha Avenue.

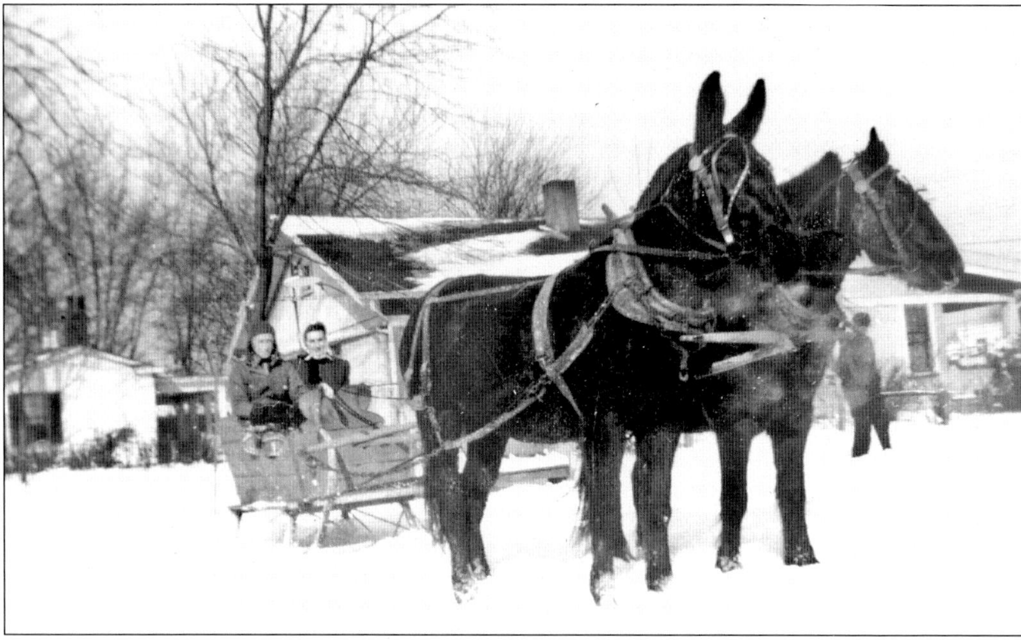

On a snowy winter day, Dan Carpenter invited Mary Bresser to join him for a sleigh ride down U.S. 25 to Main Street in Florence. The sleigh proved to be a popular attraction, and many residents of Main Street came out to wave and ask if they could also have a ride. Powering this excursion were Dan's mule, Old Jack, and his horse, Dick.

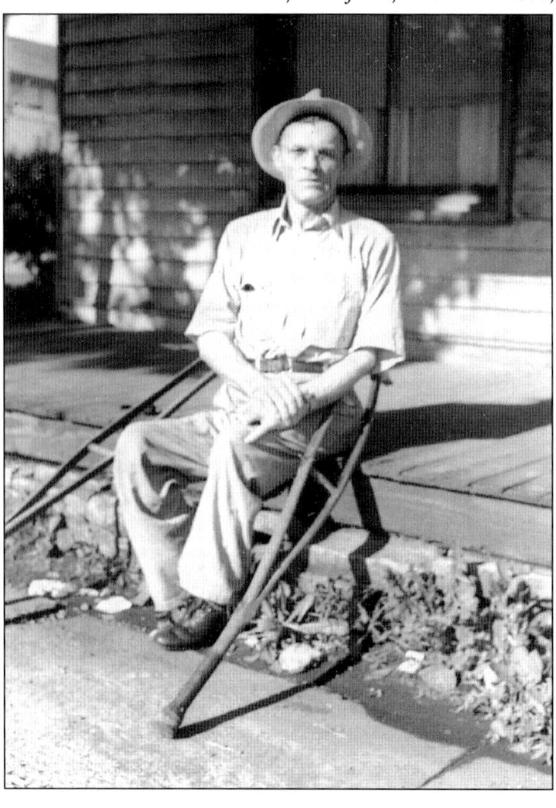

Seated here is Joe Littrell. For many years, Joe, along with his wife, Goldie, operated a shoe repair shop on Main Street. Joe was the nephew of Miss Kate Adylotte, a well-known member of the Florence Christian Church at that time. Both Joe and his wife suffered from the crippling effects of polio.

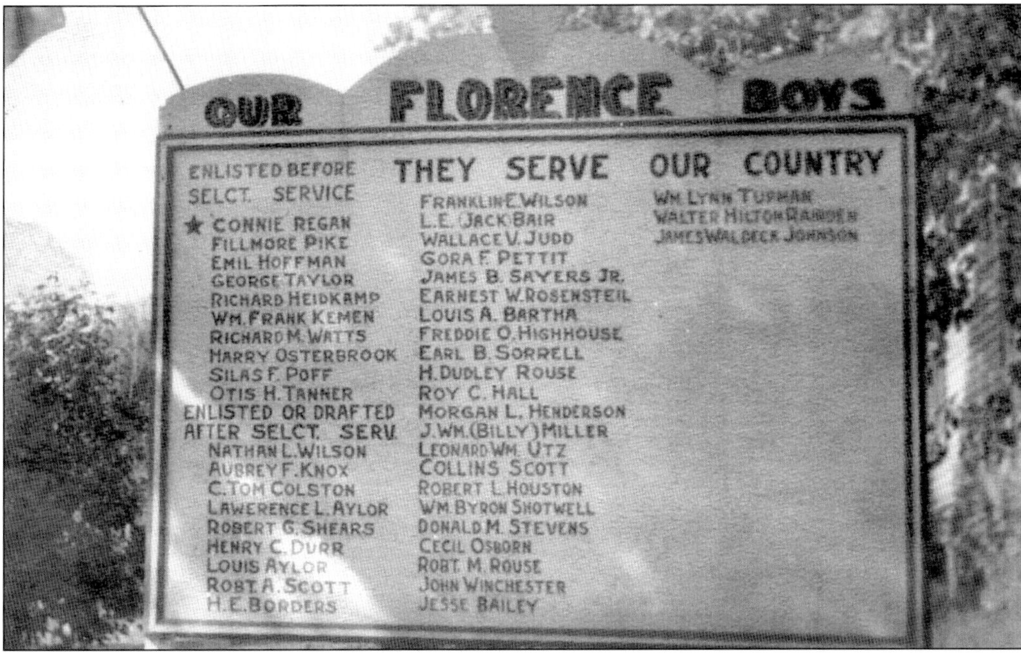

After December 7, 1941, the young men of the Florence community answered their country's call and joined the armed forces. To remember and support them, the town erected a service board at the corner of Main and Youell Streets. As the war continued and more men were called to service, the board had to be expanded to include all of their names.

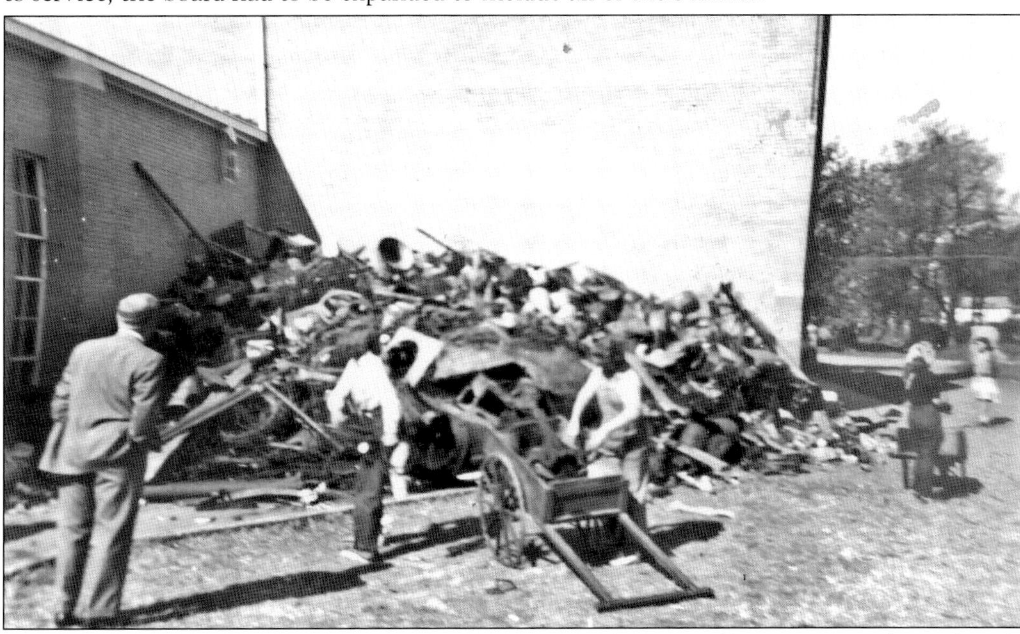

During World War II, the Florence community began a drive to collect scrap metal to aid in the war effort. The collection was piled in a corner behind the Florence High School building. To the left can be seen the school's gymnasium, and in the rear is the three-story main building. The collection must have been a success, as students of the time recall the pile reaching beyond the gym's roof.

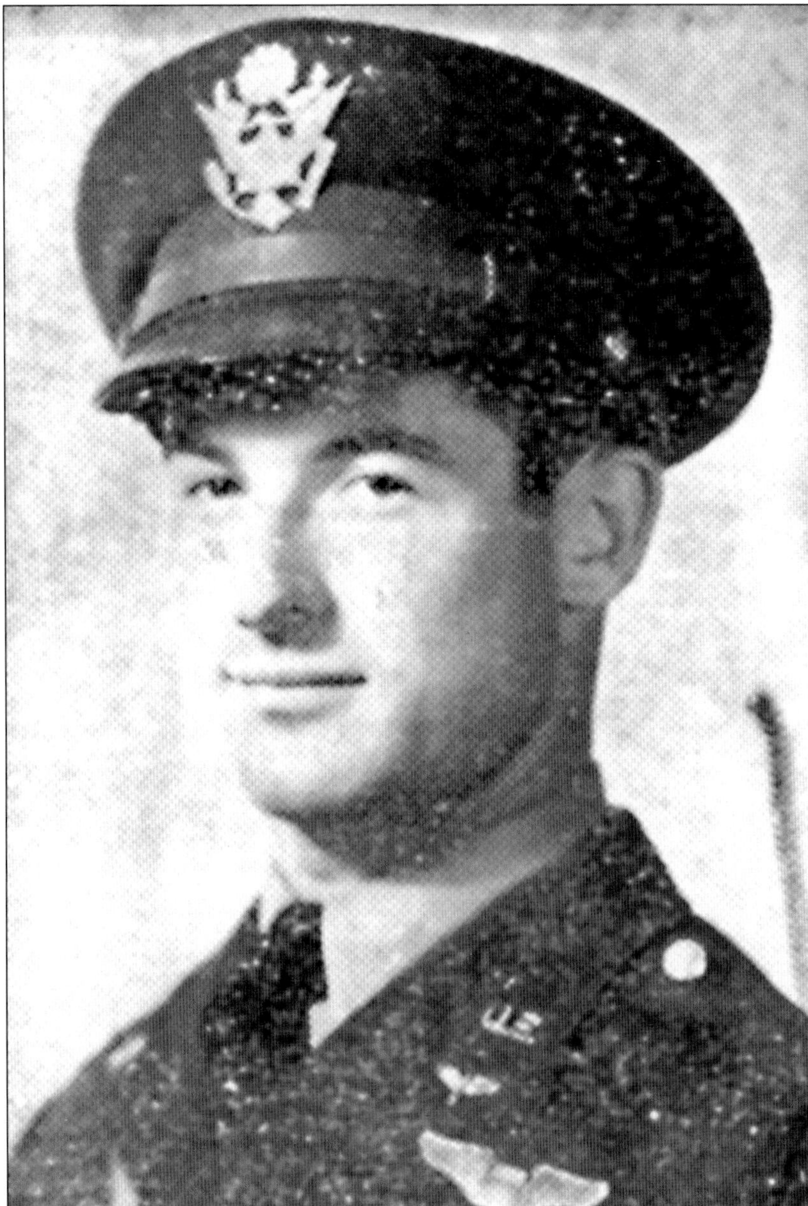

Capt. Cornelius "Connie" Reagan graduated from Florence High School in 1934 and entered the service in October 1940. Serving as a fighter pilot in the Air Corps, he flew over 85 missions. In March 1942, while on a strafing mission on the cost of Java, he was forced to crash land his P-40 fighter in a rice paddy. His mother, Mrs. Bertha Bauers, was notified that her son had been killed. For over three years, he was thought to be dead; actually he had been taken as a prisoner to a Japanese POW camp. Told that he would have to give pro-Japanese propaganda over the radio or be shot, he refused and broke up a microphone and radio set. He was not shot but sentenced to 15 years of hard labor. On his birthday, October 5, 1945, his mother received a telegram stating her son had been found alive. After returning to the United States, Captain Reagan was given an Air Corps vacation in Miami, were he met his future wife, Frances Hogan. The couple returned to Florence to be married in the Christian church.

One of the many businesses to occupy the first floor of the building on the corner of Main and Girard Streets was the Florence Dry Cleaners. Apartments occupied the second floor. The street to the right is Girard. Notice that there were no houses on the right-hand side of the street when this photo was taken in the 1940s.

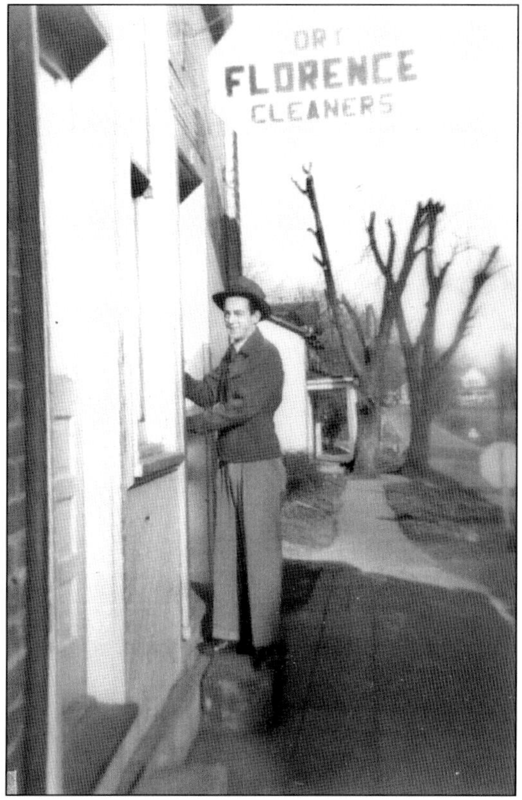

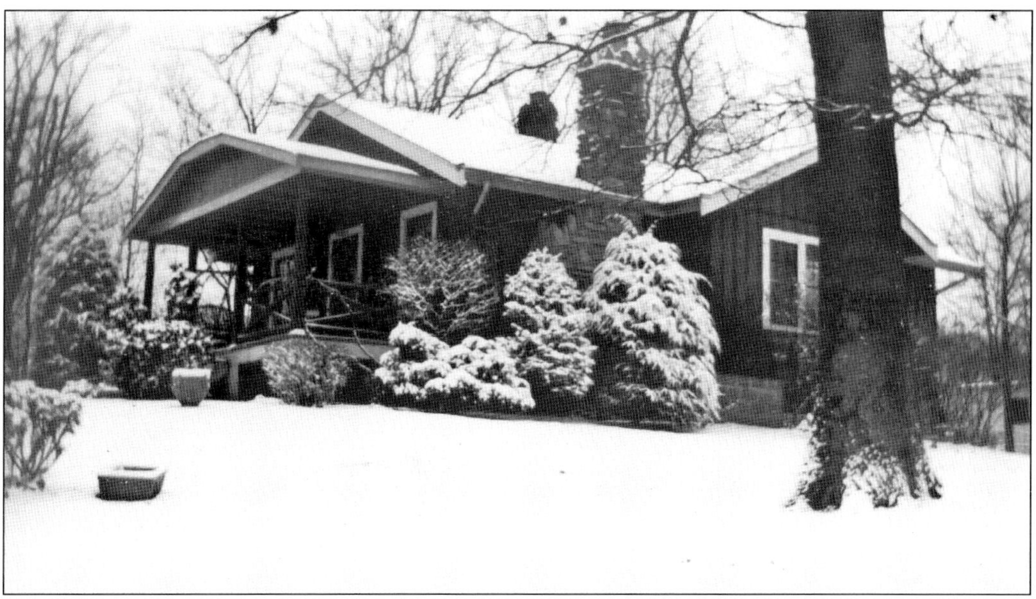

Located on U.S. 42 approximately two miles west of Florence as the highway descends towards Gunpowder Road, this house was the home of the Kessler family when this picture was taken in the 1940s. Today the Key Bank occupies this site, and a McDonald's is just across the road. It is quite a change from the peaceful landscape seen here.

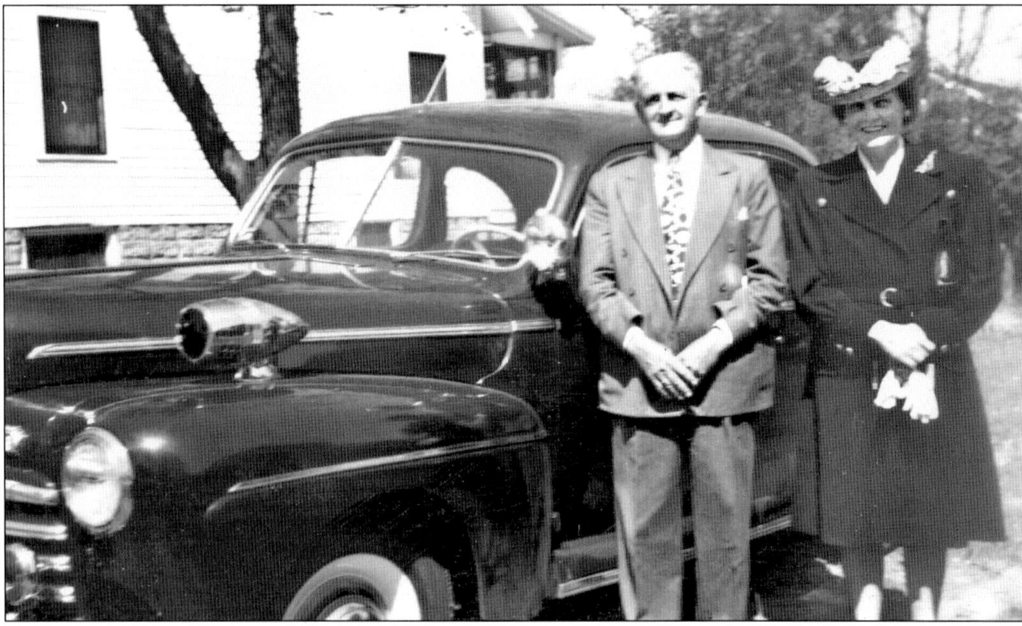

Florence's first fire chief, Albert Hue Sr., and his wife, Emma, pose here in front of their family car. As befits a fire chief, the car was painted red, and a siren was mounted on the front fender. Mr. Hue purchased the city's first fire truck himself in 1935. His daughter Wanda remembers her father coming home at the end of a week of work and saying to her mother: "I don't have a full paycheck this week. I bought a fire truck for $75."

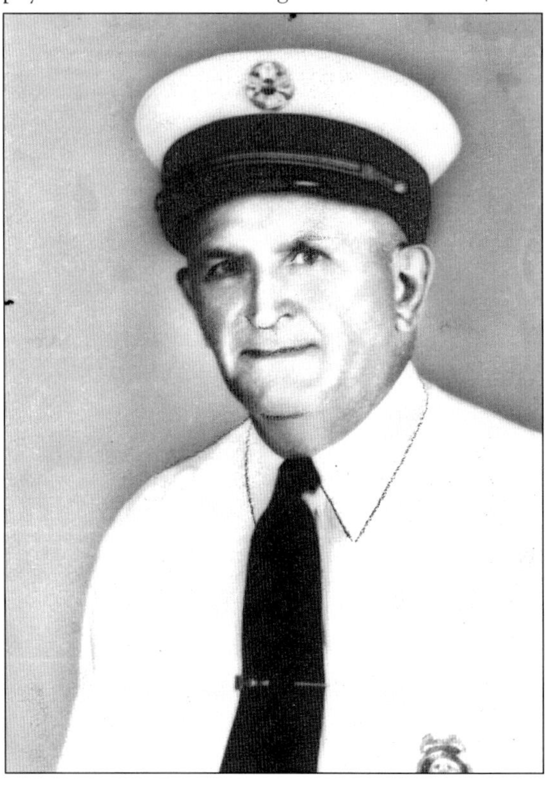

Albert Hue Sr. was the first fire chief of the Florence Volunteer Fire Department. He began organizing a squad to fight fires in 1934. In 1936, the department was organized with a 1913 Ahrens-Fox pumper and 500 feet of hose borrowed from the Elsmere Volunteer Fire Department. Hue remained chief until his death of an apparent heart attack while on the way to fight a fire in 1957. The fire station on the corner of U.S. 25 and Industrial Road is named in his honor.

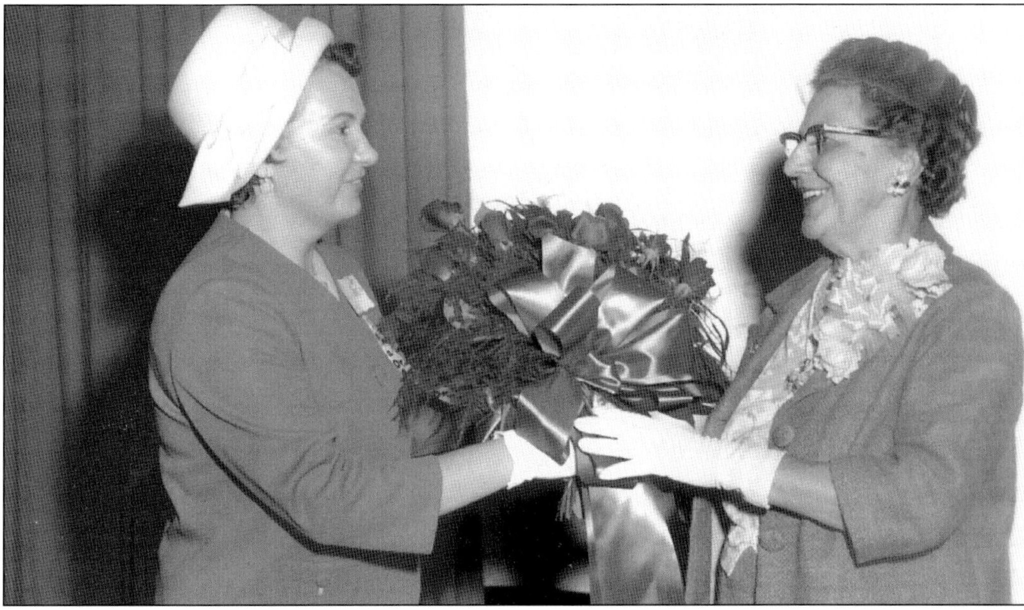

In the days when doctors were overwhelmingly male, Dr. Gladys Rouse made the decision to enter medicine. A graduate of the University of Cincinnati Medical School, Dr. Rouse returned to her native Florence and began her long practice at her office on Main Street. Following her retirement in the 1960s, Dr. Rouse was honored officially by the city of Florence with "Dr. Rouse Day." She is seen here receiving a bouquet of flowers from Betty Pierce, the first baby Dr. Rouse delivered in Florence.

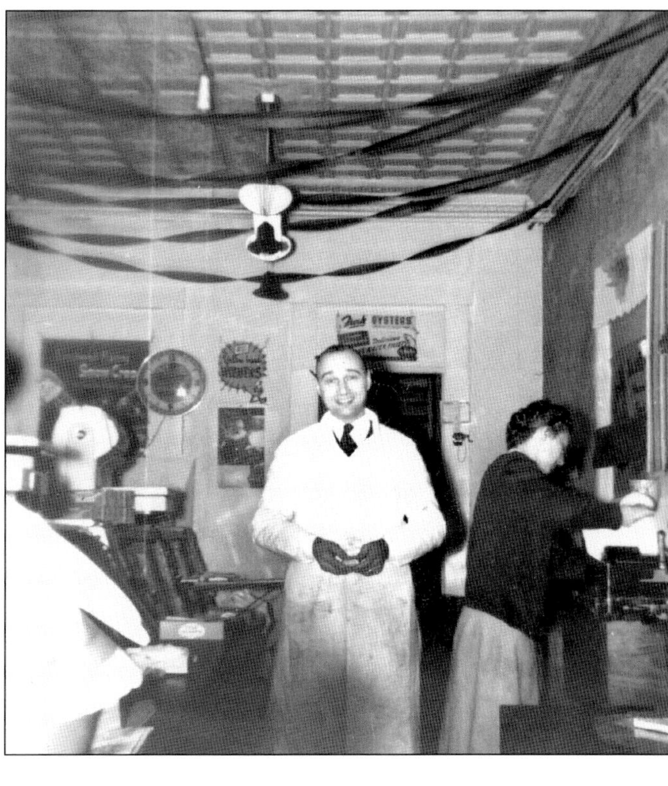

Carr's Market was one of the many small markets that served the outlying Florence community. Located on the corner of today's Ewing Boulevard and Burlington Pike, the store stood on the approximate site of the modern skateboarding park. Seen here are owners Dick and Nina Carr.

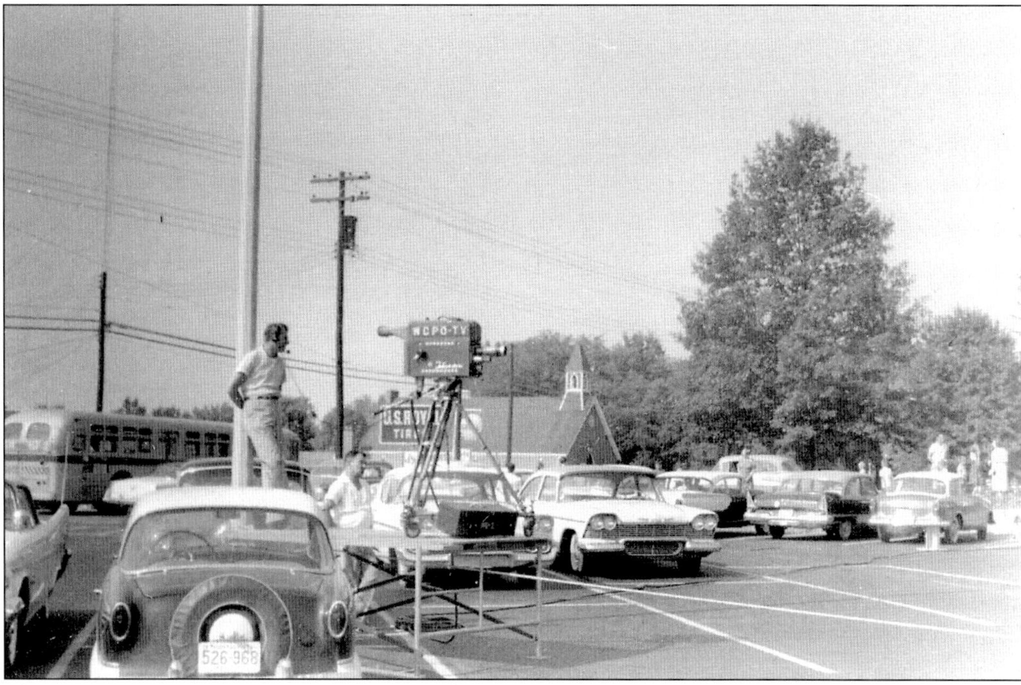

The opening of a large new store in any small town is big news. When the new Albers Supermarket opened in Florence in the early 1960s, WCPO sent a news team to cover the event. To the delight of the children, popular television artist "Uncle Al Lewis" and his wife, "Captain Windy," hosts of the *Uncle Al Show*, also attended the event. The enormous camera seen in this snapshot is a far cry from the small digital television cameras used today.

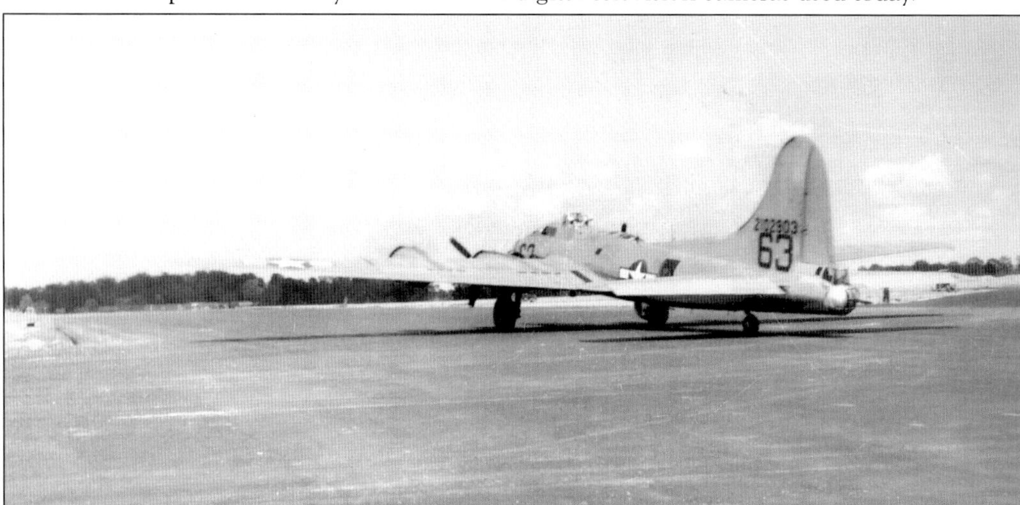

Shortly after World War II, a group of enterprising Northern Kentucky businessmen took the initiative and promoted the development of what would eventually become the Greater Cincinnati/Northern Kentucky International Airport. Lunken Airport, which had served the Cincinnati area prior to World War II, was proving to be to small to handle the increased traffic and size of postwar aircraft. By 1947, construction began on the new airport just outside of Florence. The airport would spur dramatic growth in the Florence economy.

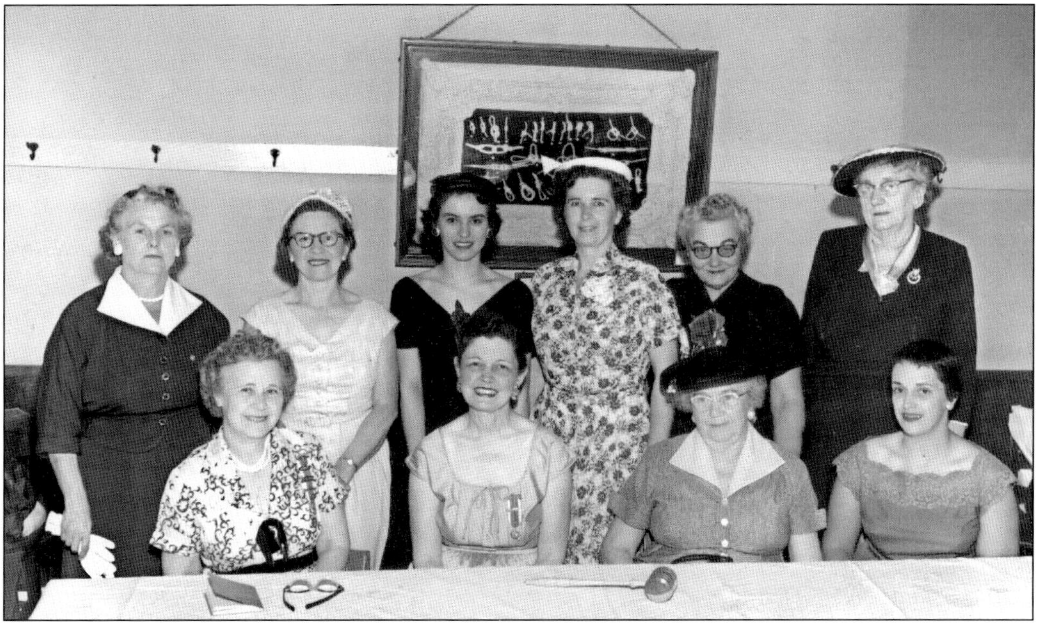

Seen here are the early members of the Boone County Chapter of the Daughters of the American Revolution. Seated second from the left is Elizabeth Goodridge Nestor. Mrs. Nestor was also an active member of the Boone County Historical Society and served as president. Students of Florence history owe a debt of gratitude to Mrs. Nestor for her efforts to record and preserve local history.

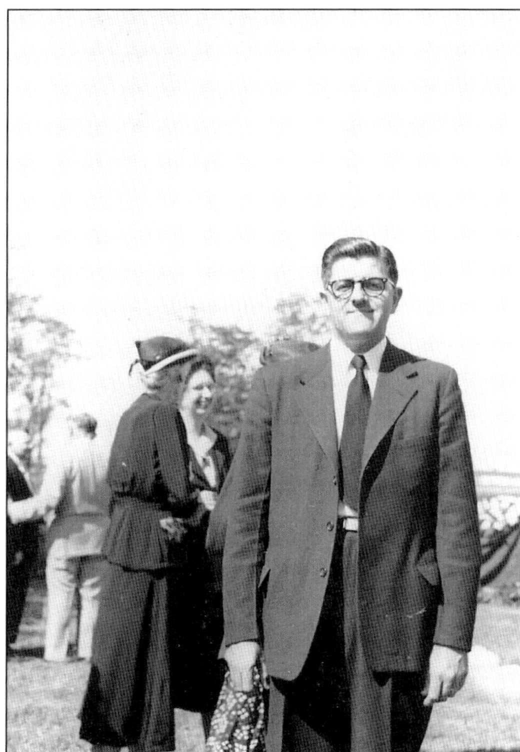

After his arrival in 1948 as the pastor of Hopeful Lutheran Church, the Reverend Herman Andres became a well-known member of the Florence pastoral community. At that time, Hopeful Road, just outside the boundaries of Florence, was a narrow, winding two-lane road. The church was still surrounded by fields and farms. Pastor Andres served the church until 1953.

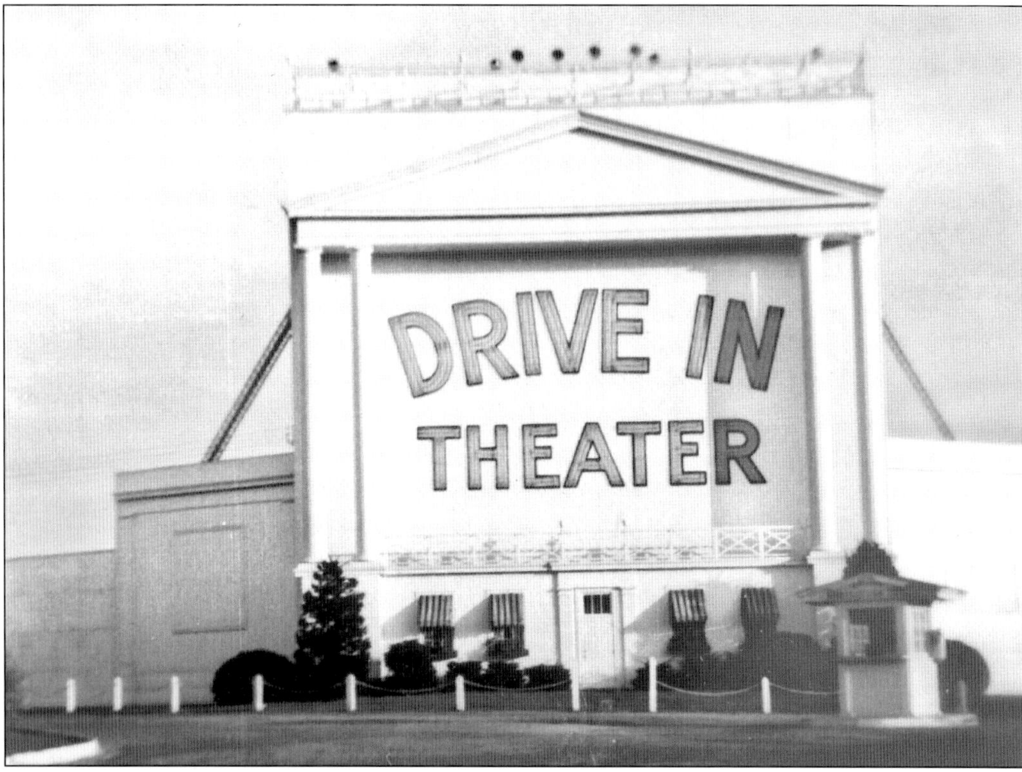

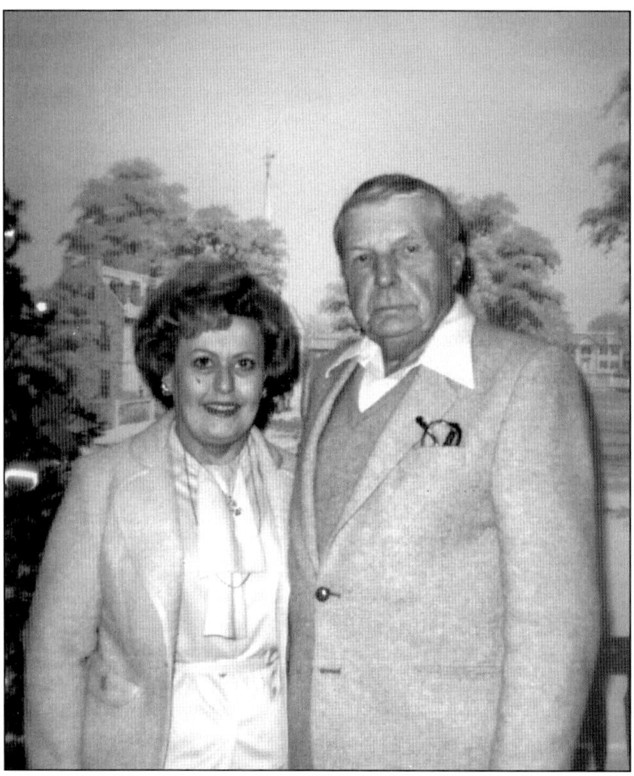

What Florence resident cannot recall a warm summer's evening at the Florence Drive-In Theater? Beginning in the 1940s, the convenience of viewing the latest Hollywood hits from the comfort of one's own car came to Florence. Parking the car, attaching the speaker to the window, and waiting for twilight to end have now become only pleasant memories. Today a condominium complex occupies the site.

The Florence Building and Loan was established in 1925 and was originally located in the Meyer's Building on Main Street. By the 1940s, the Building and Loan office had moved across the street to share quarters with the post office. Seen here in the newly redecorated lobby are Marilyn Goley and John McEvoy.

No trip to the Florence Drive-In Theater would be complete without a trip to the concession stand. Seen here is Kay Hammbrick smiling for the photographer. The concession stand was later enlarged to provide more than just the traditional hamburgers, hot dogs, and popcorn.

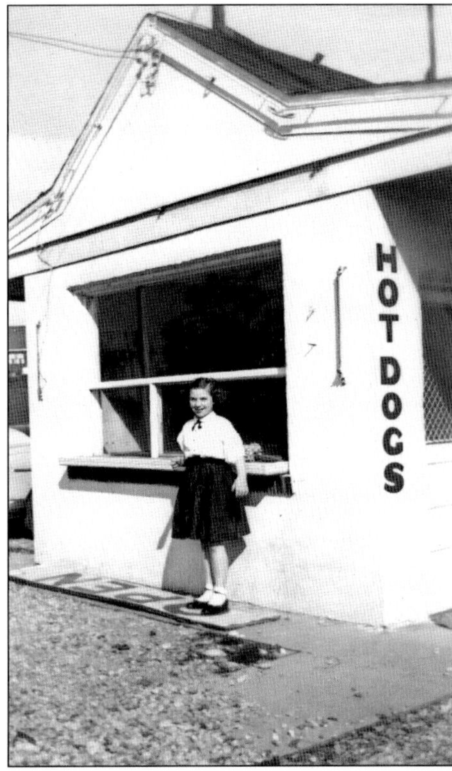

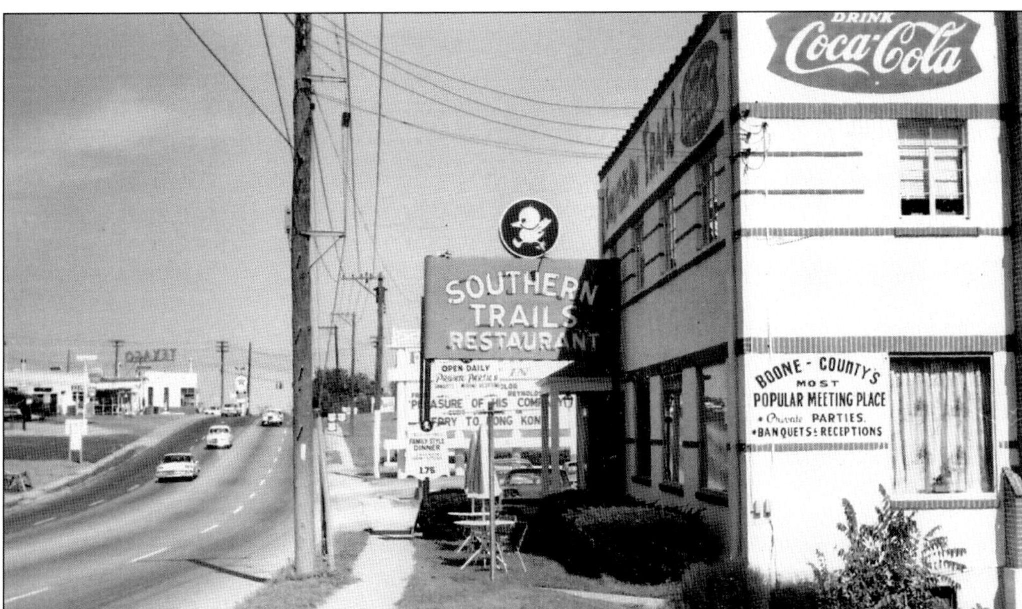

After the construction of the Dixie Highway Bypass, numerous businesses sprang up along the highway. Perhaps one of the most visible was the Southern Trails Restaurant. As the sign on the corner of the building indicates, it was considered by many to be Boone County's most popular meeting place. While much of its business was derived from catering, Southern Trails was famous for their delicious Sunday dinner, complete with Southern fried chicken.

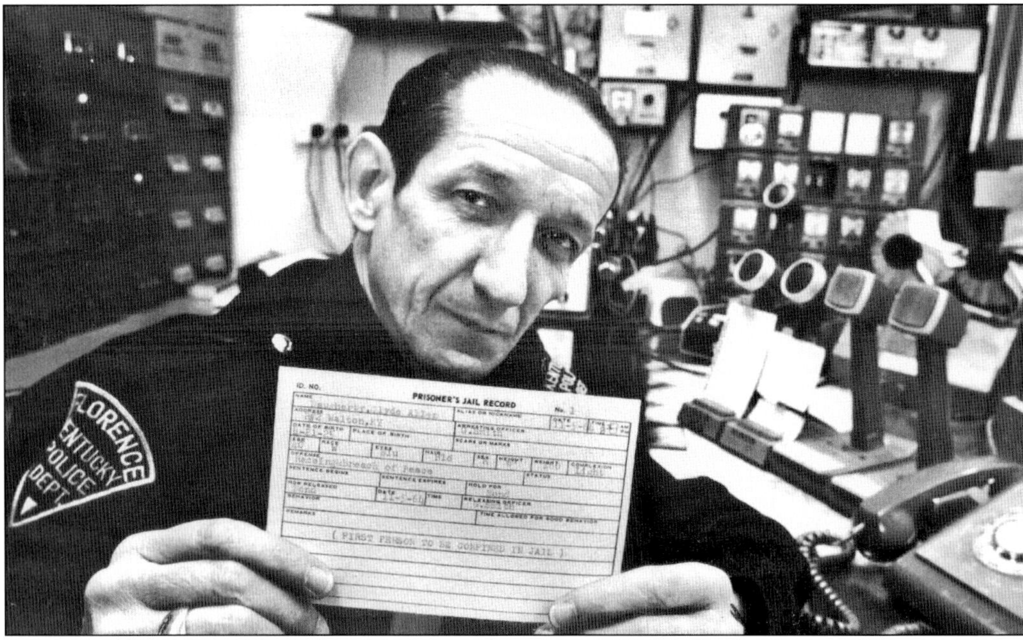

In 1964, the Florence city government moved to its new home on U.S. 42. Pictured here in the communication center of the Florence City Building is dispatcher Wendell Cooper. As well as the calls for the Florence fire and police departments, those of Boone County were also channeled through his center. In his hand, Mr. Cooper holds the file card for the first prisoner in the new jail.

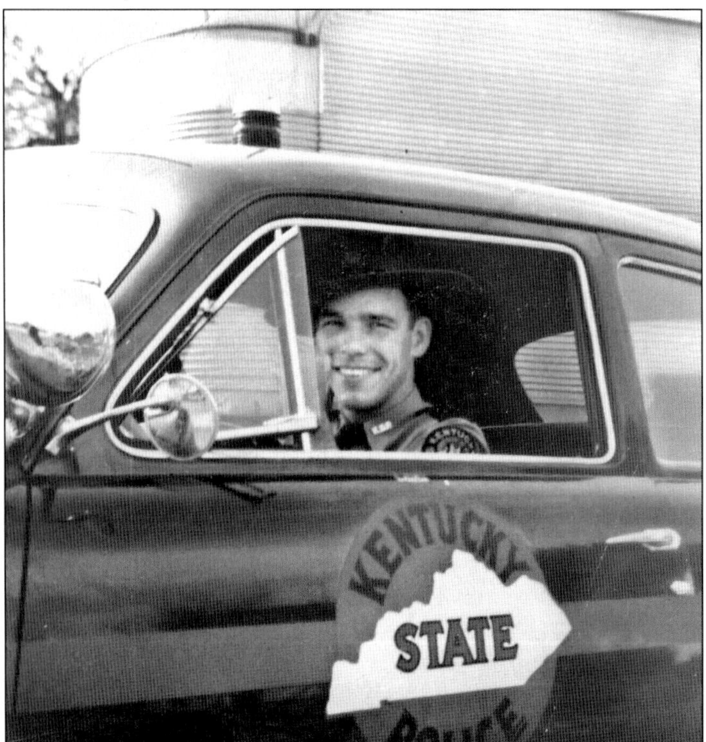

Seated behind the wheel of his cruiser is Kentucky state trooper Robert Renaker Miller. Trooper Miller, a graduate of Florence High School in the class of 1945, was the son of Robert and Eva Miller. He had served on the state force for three years when, while checking the conditions of icy roads on U.S. 25 near Cabindale, his car skidded on a turn and collided with a utility truck. He was killed instantly. A highly esteemed member of the Florence community, he had over 3,500 people call during his visitation. One hundred state troopers from around the commonwealth attended his funeral.

Nine

BUSINESSES

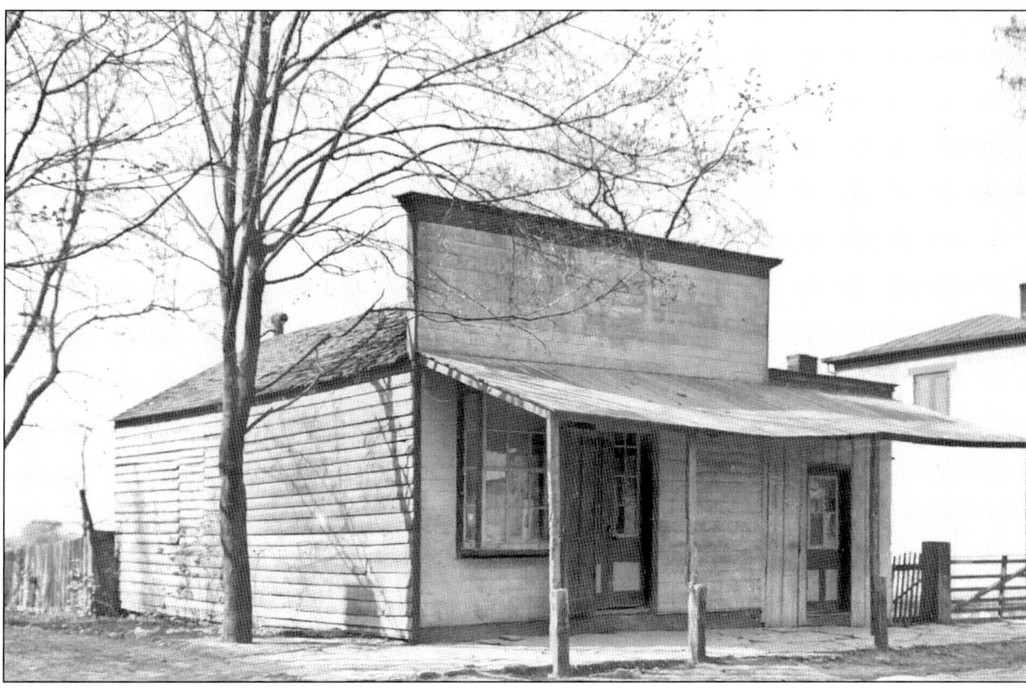

This general store, located on the north side of Main Street opposite Banklick Street, appeared in John Lloyd's book *Stringtown on the Pike*. Jim Carpenter later operated a butcher shop in the building, which he had moved across Main Street. During its history, the building also housed the U.S. Post Office. Mr. E. T. Sine and his daughter, Carrie, operated a grocery there in the late 1930s. The building was dismantled around 1945.

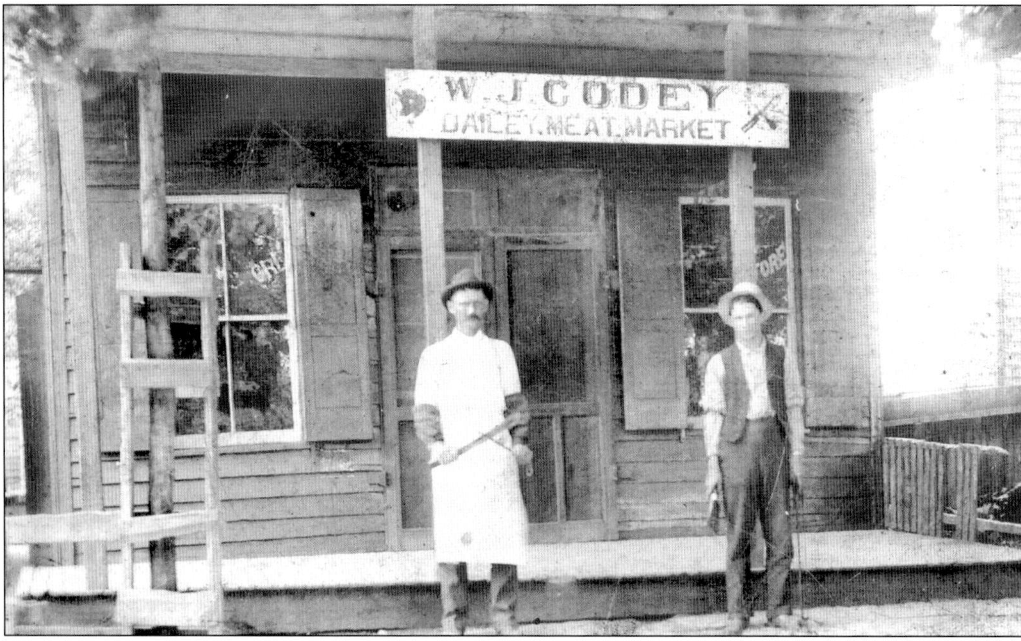

W. J. Codey's butcher shop was located on Main Street near the Christian church. Two employees stand in front of the shop ready for a day's work. To the left, sharpening his knife, is David Osborn. His son, Ed, stands to the right holding a cleaver and a meat saw. The Osborns were a well-known Florence family and active in community affairs. Benjamin Osborn, David's other son, served as town constable.

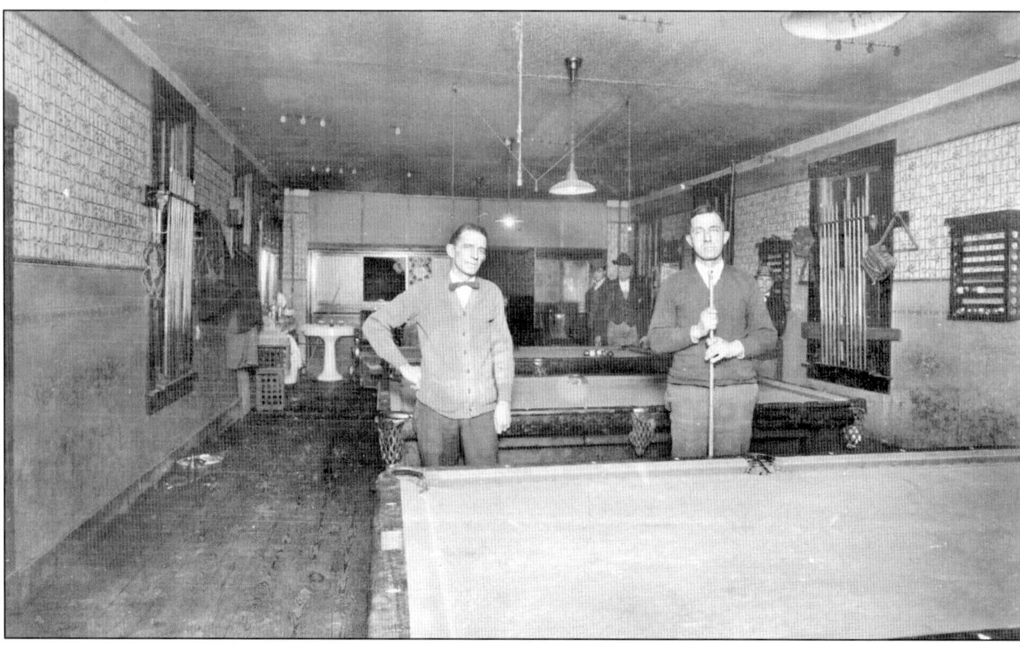

Enjoying a game of billiards at Ed Osborn's store are Ed Osborn (left) and Charlie Popham. The billiards parlor was a very popular gathering place in the 1930s for many of the men of Florence. In addition to the billiards parlor, Mr. Osborn ran a barbershop, department store, and a soda fountain on Main Street, thus making him one of the leading merchants in town.

In the days before self-serve gasoline stations, attendants routinely checked the oil and washed the windshield of every car pulling into the station. Included in this picture of Lloyd Rouse's Standard Oil Station are Bill McEvoy and Winfield Aylor. Mr. Rouse's service station was located at the busy corner of U.S. 25 and U.S. 42.

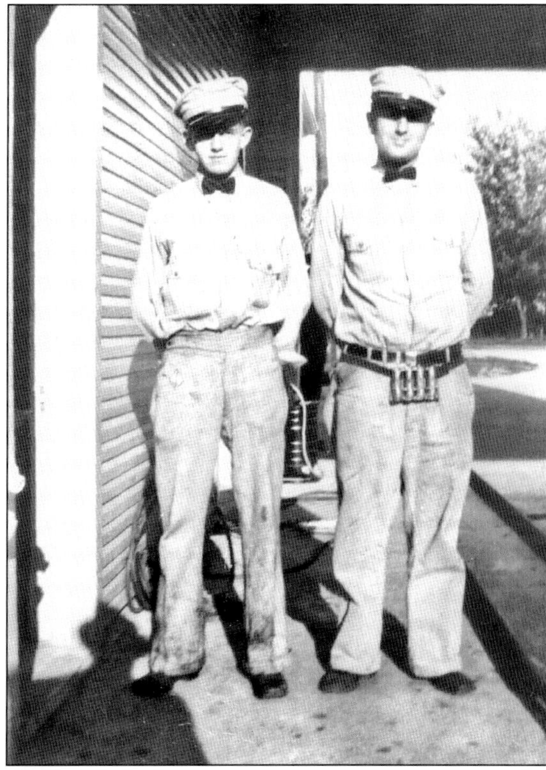

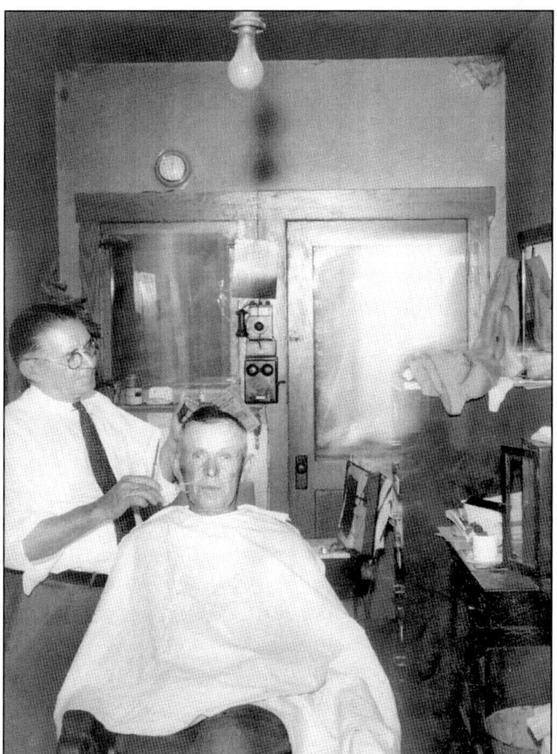

Ed Osborn's barbershop on Main Street was the place to exchange local news and get a good haircut. Lonnie Tanner was in the barber's chair when this picture was taken. Notice the hand-crank telephone on the rear wall. At that time, Florence residents would have to place all calls through Consolidated Telephone's switchboard operators. Mr. Osborn's telephone number was 133.

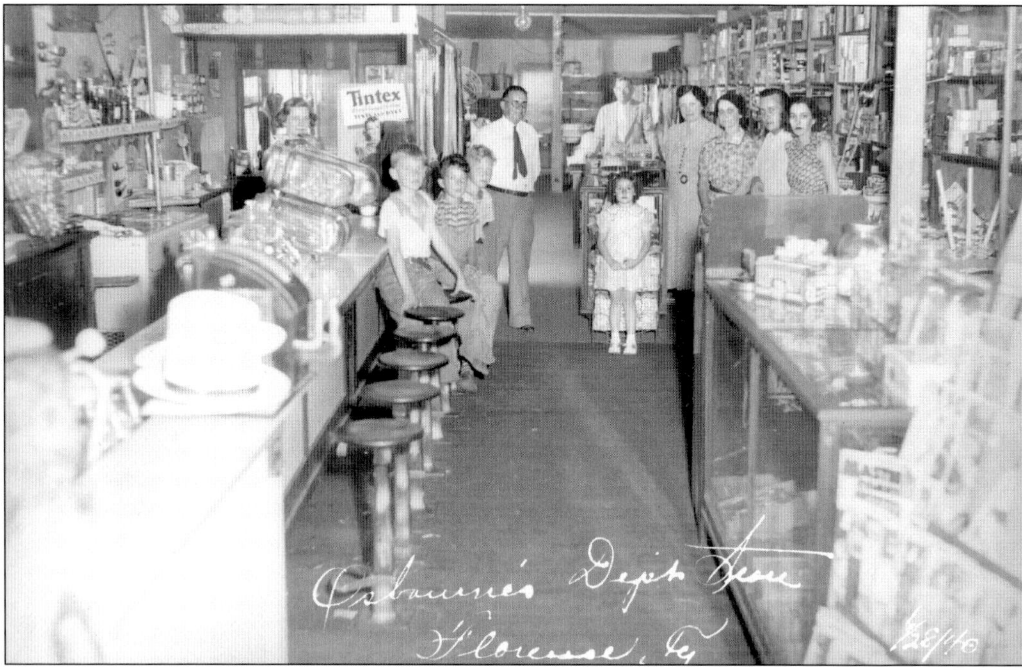

A group of employees and patrons paused to have their picture taken in Ed Osborn's store in 1940. From left to right are (seated on the stools) George Houston, Bobby Martin, and Dan Houston; (standing) Carrie Martin, Ed Osborn (wearing the tie), Hal Highhouse, Virginia Osborn, Sally Highhouse, Eva Osborn, Elmer Corbin, and Mary A. Tupman.

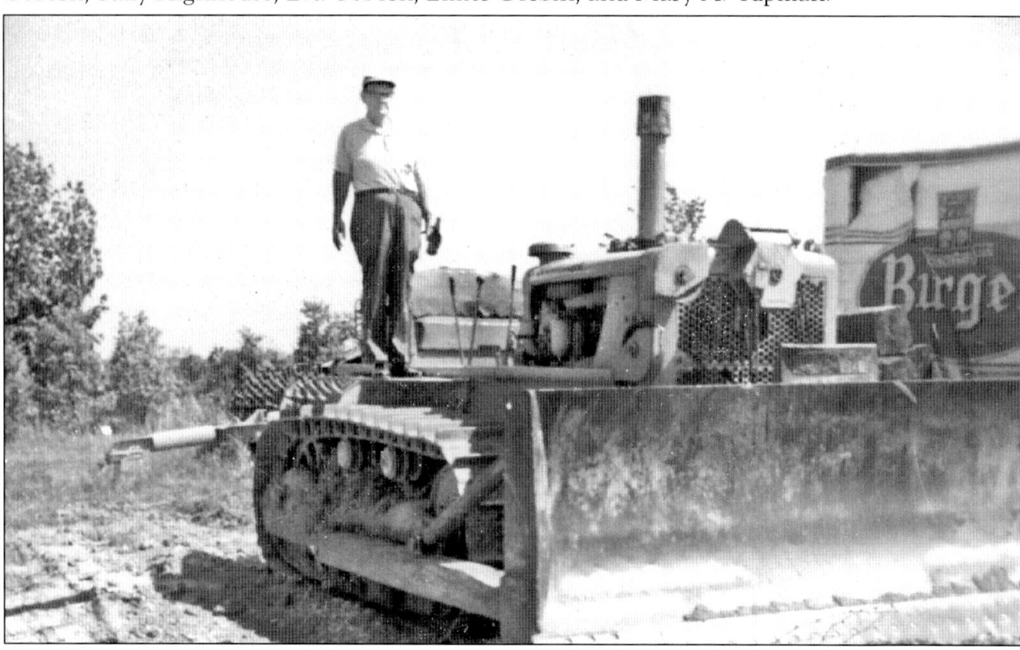

Standing on the bulldozer is R. B. Taylor, founder of R. B. Taylor and Sons Construction. Mr. Taylor, along with Dr. Harry Daughtery, developed the Sweetbriar Subdivision, one of the first to spring up in Florence after the Second World War. Mr. Taylor purchased the first bulldozer in Boone County. Today his sons Bob and Tom continue the family business.

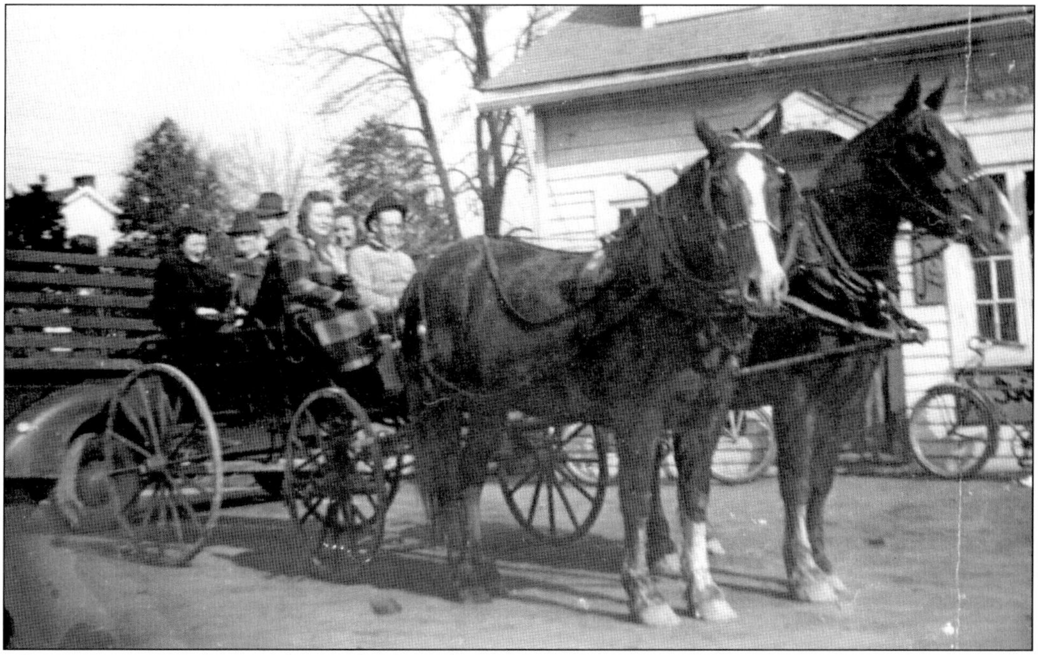

This picture was taken in front of Bob and Jean's Restaurant in February 1941. In the front seat of the wagon are Dot and Buck Easton. They had driven the wagon from the Easterdale Stock Farm on Price Pike. Seated in the rear of the wagon are, from left to right, Naomi and Jess England and Jim and Lula Mae Tanner. Bob Eades, the owner of the restaurant, took this picture.

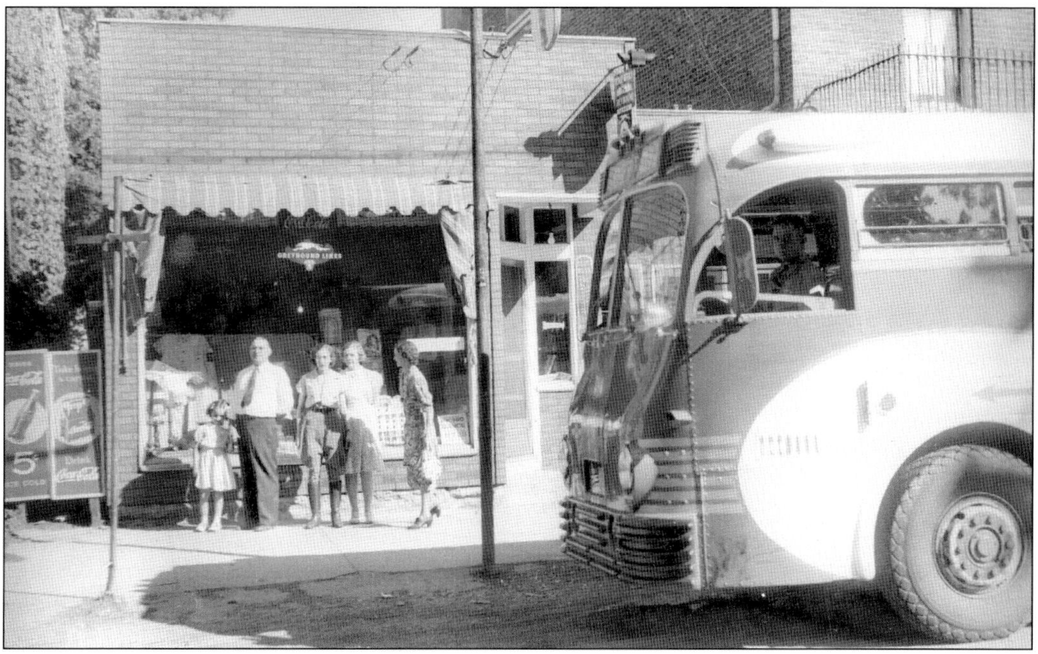

Ed Osborn's store on Main Street was also a bus stop for the Greyhound bus line. Gathered in front of the store are, from left to right, Virginia Osborn, Ed Osborn, Mary Tupman, Eva Osborn, and Carrie Sine Martin. A northbound bus has just stopped. A sign in front of the store had a light on each side that could be turned on to alert the drivers if there were passengers to be picked up.

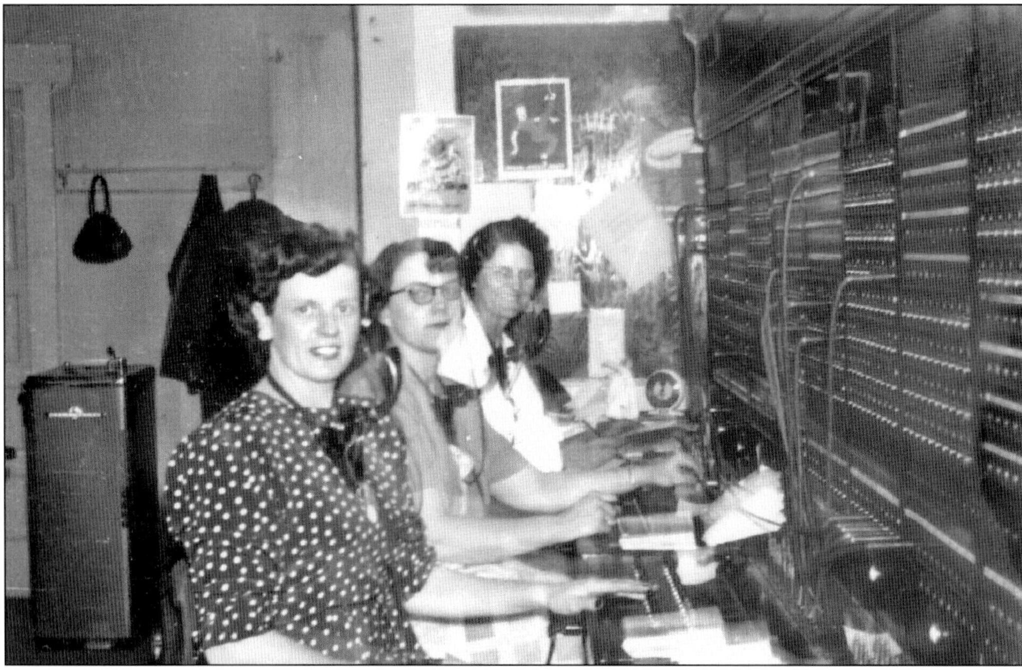

The switchboard for the Consolidated Telephone Company was located on the second floor of the Meyer's Building at the corner of Shelby and Main Streets. Seated at the switchboard are, from left to right, Ruth Wingate, Helen June Gatewood, and Bertha Jack. The phone company operated in the Meyer's Building before moving to its own building on Girard Street.

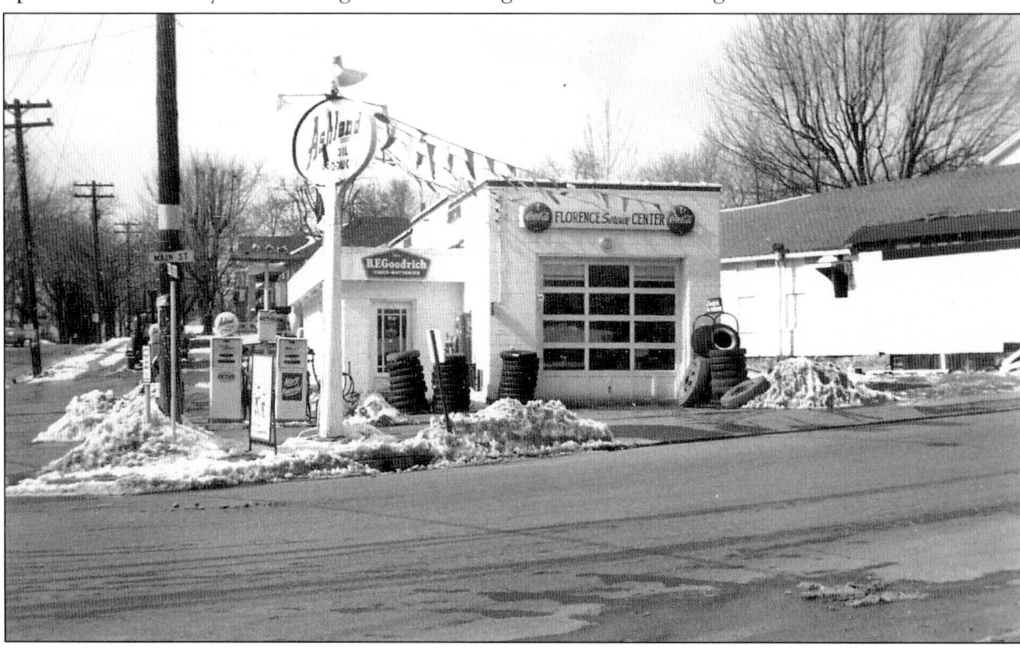

Bradford Brothers Carriage Shop began on this corner of Shelby and Main, but as the automobile slowly replaced horse-drawn vehicles, they became an automobile and carriage company. The transformation was finally completed in the 1920s, when a service station took over the location. The Florence Service Center is seen here in the late 1950s.

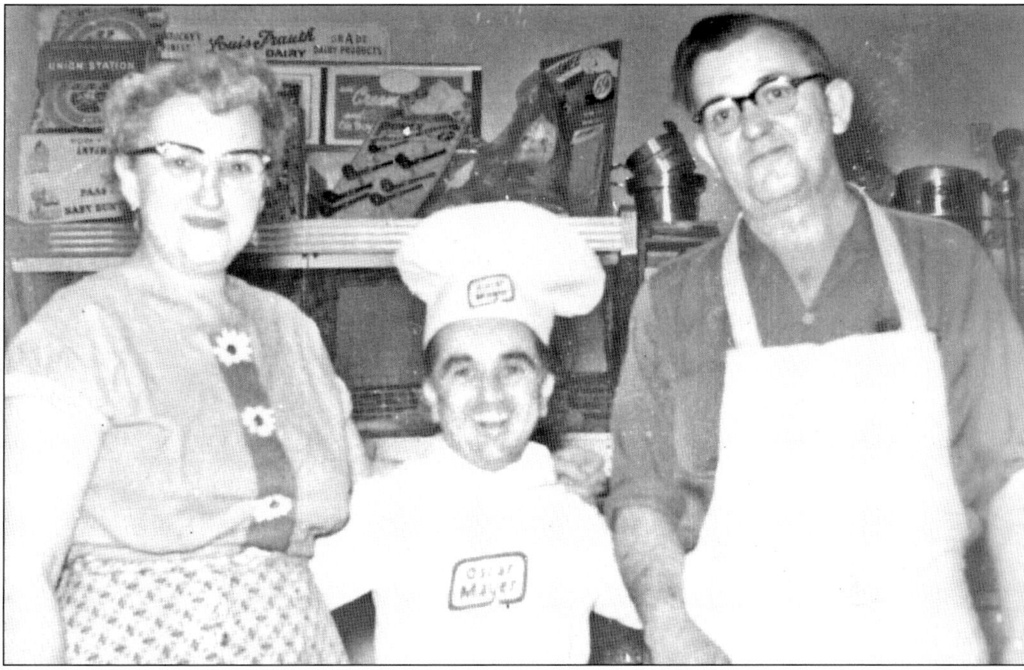

Ernie Godsey operated a small grocery store on Dixie Highway near where today's United Dairy Farmers store is located. Pictured here from left to right are Ruth Cooper, the Oscar Mayer Weiner Man, and store owner Ernie Godsey. Many small markets operated successfully in and around Florence before the advent of the larger chain stores.

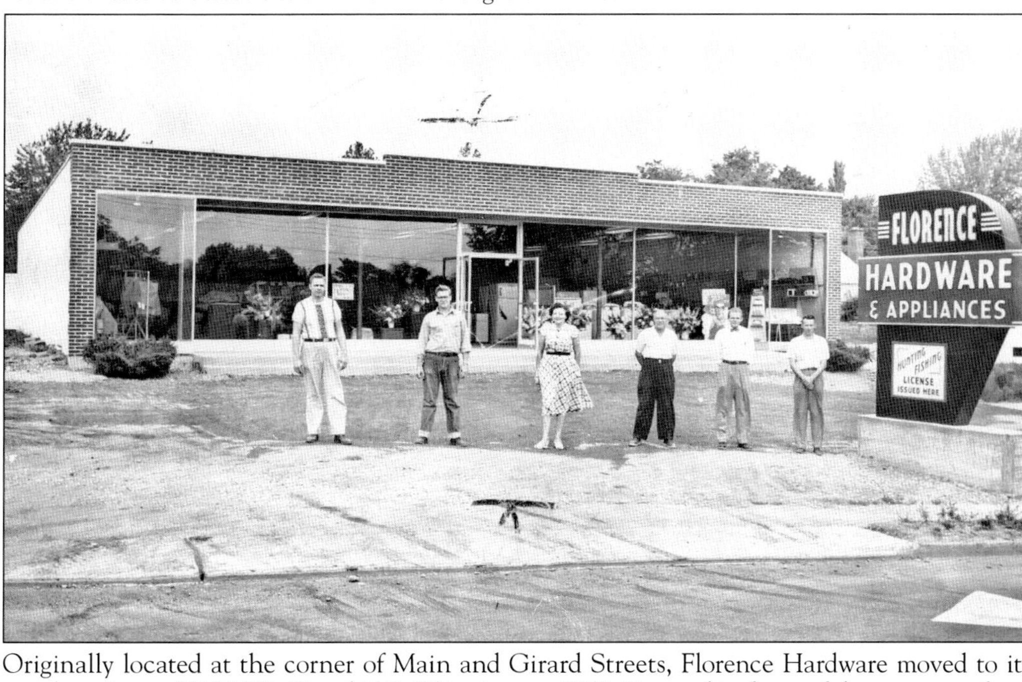

Originally located at the corner of Main and Girard Streets, Florence Hardware moved to its new location at 7110 U.S. 42 and U.S. 25 in August 1953. Pictured in front of the new store from left to right are Bob Nee, Charles Markesbery, Lucille Souther, Bill Campbell, Russ Wilmhoff, and Bill Shotwell.

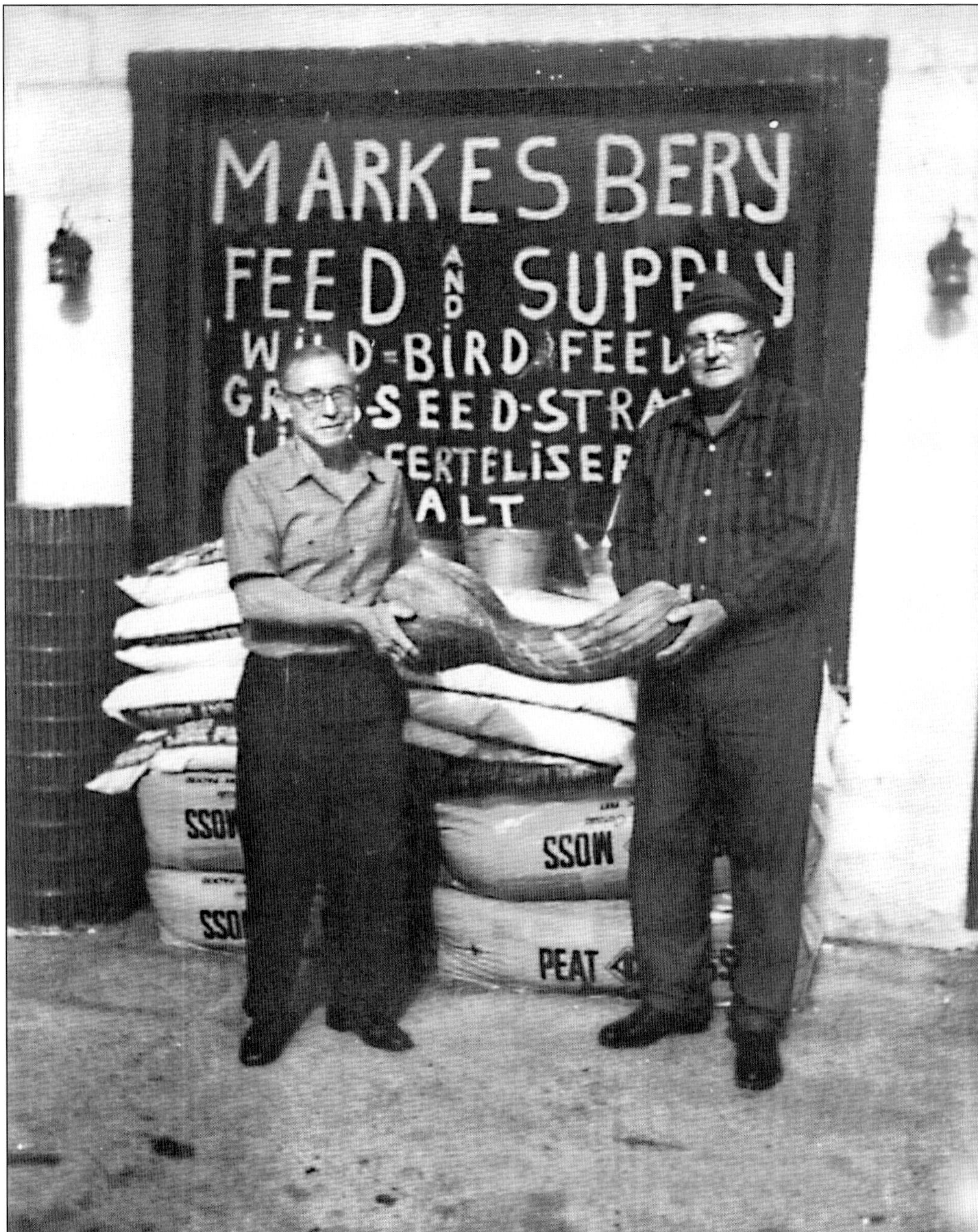

Nelson Markesbery, pictured here on the left, could often be seen standing outside his feed and supply store on Girard Street. Mr. Markesbery also operated Markesbery Movers out of the same location. Today his son Don operates Don Markesbery Construction, Inc., at the same location. Seen here along with Nelson is Raymond Gross.

Ten

SURROUNDING COUNTRYSIDE

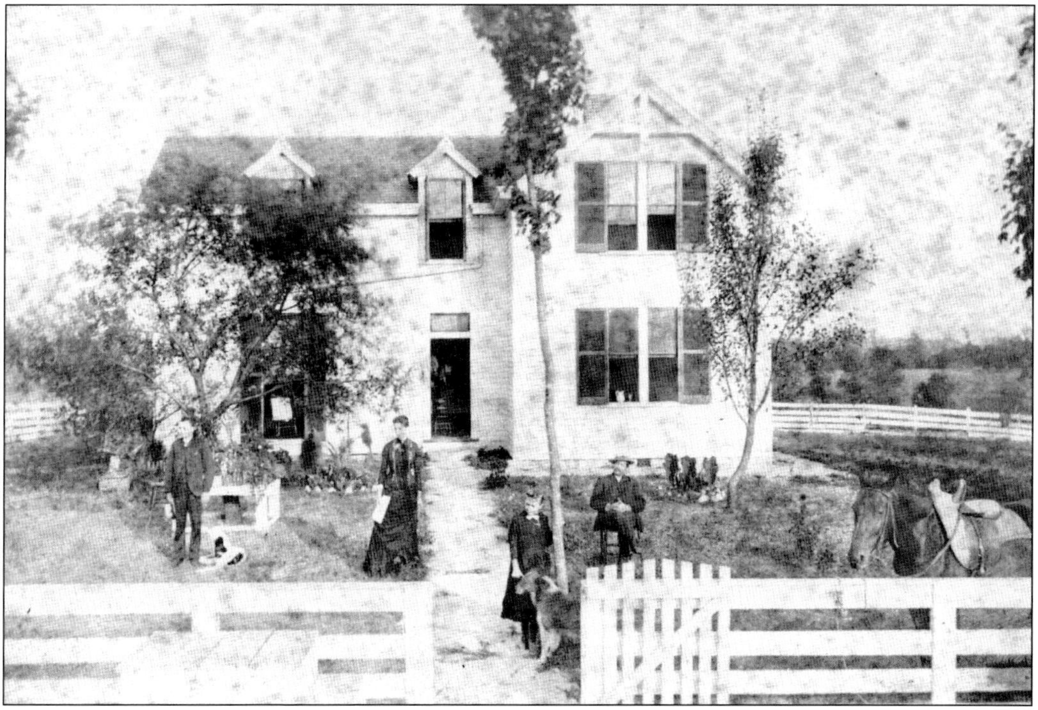

The Benjamin Surface farm was located about two miles west of Florence on the Florence-Union Pike (U.S. 42). Standing in their front yard are, from left to right, Willie, Ada, Minta, and Benjamin Surface. Just visible in front of the fence is a style block used for getting in and out of wagons and carriages. The Boone County Board of Education office currently occupies the site.

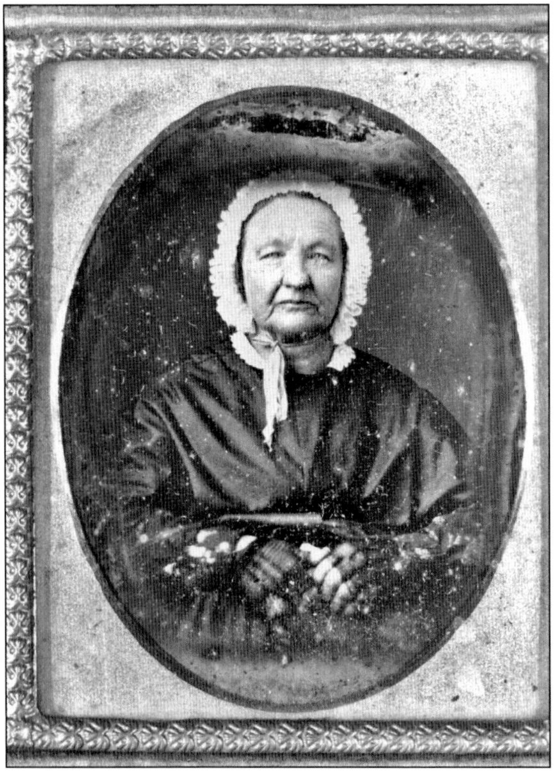

The matriarch of one of the Florence area's earliest families, Susannah Tanner, seen here around 1860, arrived with her husband, Ephraim, in November 1805. They settled on a farm just west of Florence near the present intersection of Industrial Road and U.S. 42. Their family included 14 children and 112 grandchildren. Many of their descendants are members of the Florence community today.

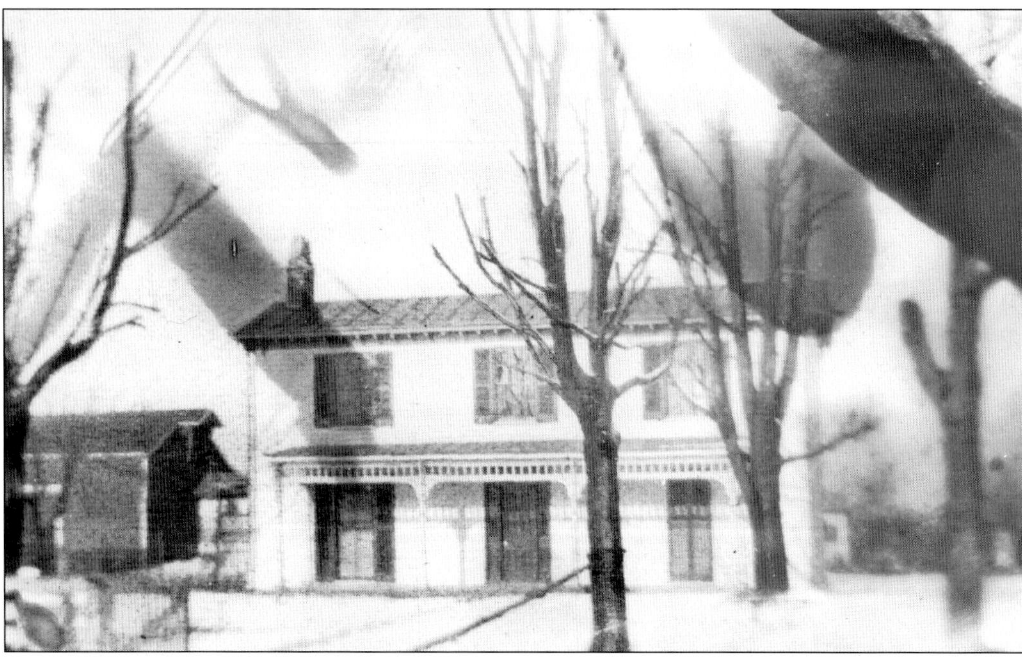

This farmhouse, located on Burlington Pike near the end of Shelby Street, was home to the Tom Easton family. It was an example of how close farms were to the center of town. The Easton family continued farming their land through the first half of the 20th century. The development of nearby Wallace Avenue in the 1950s signaled the beginning of change from rural to suburban.

One of the larger farms near Florence was owned by Joshua Zimmerman Tanner, seen here. His land stretched along Burlington Pike from today's Utz Drive to include today's homes along Kathryn Avenue and Wallace Drive before ending near the junction of Shelby Street. His home was located near the entrance of today's Stringtown Park.

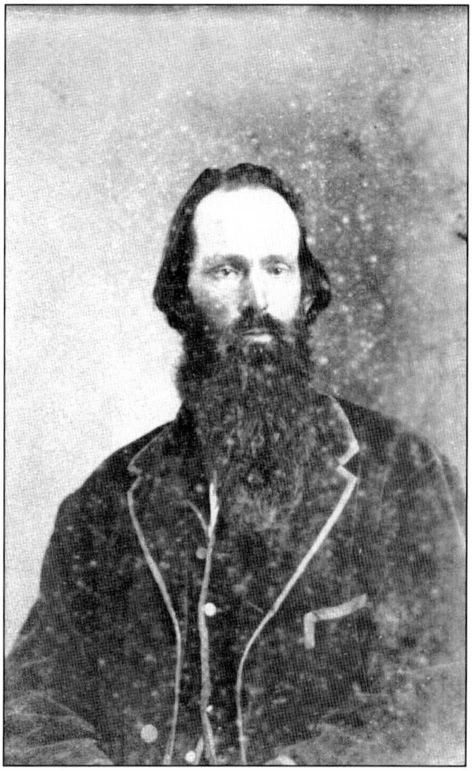

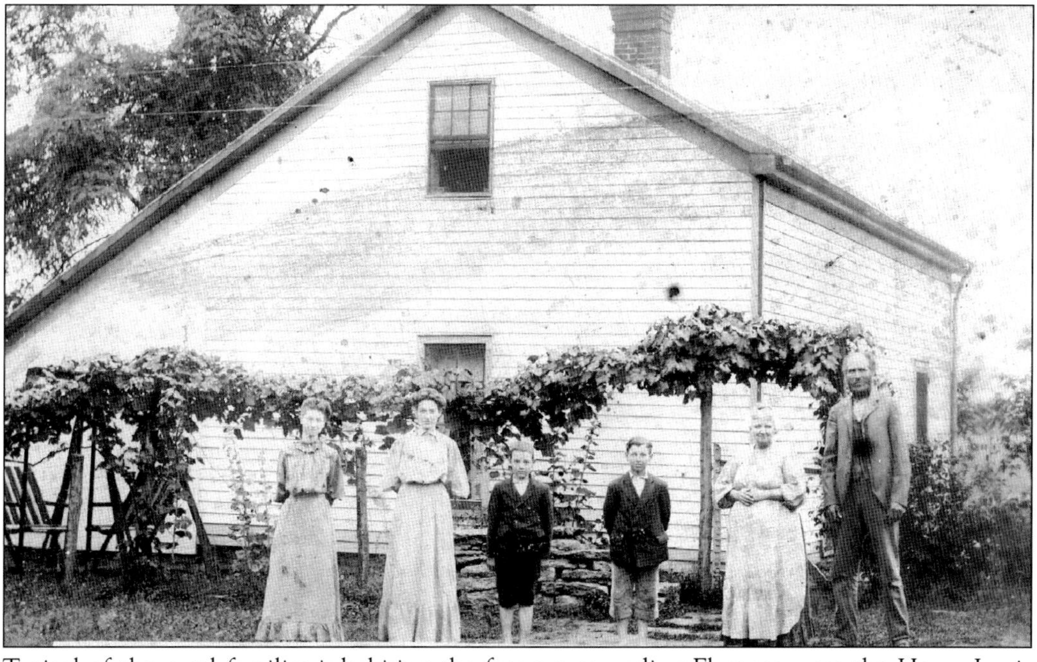

Typical of the rural families inhabiting the farms surrounding Florence were the Henry Louis Tanners. The 100-acre farm was located just off Hopeful Road. The imposing figure of six-foot-three-inch Henry Louis Tanner stands at the right. The other family members in the picture are, from left to right, daughters Ethel and Kitty, sons Lloyd and Fitzhugh, and wife Carrie Naomi.

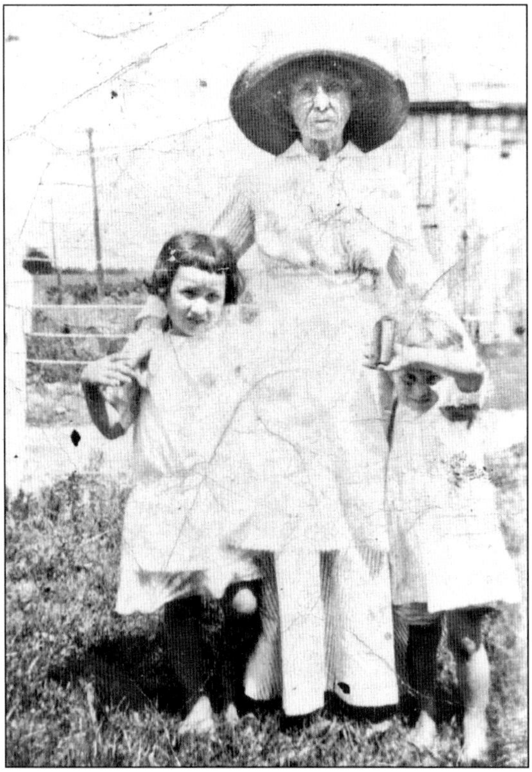

Florence resident Elizabeth Bartell often visited with her relatives living in the surrounding countryside. Seen here at her cousin Charles H. Tanner's farm on Burlington Pike, she appears ready for a day in the country. From left to right are Cora E. Tanner, Bartell, and Evelyn Tanner. "Aunt Liz" experienced much of Florence's history before her death at age 83 in 1937.

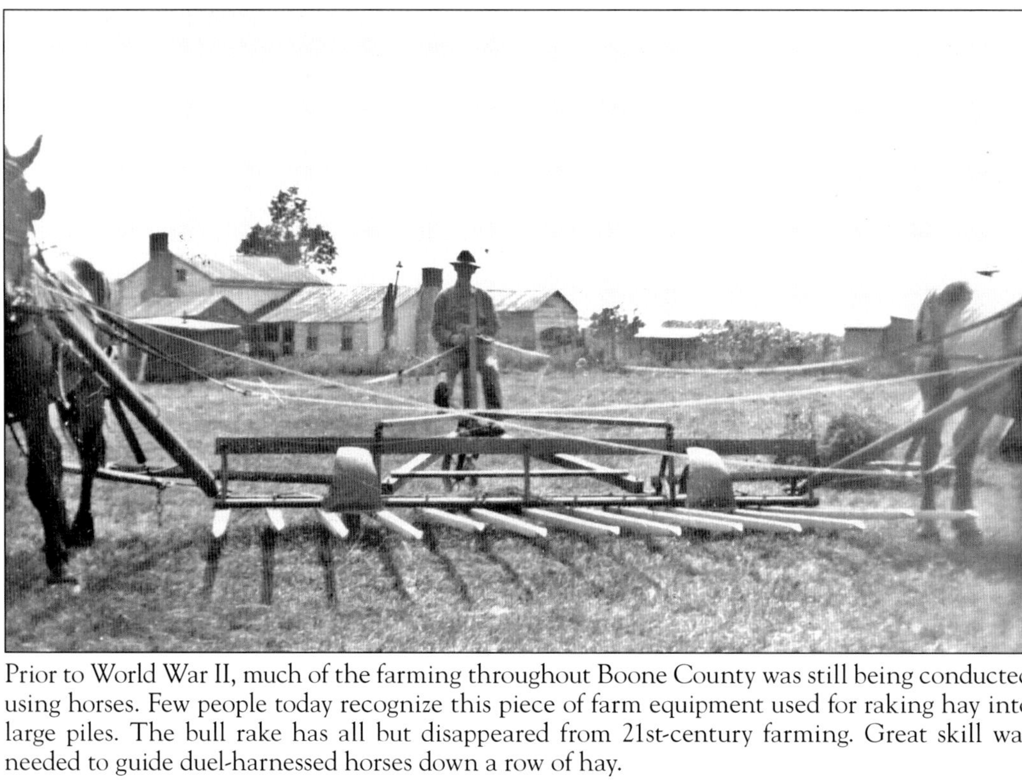

Prior to World War II, much of the farming throughout Boone County was still being conducted using horses. Few people today recognize this piece of farm equipment used for raking hay into large piles. The bull rake has all but disappeared from 21st-century farming. Great skill was needed to guide duel-harnessed horses down a row of hay.

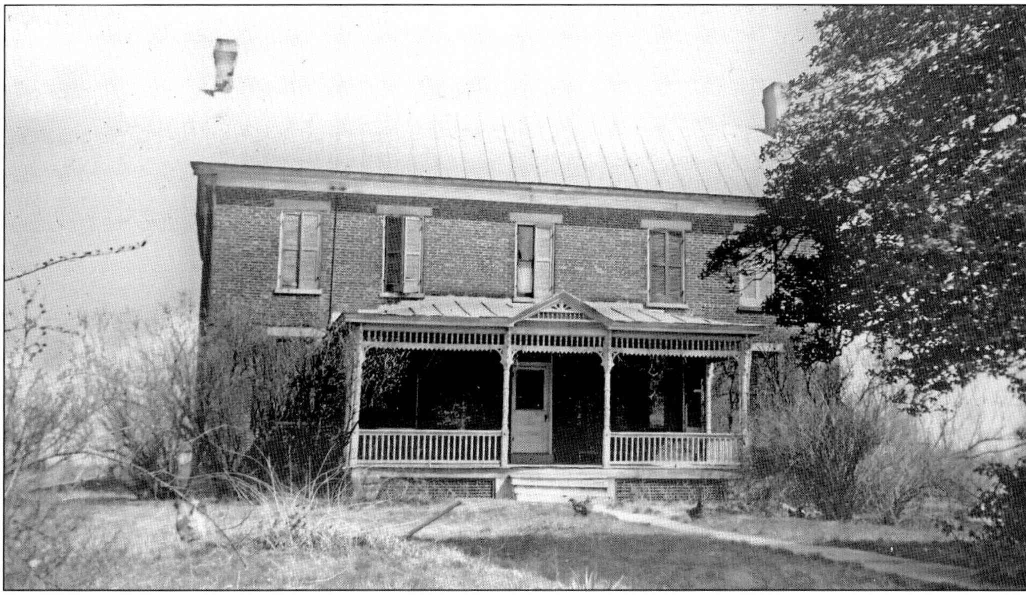

Heading west on Price Pike just after leaving Florence, one passed the Butler Carpenter home. In the late 19th century, one of the tollbooths on Price Pike was located directly across from the Carpenter home. This was the home of Stella Carpenter, a member of the Florence School faculty in the early 20th century. Today I-75 runs to the immediate left of the property.

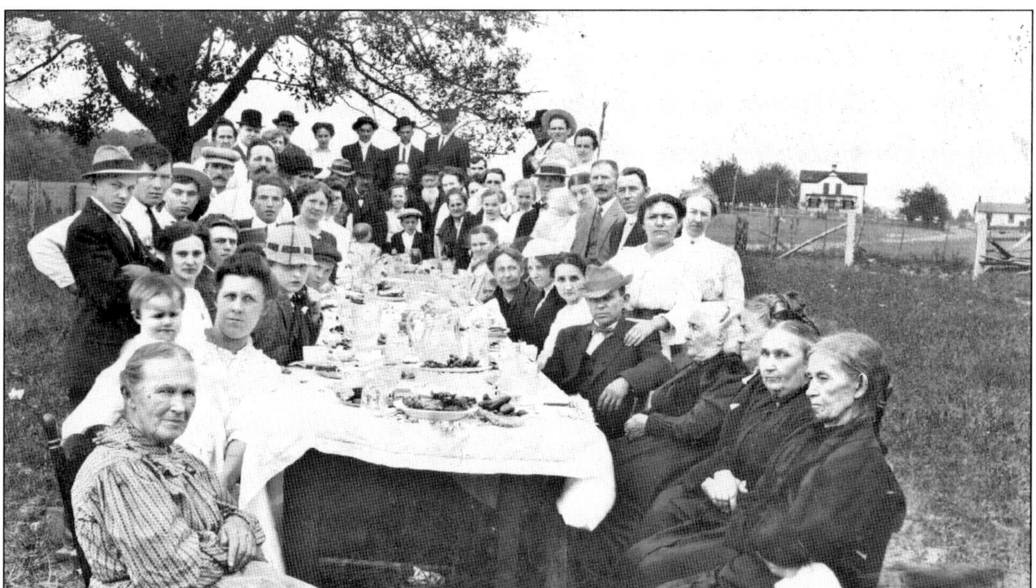

Members of the Clutterbuck family are seen here in the front yard of their home on Price Pike at a family reunion in the early 20th century. Seated at the end of the table at right is family matriarch Sarah Francis Clutterbuck. Today the Clutterbuck farm is part of the growing Greater Cincinnati/Northern Kentucky International Airport.

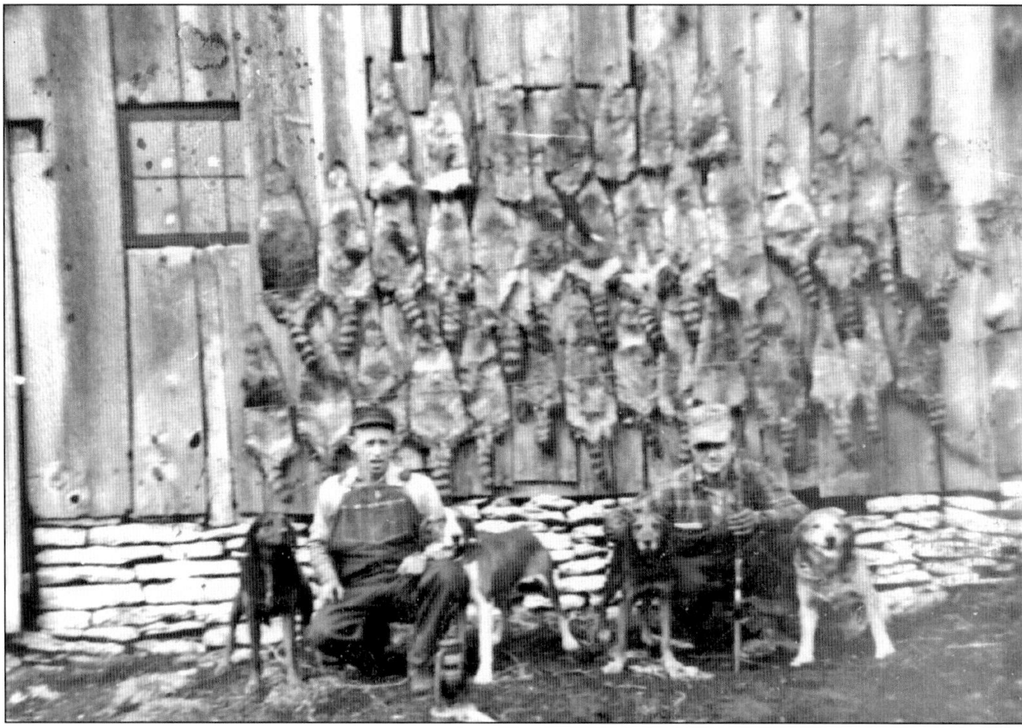

For years along the ridges and valleys surrounding Florence, coon hunting was a popular pastime of local residents. The numerous pelts displayed by Dan Carpenter (left) and Ken Griffith is a testament to their skill as hunters. To many, the joy of the hunt was the sound of the baying coonhounds, seen here with their proud owners.

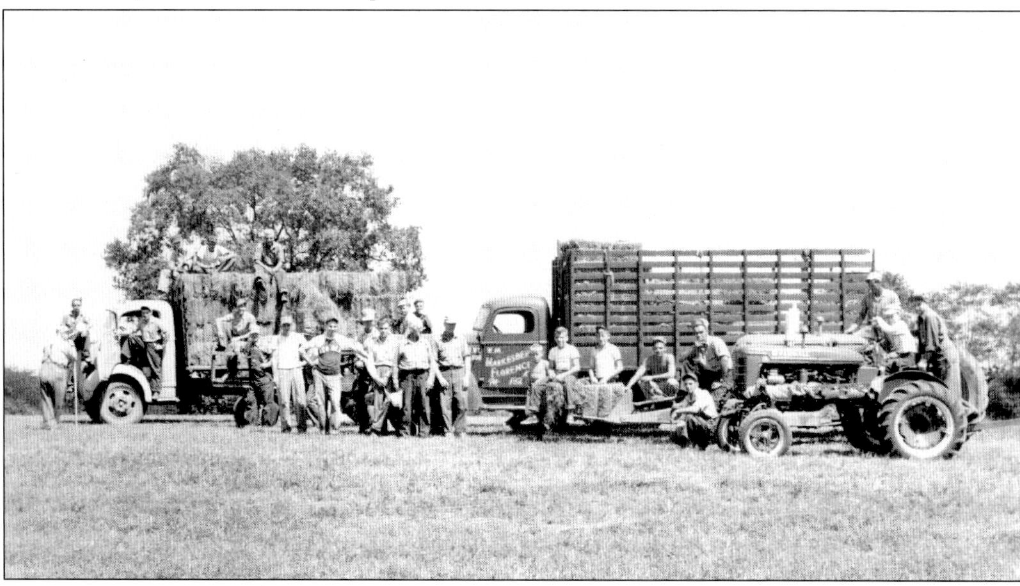

In August 1949, around 30 men from the American Legion's Boone Post No. 4 in Florence gathered at the farm of fellow member and World War I veteran Kenneth Stamper to help him put up hay. Tom Easton, John Middendorf, and Charles Forder furnished tractors. Over 500 bales of hay were hauled on the trucks of Bill Markesbery, Bob Eads, and John Middendorf.

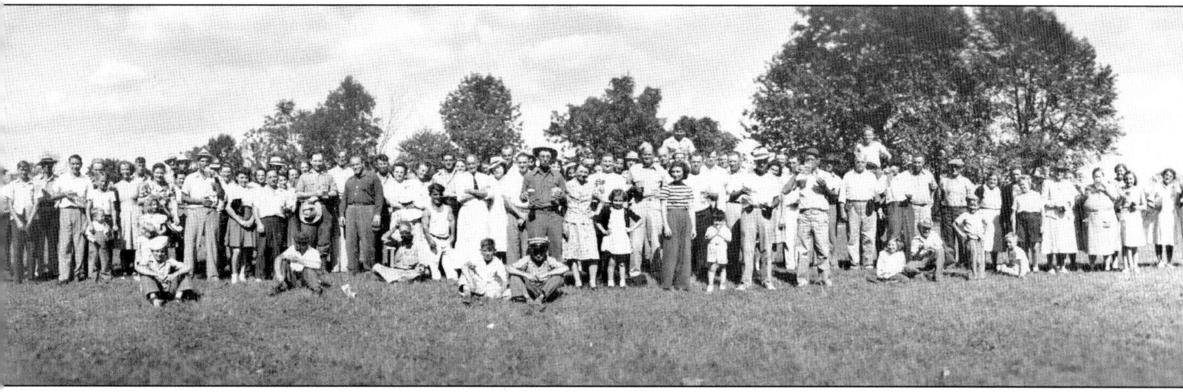

Pictured here are the friends of Dan Carpenter. Dan stands in the center of the photo wearing a hat and dark outfit. The picture's story begins with Dan, an avid fisherman, having a slight altercation with the local fish and game warden. When his friends heard of his case going to court, they all chipped in to help pay for the lawyer. On the day of the trial, the fish and game warden failed to appear and the judge dismissed the case. After paying the lawyer's $25 fee, Dan still had a good amount of money left over. He decided to use it to hold a fish fry to thank all of his supporters. They are pictured here. No one can say Dan Carpenter did not have a lot of friends!

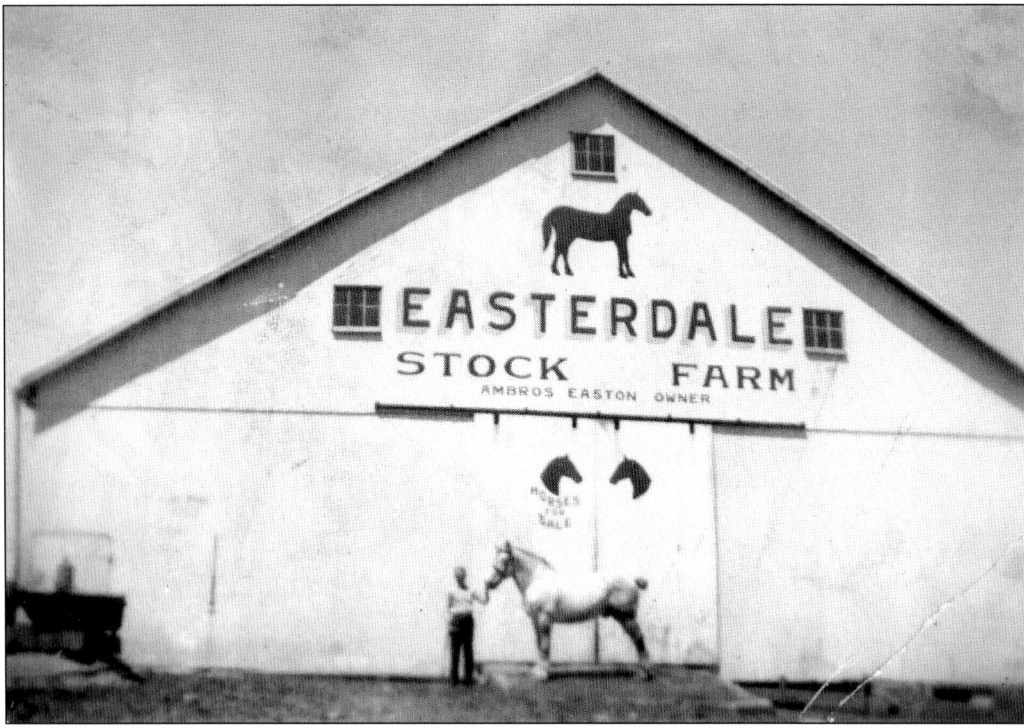

Easterdale Stock Farm, located on Price Pike, was the home to championship racing stock. Thoroughbreds from the Easton stable raced at the old Latonia Race Course as well as in the Lexington and Louisville areas. The farm was owned by Ambrose and Linnie Easton.

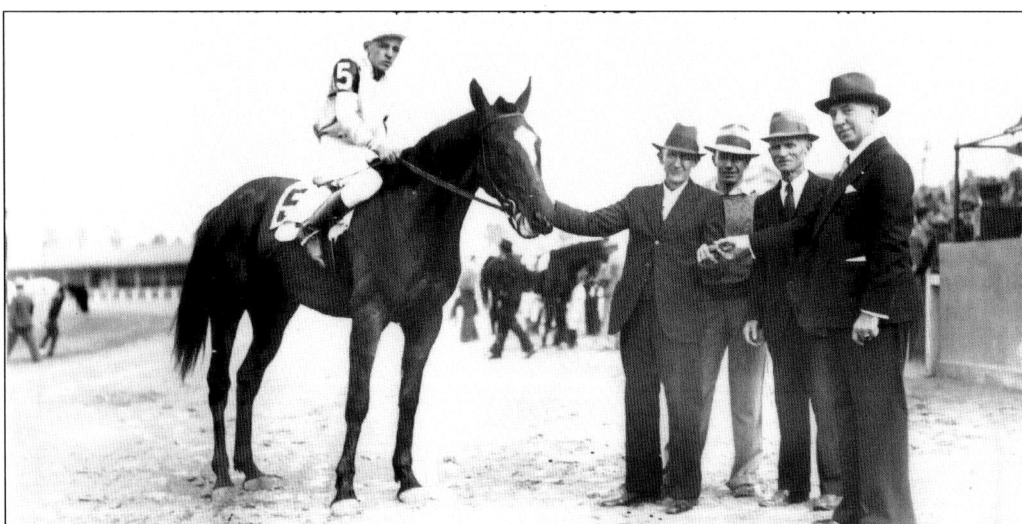

Proud owner Ambrose Easton holds the reins of his thoroughbred Kentucky Flyer following his winning the Joseph M. Cousins Purse at the Kentucky State Fairgrounds. Mr. Easton and his wife, Linnie, were the owners of Easterdale Stock Farm on Price Pike.

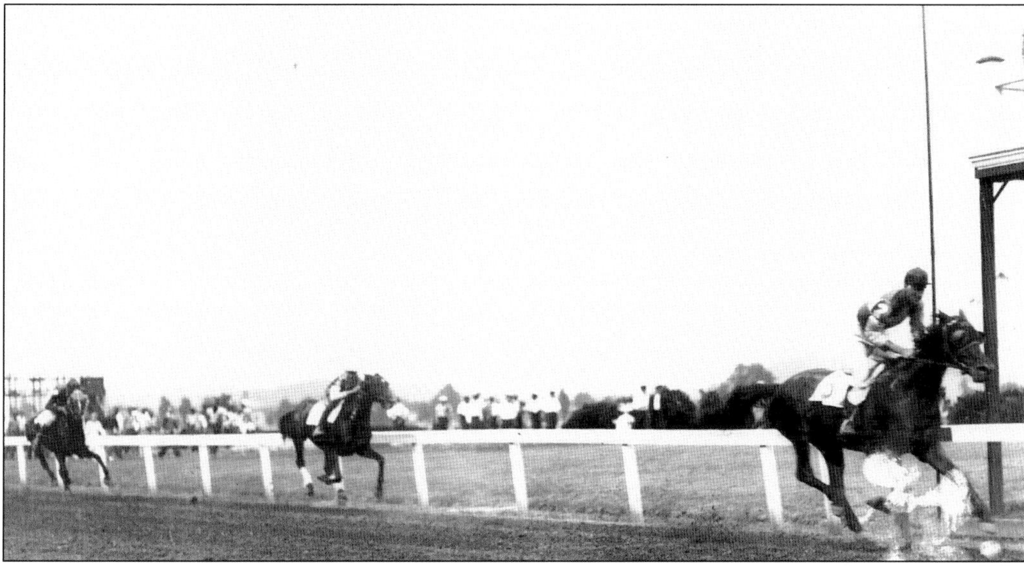

On June 27, 1936, Easterdale Stock Farm's thoroughbred Busy Vew came in second in the running of the Gentleman's Cup at the old Latonia Race Course. The jockey was Mr. Arnold "Buck" Easton. The winner of the race was Rope Walker, while Lucky Amelia finished third.

When silos were raised on the Buck Easton farm in the early 1950s, the Martin Brothers Garage was called in to assist with the project. As noted on the door of the wrecker, most telephone numbers in the Florence area began with AT3 (Atlantic). Martin Brothers Garage was an institution on Main Street.

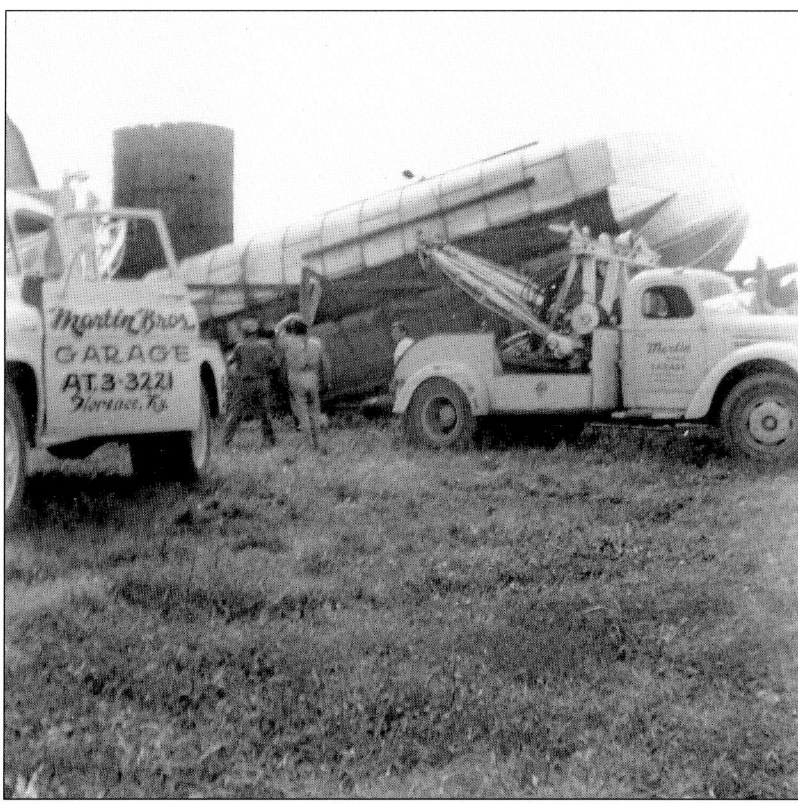

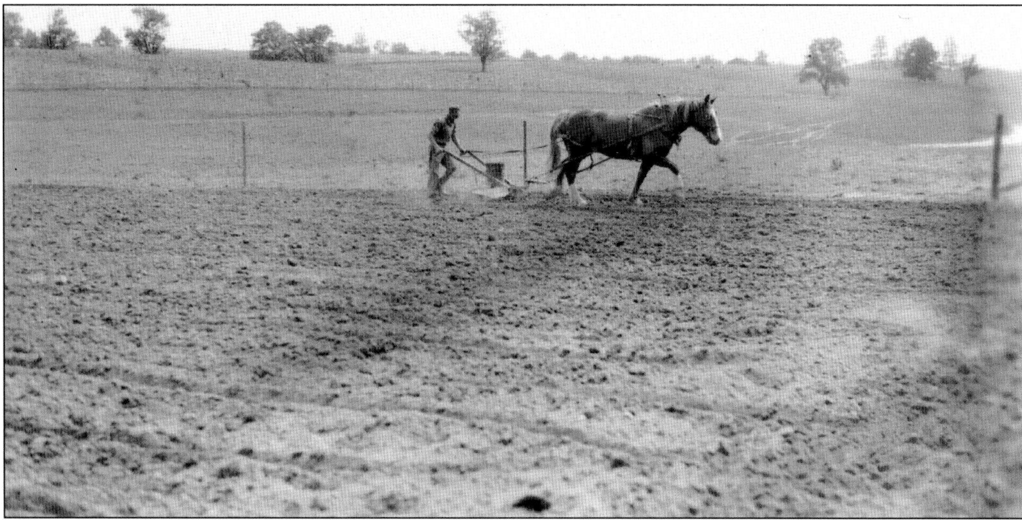

This beautiful snapshot of the bygone farming era of Florence was taken on the Buck Easton farm on Price Pike. Today this field is at the end of the east/west runway of the Greater Cincinnati/Northern Kentucky International Airport. In addition to fine thoroughbreds, the Easton family raised quality draft animals.

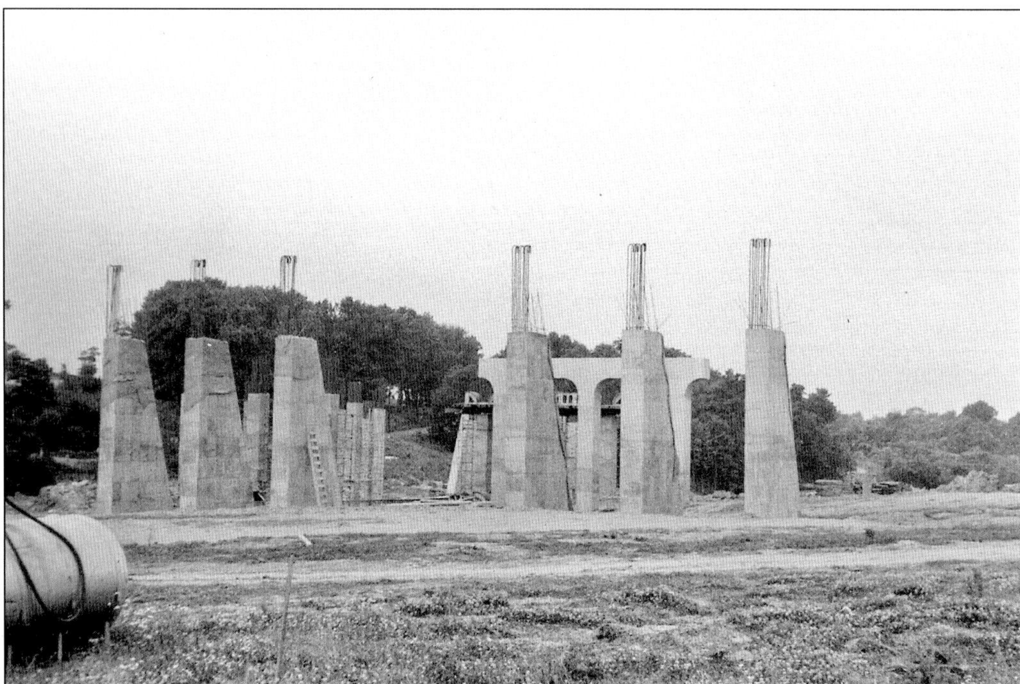

Like so many small towns, the eventual construction of I-75 altered the local landscape of Florence forever. This picture shows the construction of the I-75 overpass along U.S. 42. The completion of I-75 would redirect the commercial center of Florence from Main Street to the express interchanges at U.S. 42 and Route 18.